# What people saying about
## *The Harder I Fall, The Higher I Bounce*

"I love how Max demonstrates the rewards of overcoming seemingly impossible obstacles. He fought through tremendous disappointments to succeed not only in business but also to become a world-class philanthropist. **He is an MVP in the entrepreneurial arena**."

—**Steve Young**, NFL Hall of Fame Quarterback

"This is a fascinating book and should be on the reading list of every young aspiring entrepreneur. Max vividly captures his early experiences as a cadet at the Air Force Academy and how they shaped and guided him for a very successful business career years later. With a good deal of humor and humility, he describes how failures in life, if honestly recognized, can be a powerful learning tool ultimately leading to success in whatever endeavor one chooses."

—**Harry Pearce,** Vice Chairman of General Motors (Retired)

"Max James' *The Harder I Fall, The Higher I Bounce*, is a wild and hilarious ride thru the challenges of growing up as a disadvantaged young man in Tennessee thru the tremendous challenges of the Air Force Academy thru Vietnam combat to the peak of the business world. I could not put this book down as Max winds his way thru one spectacular adventure after another. You will love this book. I strongly recommend Max James' new book *The Harder I Fall, The Higher I Bounce*. It's a great read!"

—**Paul Madera,** Co-Founder, Managing Director, Meritech Capital Partners

"The storied career of Max James jumps from his heroic actions as a rescue pilot in the jungles of Vietnam to the highest board rooms of entrepreneurial America. In all cases, Max has been on the leading edge, whether it be failure or success. His unvarnished accounts of his failures are educational grist for all and his many and varied successes. Interwoven in his story is a legacy and practice of honor and character we all can aspire to. This is not a complicated read but a man reflecting the "old fashioned" basic American values in fascinating personal history. This book is hard to put down with wide-ranging and pervasive lessons for all.

"Please feel free to recommend this book to anyone. I enjoyed it, and it spurs me to talk further with Max to know more about his successful and quirky career."

—**Dick McConn**, Chair Emeritus, National Defense Industrial Association (NDIA), Chair, Emerging Technologies Institute (ETI)

"In my career in the Venture Capital business, I witnessed much success and much failure. People often ask, "What is the most important quality for a successful entrepreneur to have?" In my opinion, unfailing resilience and ceaseless determination rank right at the top. The title of Max James' book says it perfectly. He shares with the reader invaluable real-world lessons on how to succeed by never giving up. Everyone who has undertaken an entrepreneurial venture or is thinking about doing so will learn greatly from reading this book."

—**Bart Holaday**, Oxford Scholar, Former Managing Director of the UBS Private Markets Group, Former Officer and Board Member of the National Venture Capital Association

"In *The Harder I Fall, The Higher I Bounce,*" Max James has written an immensely readable account of a young farm boy, wearing shirts made from old flour sacks, who becomes a highly decorated Air Force officer and later a remarkably successful businessman. His narrative explores not only the highs and lows of an extraordinary career but lessons learned along the way. It is required reading for anyone who wants to achieve more than what seems possible. A truly inspiring story."

—**John Fox,** Distinguished Graduate Award
from USAFA and Founder, Chairman,
and CEO of Markwest Energy Partners, LLC

"For those that think they cannot overcome adversity, Max James will teach you how and why you can rise to success despite the seemingly endless barriers. I watched him do it in the late 1980s at Days inns. His career will help anyone who wants to make it happen. Read and learn."

—**Mike Leven,** former President of the Las Vegas Sands
Corp, Holiday Inns and Days Inns

"Extraordinary! Follow the adventures of Max James, a modern-day Odysseus, as he careens from one improbable, impossible situation to another, and another, and another . . ."

—**William Wecker, Ph.D.,** Professor University of Chicago,
Stanford University, and University of California,
Davis (Emeritus), Chairman, Wecker Associates, Inc

"In his book, Max James, my dear friend for over sixty years, lays bare the highs and lows of his business and financial life with brutal honesty and humble humor. Intertwined are pithy "Max's Maxims" applicable not only for would-be entrepreneurs but as sage life lessons."

—**General (Ret) Michael E. Ryan,** 16th U. S. Air Forces
Chief of Staff, former Board Member USAA

"*The Harder I Fall, The Higher I Bounce* is a very engaging book! Max James has lived an interesting and adventurous life that most readers will enjoy. Learning about his folksy writing style adds to the enjoyment of learning the lessons Max teaches, and I believe entrepreneurs will especially find it interesting and helpful. Max is candid about his failures—and there were a number of them! Most entrepreneurs need to learn the lesson that the number of their failures may exceed their successes, although one big success can overcome a lot of failures."

**—Darryl Bloodworth,** Attorney, Author, Fellow of the American College of Trial Lawyers, Retired President, Central Florida Chapter of American Board of Trial Advocates

"Max and I were classmates at the Air Force Academy, and we were both Founding Directors of the AF Academy Endowment – now the AF Academy Foundation. We experienced many situations in common, and he provides an excellent (accurate, understandable, and enjoyable) description of those situations, adding a perspective that I often missed. He also shared several experiences that we didn't have in common, and I learned new things - including several remarkable things about Max. This is an extraordinary story about an extraordinary guy."

**—Honorable Dr. Paul G Kaminski,**
Chairman and CEO of Technovation,
Inc. Former Under Secretary of Defense, National Medal
of Technology and Innovation recipient,
Member National College of Engineering

"Insightful and fascinating autobiography of Max James, a gifted and heroic young military officer whose professional aspirations led him to the less structured career of an entrepreneur in the private sector. With exceptional candor and focus on character, he describes the highs and brutal lows of his professional and personal voyage."

**—Dr. Erv Rokke,** (Lt. General, USAF Retired)

"Max, early in his life, encountered many forks in the road and chose paths not normally considered the right thing to do. His success is based on his assessment, not just on immediate issues but also on a unique ability to look far ahead and anticipate and prepare for future needs. He's done all of this while demonstrating exemplary integrity and character. *The Harder I Fall, The Higher I Bounce* certainly is a source document for entrepreneurs but has equal application to any field of endeavor. I highly recommend that you read and refer to this book repeatedly throughout your career."

—**Honorable Fred Gregory**, NASA Deputy Administrator, NASA Astronaut, USAFA Col (ret), Helicopter Combat Rescue Pilot

"In *The Harder I Fall, the Higher I Bounce*, my classmate Max shares his many life lessons learned growing up on a farm, persevering through four years at the Air Force Academy, and serving as an Air Force air rescue pilot in the Vietnam war. Then, by expertly applying those experiences to his numerous business exploits, he provides several meaningful lessons to those pursuing their entrepreneurial dreams."

—**Hugh H. Williamson**, Past Fortune 500 Chairman and CEO, Chairman and CEO Finna Sensors, Inc

"Profound thoughts from someone who has 'been there, done that, has the T-shirt.' As a public company CEO for 56 quarters (14 years) and a member of ten public company Boards of Directors over the years, I've met some extraordinary entrepreneurs, managers, leaders, and mentors. Max James is among the best. Words and ideas worth heeding!"

—**R David Yost**, Founder, and retired CEO, AmerisourceBergen Corporation (NYSE: ABC)

"Sitting side by side with Max through the years of one of his more personal pursuits, I learned many lessons of leadership, success, and values. Whether you are looking to be better in business or life, Max James walks you through a true American entrepreneur's many challenges and lessons. As important as the business lessons are, so are the stories of his life. Through his personal stories, Max demonstrates what it is and takes to be a good person and a leader, and these stories will fascinate, inspire, and humble you."

—**David M. Paltzik,** Paltzik Law, PLLC

"An extraordinary book by an extraordinary entrepreneur. Max James inspires us to reach higher and achieve more while learning to embrace and laugh at our failures. A must-read!"

—**Steve Harrison,** Publisher of *Radio-TV Interview Report* Magazine

"Nuggets from a Storyteller"

"Max James has written a narrative about his life, from dirt farmer in Tennessee through a career as an international business consultant to some of the world's wealthiest individuals, into real estate development and brokerage, and ultimately into retail, the industry in which he, his wife and colleagues built a "billion-dollar business." Max has always been a natural storyteller; it is one of his "people skills" that enable him to engage many individuals in his career. He had successes and failures, hence the title of his book, *The Harder I Fall, The Higher I Bounce.* And in his "down home on the farm" storytelling style walks you through each of them in order of occurrence.

"His stories are engaging and fun, but that is not the purpose of the book. Each story contains a "nugget of wisdom," a philosophy, a management skill, a people skill," the wisdom of the lessons learned from success and failure and success again in a series of different enterprises. These "nuggets" outlined in brackets in each chapter of the book, sometimes more than once per chapter, make the book worth reading and the nuggets worth remembering. It is the stories that set the stage for the nuggets of learning and paint the background picture enabling the reader to remember. So enjoy a reading of "Max's habits learned from years of serial entrepreneurship."

—**Ron Fenolio,** CEO and Proprietor-Veedercrest Estates,
Chair - Family Winemakers of California,
Attorney at Law (Retired) Practice Emphasized Entrepreneurship

"For ten years, I had the opportunity to ride the " Roller-coaster" with Max on a couple of his ventures; no one could have asked for a better friend and Mentor. In addition, my son-in-law just graduated from the BYU entrepreneurship school and Max's book will be a "Must-Read" for him, great real-world experiences and lessons. . ."

—**Steve Stratton**, President (ret), Redding Development Group Inc

"Max and a few of his friends started an investment group to evaluate deals and invest in the best we could find.  The group was called AMBIZ (The American Business Associates), and I was eager to join since I was an active Angel investor like Max. I found Max to be a man of his word and generous to everyone around him. People truly loved Max, and I did too. I had made a pledge to Max over a several-year period to share the profits of an investment that we had made.  It was a five-figure donation to his camp, and I kept my pledge.

"Max taught me a lot about character and commitment, and I thoroughly enjoyed knowing Max and being a member of his circle."

—**Harvey Ring,** Former Senior Executive with IBM,
Angel Investor/Consultant

"Max James is a true entrepreneur. And a great storyteller. We worked together for over a decade, and he always made it fun, unpredictable, and lucrative. So if you like entrepreneurship or good stories, you will enjoy this book—and you will find yourself smiling a lot!"

—**Ben VandeBunt**, former CEO of Guthy|Renker

"Max sent me a manuscript of his new book (which I thoroughly enjoyed). As I read Max's new book, it seemed like we were sitting down across a bar table, reminiscing about our shared times together from the AF Academy, Vietnam, Stanford Biz School, and our real estate careers. As an entrepreneur, I was struck by the honesty, humility, humor, and even embarrassment of Max's failures, but I also felt the shared euphoria of the highs. A helluva storyteller, Max shows the road to entrepreneurial success is rarely an easy one. Still, the lessons learned here suggest that a mix of diligence, character, and integrity can overcome the obstacles.

"Max is one helluva storyteller, and he has added the principles that he learned in each of his entertaining adventures. You just gotta read it."

—**Bill Mitchell,** Owner/Managing Director
of Carmel Realty Company

"I have worked with Max for the last 20 years in his role with developing our Proactiv Kiosk business, an enormous success. Looking back, I wasn't sure why we hit it off so well personally as well, but we did. After reading *The Harder I Fall, The Higher I Bounce,* I now know why—a fascinating telling of a man who never gives up and is always in pursuit of the good.

"If you ever get to meet Max, he's even better in person but this book is the next best thing. I highly recommend it."

—**Kevin R. Knee,** Former COO/CFO of Guthy|Renker,
LLC, Co-Founder of Cypress Creek Renewable,
LLC, Private Equity Investor

"I have traveled with Max on his entrepreneurial journey since 1995, not every day, but on enough days to be able to confirm the spirit and accuracy of the most recent 26 years of his remarkable story, some of which is new to me. I fortuitously met Max when he was first involved in network marketing, and something clicked between us, most probably a common devotion to integrity and leadership. His hallmark entrepreneurial story has been told in 25 chapters, but 50 chapters would still have been too short. The book cannot fully convey to each reader the devotion he had for making life better for physically disadvantaged kids while experiencing the many sleepless nights, 24 hour days, gut-wrenching disappointments, and everyday living challenges that the ultimate entrepreneur must face and overcome. The guidance of his father's legacy, his Christian faith, his military training, the teamwork with Linda, his choice of close confidants, and his deep roots in Tennessee soil constituted the recipe for his success."

—**Jim Prochnow**, Senior Partner, Greenberg
Traurig Denver, Former White House Fellow

"Max James has led a life as rich and complicated as anyone I know, complete with the highs and lows that create a true leader. Max's humility shines through on every page, along with a level of grit earned only through surviving and thriving through extreme adversity. It is easy to know Max James as an aviator who pursued the most difficult missions in Vietnam as a rescue helicopter pilot. He is also easy to know as a profoundly successful businessman who has made and lost and remade fortunes several times. Finally, I came to know Max as a philanthropist who dedicated his wealth and time to developing adolescents and adults into leaders of character in service to their communities, our nation, and the world. All of those experiences are captured in this book. If Max didn't write it, I would have asked him to; you will not only enjoy this book, it will make you a better leader, follower, and person."

—**Dr. Mark Anarumo**, President, Norwich University,
Former Director and Permanent (Full) Professor,
Center for Character and Leadership Development,
US Air Force Academy

# THE HARDER I FALL, THE HIGHER I BOUNCE

Life Lessons from the Entrepreneur
Dubbed the King of Kiosks
by *Fortune* Magazine

MAX JAMES

MADE FOR
SUCCESS

Made for Success Publishing
P.O. Box 1775 Issaquah, WA 98027
www.MadeForSuccessPublishing.com

Distributed by Made for Success Publishing

First Printing

**Library of Congress Cataloging-in-Publication data**
James, Max
　　　THE HARDER I FALL, THE HIGHER I BOUNCE: Life Lessons from
　　　the Entrepreneur Dubbed the King of Kiosks by *Fortune* Magazine
　　　　　*p. cm.*

LCCN: 2021942682

ISBN: 978-1-64146-671-4 *(Hardback)*
ISBN: 978-1-64146-673-8 *(eBook)*
ISBN: 978-1-64146-672-1 *(Audiobook)*

Printed in the United States of America

For further information contact Made for Success Publishing
+14255266480 or email service@madeforsuccess.net

# CONTENTS

# DEDICATION

I'VE HAD MANY friends over the years who have listened, sometimes repeatedly, to my stories and they often have the same response:

"Max, that's hilarious! You need to write a book!"

So, to all of you who have endured my stories, and especially to those like my wife Linda, who has heard them a thousand times: Thank you for your encouragement. I hope you will find some of the ones repeated here just as entertaining as before—and maybe you'll see them in a different light, even learning something that might be beneficial.

Most of the humorous stories you'll find in these pages came from my entrepreneurial journeys, seemingly always tied to some business venture I had pursued. In a video interview I did with Jack Canfield a short time ago, I told him that I had retired, or so I thought, and that now I wanted to see if I could put some of these stories on paper. Maybe there was something I could share that would help others, particularly entrepreneurs, learn from all my mistakes… and hopefully from my many successes.

The mission of this book, therefore, is to help entrepreneurs who are struggling with failures or limited successes, a lack of motivation to keep on keeping on, wondering if they have chosen the right market targets, or worrying about failing to sustain their venture.

I believe I can help because I've been there, having overcome a series of failures as well as achieving great successes, including a venture which achieved almost $1.8 billion in sales over a 15-year period.

Sometimes it seemed that I learned more from my failures than even my most successful ventures.

That is precisely why I titled my book, *The Harder I Fall, The Higher I Bounce.*

# FOREWORD

WHEN MY GOOD friend Max told me he was writing his business memoir, I thought, "Now THAT will be one helluva read!"

Max and I were roommates at the Air Force Academy (Class of '64). His life and career have been an energetic race through many ventures and bold risks. We are similar in many ways: we both came from humble beginnings, were natural leaders, risk-takers, and fun-loving. Maybe that's why Max and I became close friends over six decades ago. And we haven't stopped laughing yet!

I have truly enjoyed Max's memoir *The Harder I Fall, The Higher I Bounce*, which recalls some of his personal stories and business adventures in a way that gifts the reader with the tools they need in their entrepreneurial journeys.

Max dares to bet on his ideas. (This is a trait of leadership I try to instill in young executives.) He also has an unwavering moral compass and a genuine commitment to charitable causes and has earned the respect of those who know him. They would describe

Max with words like smart, witty, trustworthy, courageous, funny, loyal, committed, and successful.

Max was a heroic rescue helicopter pilot in Viet Nam (and shot down twice). This resilience under pressure and tenacity propelled Max into the title of Original Founder and CEO of American Kiosk Management, a billion-dollar global presence in North America, Canada, Australia, and New Zealand with 5 million repeat customers, 600 staffed locations, 1,000 automated stores, and 54,000 employees.

In recognition of his groundbreaking contributions to the specialty retail field, Max James became the first inductee into the $25 Billion Specialty Retail Hall of Fame, as well as holding the honor of being an Al Kushner Breakthrough Innovation Award recipient and receiving the Distinguished Graduate Award for the year 2010 from the Air Force Academy. In addition, Max has been featured in *Fortune* magazine and dozens of media publications and television appearances for his work in business and charitable contributions.

Max has spent the past decade leading the charge as the Chairman of the Air Force Academy Foundation committee for the CCLD (Center for Character and Leadership Development), now Polaris Hall.

With a list of accomplishments and accolades like this, I think it goes without saying that you'll want to take notes as you dive into these pages. You'll find humorous and entertaining stories, yes, but more importantly, you'll find life lessons from Max's failures and successes alike—and you'll do well to heed his advice. Breaking the mold of a typical business book, Max's writing will make you feel as if you're sitting on the porch with an old friend, listening to the retelling of events past and being inspired to live out your own success story (and prepared for the falls and subsequent bounce-backs).

There's no doubt in my mind that the book you hold in your hands is a special one, and I know you are going to truly enjoy Max's recount of life, war, and business.

T. Allan McArtor
Chairman Emeritus, Airbus Americas

# PREFACE

HOW IN THE world did I, the son of a Tennessee sharecropper, end up here on this 195-foot private yacht of the "Richest Man in the World," watching the sun slowly settle over the horizon as we slide back into the port of Malaga after being at sea on the Bay of Majorca?

It's hard for me to even imagine this country boy in such "tall cotton." I had spent the last couple of years traveling all over, including New York, Boston, San Francisco, Beverly Hills, London, Paris, Beirut, Riyadh, Acapulco, and Monaco. Wow!

Yet, here I am, a farm boy who spent his preteen years following two gray mules in the dusty, plowed fields of a row crop in the Deep South!

At that point in my life, though I certainly didn't know it then, I was embarking on a great lifetime journey of entrepreneurialism. This journey has led me through some wonderful successes and some painfully disappointing failures. But the harder I fell, the higher I bounced.

So, let's back up and share the entrepreneurial journey to Malaga—and far beyond.

# *Introduction*

## IF YOU'RE THINKING ABOUT BECOMING AN ENTREPRENEUR...

JACK CANFIELD, AUTHOR of the *Chicken Soup for the Soul* series, asked me this question: "Max, if there are others who are thinking about becoming an entrepreneur, what would you tell them?"

Without hesitation, I responded, "Do it! Get to it! Go for it!"

However, if you were to ask me that same question now, I would add an important caveat. I would tell you that you need to know that going for it is not only what you kinda, sorta, maybe would like to do, but that it is something you feel you just *have to do*. Then, having passed the "I have to do it" test, you must dig deeper to determine the answer to the next question:

"*Why* do I have to do it?"

Perhaps the following will help answer the "Why" question.

There's a freedom about being your own boss and a great joy in having created something important to you. Plus, there are good measuring sticks for success. It's either the needed services or products that you provide to other people, or it's the money that you make. And money is a great measuring stick in the world of business. It's a chance for you to run your own life, take the risks, step out, build something unique, and enjoy the rewards in several ways. Additionally, if you do it really well, you'll be able to become a great philanthropist, giving back where your heart and your conscience lead you. And of course, you will also be able to do the personal things that you would like to do, the things that your dreams are made of.

For me, those are great and sufficient reasons for taking the risks, making the plunge, climbing the mountains from one peak down through the valley to the next peak. There are no automatic winners in the world of entrepreneurialism. The mountains are steep and rugged, sometimes unforgiving as you attempt the climb. And often the failures and falling down the mountain to where you started, or even below where you began are terribly painful. The winners who reach the peak work harder, longer, smarter, and are blessed with good luck leading to good fortune. Climbing as high up the mountains as possible, knowing that you gave it your all, is a reward unto itself. Doubt your doubts; don't doubt your dreams.

My version of Kurt Vonnegut's book *Cat's Cradle* is this:

"Of all the dreams of *women* and men, the saddest are 'It Might Have Been.'"

### Do it! Get to it! Go for it!

# Chapter 1

## ON THE FARM

"GET AWAY FROM that wheelbarrow! You don't know anything about machinery."

My first mentor was my dad. We lived on a farm in West Tennessee, and my early summers were spent working in the row crop fields. Come to think of it, it never was just summer. It was also spring, fall, and winter! In the early years, our only way to grow crops was to use mules to prepare the land for planting, pull the planters, and hopefully do whatever was necessary to haul in the results of the plowing and planting. It might be corn, cotton, strawberries, or soybeans.

With my high-top plow shoes, a straw hat, and a pair of gray striped overalls over a white t-shirt, I started my work in the fields by riding a drag behind a mule named Old Tom. I'll never forget his name for the rest of my life, nor will I forget the view from behind him I looked at all those years! *Side note: a drag is a platform of boards nailed together, used to flatten down the rows that the "turning plow" turns up before planting.*

A couple of years later, I attempted to drive the mules (we added another one named Jack to the mix) and pull the turning plow. I'm afraid I wasn't very good at it, so I was promoted to the harrow. Since that particular plow didn't dig deeply into the dirt, it was easier to manipulate, and therefore, I often was able to satisfy my dad with my efforts. Later, I was promoted to riding a piece of equipment called the planter. The planter was drawn through the dusty fields by the two mules, and you sat right on top of it. The iron wheels rolled down the sides of the rows, dropping seeds into the now-flat row top of prepared dirt.

I wasn't tall enough to put all the harness leathers on the mules that were hooked up to the plows, so I would have to pull up a wooden bench to lift the heavy leather and metal harnesses onto their necks, praying that the mules wouldn't sway over in my direction and knock me off the bench right into the mud. Thankfully, I discovered if you gave each of them an ear of corn, they would be content, and I could get it done.

Eventually, we bought an old tractor to do some of the work, thank the good Lord. However, for quite some time, and much to my chagrin, Dad was the one who drove *that* machinery advancement.

One of the best parts of the job in the fields was the lunch break. Usually, we packed up our lunches at the house before heading off to the fields and ate them under whatever shady trees we could find. I looked forward to my mom's great sandwiches, some of which I have later learned were not all that common around the country. I had two favorites: peanut butter and banana, and pineapple slices and mayonnaise. Occasionally, I would find a sandwich of bologna and mustard or maybe even a can of Vienna sausages with saltine crackers.

After I gulped down a sandwich with a jar of cold water, it was time for my second favorite part of the job: a little rest break. I would lie down under a big oak shade tree, staring up at the white puffy clouds blowing through the bright blue sky. Often my eyes would close, and I would wander off into a quick nap. After about 15 to 30 minutes of this pastoral break, and when the mules would have finished eating their corn and hay, it was back to the fields for the rest of the afternoon. Either Dad or Mom would bring big half-gallon jugs of ice water to the fields in midafternoon. As the sun started to disappear behind the wooded areas of the pastures, we would unhitch the mules from the plows and head for the barn. I would get to ride the mules when it became too dark to keep on plowing.

The other welcomed break was when a thunderstorm would blow in, so I would watch the horizons for those puffy white clouds to grow tall and dark. You see, you can't plow a wet field. Man oh man, did I used to pray for rain!

When I was about 13 years old, my dad sold the two gray mules that I had followed for years, struggling up one dusty row and down another in the fields of West Tennessee on our small farm. Finally, I "graduated" from staring at the backsides of Old Tom and Jack to staring at the far end of those same dusty rows, except now I was on a beat-up old tractor. I would have preferred almost any job over working on that farm, and to be fair, I wasn't very good at it anyway. But my bad attitude probably didn't help!

> Looking back, I now see the lesson at hand: If you don't like the job that you're doing, most likely, you are not doing it very well.

Looking back, I now see the lesson at hand: If you don't like the job that you're doing, most likely, you are not doing it very well.

Then came the day when my experiencing the dislike of farm work would all change.

That old tractor broke down in the middle of the field. I mean, it just quit running! I did everything I could to get it restarted: I cleaned the carburetor, checked the sparkplugs, and double-checked that there was plenty of tractor gas in the tank. It was hot around that motor, and I burnt myself several times trying to reach stuff I knew little or nothing about. Choking on dust, sweat running into my eyes from that beat-up old straw hat I wore, I was stumped. Nothing worked!

Oh no! Here comes Dad, bouncing across those plowed furrows in his old pickup truck, kicking up a trail of dust. I knew this was not likely to have a good result for me.

With an exasperated tone in his voice, "Now what's wrong!" he said.

"I don't know, Dad. I tried 'bout everything I know how to do. It just won't start."

"Get out of the way and let me see what the trouble is now!"

> If you don't have the skills to do a job well, then quit and get another job.

And, of course, it happened just as I expected. In about five minutes, he had it back up and running just fine.

That moment would turn into one of the first of many lessons he taught me, one that I fondly remember. With a grin he said, "Get away from that wheelbarrow. You don't know anything about machinery!"

So… what was the lesson, exactly?

If you don't have the skills to do a job well, then quit and get another job. Furthermore, if you don't have the necessary skills to venture into a new business, then don't do it! In fact, if you can convince yourself not to do it, then don't. Only start that new venture if you know somewhere inside you that you *must*, that there is NO CHOICE!

He sure was right. I was not, and never did become any good with machinery. (Well, maybe except airplanes and helicopters, but more on that later.)

Dad turned to me and said, "You really hate this farm, don't you?"

"I gotta tell you, Dad. I really do."

You see, I was always more task oriented and not excited about a long-term project. And on the farm, the work never seemed to end.

"Son, I don't much like it either, but it's the only thing I know how to do. I wasn't very good in that one-room schoolhouse where I went with my five brothers. And unlike my twin brother, your Uncle Cup who was really smart and went on to college, the 10th grade was my limit. Your granddad said it wasn't much use me wasting my time at 'book learning' and told me I needed to just drop out and come on back to working full-time on the farm."

(From everything I have learned from research, family genetics, and experience, I am quite sure my dad had attention deficit disorder.)

And then came the life-changing pivot in my early growth:

"I tell you what. I'm going to let you go. Go to town and get yourself a job there."

Now frozen in place and with what must have been a look of total shock on my face, I asked, "Are you serious, Dad? But who's gonna take my place? Who's going to do my work here? Someone has to help you out!"

With a finger pointed in my chest, he said, "That's not your problem. It's mine, and I'll handle it."

In looking back, I realize it wasn't just the work that caused my serious dislike of the farm life. The level of financial reward was extremely low, or so it seemed to me. And in no way should that be interpreted as a criticism of my dad. He started in a one-room country schoolhouse, struggled to achieve a 10$^{th}$-grade education, owned his own farm, retired at age 62, enjoyed his leisure years, lived until he was almost 95, and left a six-figure estate to his children. I judge that to be a remarkably successful entrepreneur's journey.

***

IN OUR COUNTRY neighborhood in the 1940s and early 1950s, there were no telephones. I remember the excitement of watching mules drag those long black telephone poles down the gravel road adjacent to our farm and pull them into our yard. Some sort of post-hole digger would turn up huge amounts of dirt, leaving a deep hole for the black treated poles to be lifted into. Then, the pole climbers would latch up their pole belts, put on spiked climbing shoes, and work their way to the top of the pole to attach the telephone lines. Wow!

And soon enough, that big old black telephone instrument would be in our house, sitting on a table, probably in the bedroom (which also served as our living room). It was just a plain-faced telephone, well before the rotary phone found its way into service. There were certainly no phones with a punch button dial! You just picked up the receiver and waited for an operator to ask you what number you wanted to call.

The telephone operators got to know you by your voice. "Mr. Max. How are you today? Whom can I reach out to for you?" Even now, 70 years later, I still remember my best friend's telephone number. I mean, it wasn't that hard to remember back then, either. It was "27." Yep, that was the entire number.

Our first telephones were on an eight-party line. That meant that there were seven other neighbors who might either be on the line already or were waiting to make a call. Oh, and you could listen in to their conversation, often being told unceremoniously, "Get off the phone while we're talking. What we have to say is none of your business. Hang up now!" It was hard not to listen in to the neighborhood gossip about all that was going on in our farming community. After all, gossip was the only means of communication other than meeting in person! But things eventually got much better: We were upgraded to a four-party line, and much later, a one-party line.

I also recall how we washed our clothes. At first, there was the big black kettle pot hanging over a hot fire out in the backyard. You would fill up the pot with water you hand pumped into a bucket from a well, let it heat to a boil, throw in the clothes and some soap, and stir with a wooden stick (often the handle of an old broom). Then you'd take out the hot clothes, put them in a tub of fresh water to hand-wring some dryness into them, take them to another area of the backyard, and hang them on a wire line until they were dry (hoping it didn't rain or snow that day).

Later on, about the time we installed a telephone, Dad bought a washing machine. It was set up in an outside building, constructed of concrete cement blocks. That building was known as the "well house" because we drilled down into the side yard where the old well's hand pump had been, struck water, and actually had a water tank that would pump water right out of the ground into that tank and on into the house. Egads! Running water inside the house!

The washing machine had the old dual rollers on top, into which you put the clothes to wring out the water and soap. They were then rinsed in a number-three washtub before being hung on the clothesline to dry. There were many funny—and sometimes frightening—stories of women getting a sleeve or apron caught in the rollers and being pulled toward the tight, frightening, and dangerous cylinders. Fortunately, when calmer minds prevailed, there was a lever to hit that would open up the space between the rollers to release the garment being pulled (along with its owner) into the rollers.

To iron the few articles of clothing necessary for "dressing up," an iron, shaped somewhat like the ones of today but far smaller, was placed on top of the potbellied coal stove that sat in the bedroom. When the iron was hot enough, it was taken to a table covered with a blanket that served as the ironing board. Somewhere in that process, a box of starch powder was added to water. That mixture was then poured into a glass soda bottle, which was usually an empty Coca-Cola bottle. The metal top of the bottle was punched with a nail to make small holes, and that contraption then served as a device to sprinkle the starch on some of the clothes. I hated that starch bottle for what it did to my shirts, especially the ones I had to wear to school and church.

We grew almost all our fruits and vegetables either in a huge garden or in the field, and always had sorghum molasses syrup from the sorghum cane crops. In the winter, one of my favorite breakfasts was molasses and homemade butter spread on hot biscuits. Even now, it makes my mouth water!

Mom would get up before sunrise to prepare a big breakfast. After breakfast, she would clean up the kitchen and straighten up the house. Then she would head for the fields, working side by side with the field hands, tending to whatever crop needed work that day. Around 11:30, it was off to the house to prepare what we called "dinner," which was the biggest meal of the day.

During the dinner hour, there was a favorite radio program on from the local town. It was called *Shop and Swap*. People would call in, describe something they wanted to sell, such as a handmade blanket, a plow for an Allis Chamber tractor, or newly born puppies, and name a price. On rare occasions, Dad might close his eyes and "sit for a spell." More often, however, he would go work on some machinery before heading back to the fields. Mom would clean up the kitchen again, saving all the "dinner" leftovers for the evening's "supper." Her afternoons were often spent washing clothes, mopping the linoleum floors, and sewing clothes by hand or on the old foot-pedal sewing machines. An old farmer's saying certainly applied to my mother's workday: "A man's work is from sun to sun, but a woman's work is never done."

We would then all "wash up" before bedtime. Since there was no indoor bathroom, that meant leaning over a pan of water or the sink in the kitchen and using a soapy washrag to get some of the day's field dirt and dust off. Entertainment for the evening was listening to the old radio and our favorite programs: Jack Benny, Bob Hope, *The Shadow* ("only the shadow knows"), Roy Rogers, the Friday night fights, plus the news.

The lack of an indoor bathroom was one of the really uncomfortable aspects of country living. We had an outhouse, which was about 30 yards away from the house, just past the chicken house and the rabbits' pen. To get to it, you walked on planks that Dad had placed down on the grass from the back porch to a gravel pathway. Now, going out there was not a big deal during a bright sunny warm day. But going out there at night with just a flashlight was the stuff of nightmares. Mosquitoes, spiders, snakes and who knew what else! During the day it was not that great either for all those reasons plus the roosters guarding that hen house just waiting for me to come by.

And then there was the toilet paper issue. That was an expensive item, and so other substitutes were often necessary. If we ran short before the next Saturday trip into town, we could use the good ole' Sears and Roebuck catalog. Those pretty picture paper pages of slick material were pretty rough when one wadded them up for "cleaning purposes." So, one of life's blessings was to be the first to use the catalog. You see, the few index pages were printed on a much thinner paper, which was considerably less rough.

Oh, life's little blessings on the farm.

Flour for cooking came in 25-pound cloth sacks, so Mom would take those cotton sacks and cut them into a shirt based upon a paper "clothes pattern" that would fit me. The flour sacks came in various colored designs, some with baseballs or airplanes or even tractors, but some had girly flowers—the worst, in my opinion. Every day before school, my Mom would iron and starch my homemade flour-sack shirts. It was the best my family could afford. But Mom still insisted that my clothes would be something I should take pride in. Somedays I would wear overalls, but most days I was able to wear blue jeans. When I got home from school, I immediately changed into my work clothes and headed for the fields or the barn. Those shirts and jeans would have to do for many more days at school—at least until the next clear wash day a week or so later.

Of course, it wasn't just our clothes that needed washing. Those sink baths we took before at suppertime or bedtime were totally insufficient by the end of the week. So, on Saturdays, we would leave the fields at noon, have a light "lunch," heat up some water in the old kettle pot, and pour it into a size number-three tub out on the back porch to take our weekly baths. Mom got to go first. Then when she finished, it was my turn to get in, and lastly, Dad would squeeze into the little tin tub with water that had turned cold (and not so clear) and take his bath.

Then it was off to town! There were several important things to accomplish in town each Saturday. We would pick up farm supplies like tractor parts and hog food and go to the hardware store, where we would shop for tools and maybe a new fishing lure for my cane pole to use in the pond on our farm.

The big visit was to the grocery store for another week's supply of what we couldn't grow or produce ourselves. I didn't always have to accompany my dad or mom to the stores. Often, Dad would give me a quarter for the movie theater. I would spend $.15 for the ticket, $.05 for popcorn and $.05 for an iced soda (my favorite was Orange Crush). The movie would consist of at least one cartoon, the news reel, upcoming movie previews, a serial which would entice you back for next week's installment, and two cowboy shows.

My favorites were Roy Rogers, Gene Autry, Hopalong Cassidy, Johnny Mack Brown, Lash LaRue, Bob Steele, and the Durango Kid. I remember finally being able to buy a real leather whip, one like the movie stars Whip Wilson and Lash LaRue used. I cannot begin to tell you how many times I cut my ears or back trying to learn to "pop" the whip with a loud "crack!"

After the movie, I would find my dad's old pickup truck parked somewhere along Main Street. Dad would be leaning on a parking meter, talking to the other farmers, and Mom sat in the truck with the other farmers' wives.

And here is a great observation that has served me so well over the years. Before we cranked up the old truck and headed back out to the country, Dad would come back and sit in the driver's seat next to Mom, with me riding shotgun at the window. He would lean back, put his hands behind his head, and with a great big sincere and contented smile on his face, he would say, "I wonder what the poor folks are doing."

Some might wonder about his thoughts, but I knew that he was saying that even though it was a hard life, he was fulfilled and content. He considered himself a wealthy and blessed man.

I was happy with the movies, but my perspective wasn't the same as his. I wanted more than what our farm offered for my future.

And so, I was able to start off in a new direction. Dad made the sacrifice for me so that I could find my way to a better life. He had always done so, and he continued to do so in all his years on this planet. He truly wanted me to have it better than what he had experienced in his life.

# Chapter 2

## MY FIRST MENTOR

DAD WASN'T CALLED up in the draft for WWII because he was a farmer and therefore exempt, but he still wanted to do more to contribute to the war effort. To his delight, he was able to join the Army. He actually was assigned to the Cavalry because of his skills with farm horses and mules, which led to a pretty plush extra duty for Corporal James. He was able to train the Army officers' polo ponies! (Though hard to believe in this day and age, many cavalry officers back then had polo ponies.) Dad taught the military horses tricks like kneeling, lying down, standing on stools, and rearing up for pictures.

In the Army, Dad was also a surprisingly good boxer—that is, until he ended up with a busted eardrum. Still, he felt like he needed to pass some of those skills onto me for my own protection, so I always had a striking bag hung somewhere around the house or barn.

"You have to be able to stand up for yourself, but if I ever catch you or hear about you being a bully, you'll have to put on the gloves against me!" Dad was a strict disciplinarian, but I never remember him striking or spanking me. He was very persuasive, however. He had a certain stare that sometimes brought tears to my eyes.

I do remember on one occasion when I had been tasked with taking our geese from one strawberry field to another. Now, they were pretty darn heavy for a young boy, but it should have been manageable assuming they didn't turn those long necks around and nip you with their sharp beaks! Dad would chase them (we had cut their wing feathers so they could not fly), and catch them, grab them at the base of their wings, and then hand them to me over the fence. He had to really hustle to catch each one, and the last thing he wanted to do was to catch the same one twice... which only happened this one time. I'll tell you why.

He handed me a big old gander and I grabbed it like he did, fingers entwined just behind the base of the wings. However, as soon as that "mean old bird" turned his neck and gave me a nick on the arm, I yelled as if I had been shot, dropped the goose, and away it ran. My dad was over that fence in a flash, but not to chase the goose.

Nope. He caught *me*. And he grabbed my ear with his thumb and finger and twisted it until I was on my knees.

"I'm going to catch that goose again. And I am going to give it to you, *again*. And you will not drop it again. Do you understand me?"

"Yes, Sir!"

And he did just what he said. When he handed it to me just like before, I didn't drop it, nor did I drop any of the others he handed me after that!

Lesson learned.

You see, most folks who care about you don't want to put you in harm's way. If you have built mutual trust with those close to you, then you need to seriously consider whatever they choose to suggest including materials that they truly require. Chances are, you will be able to avoid an "ear twisting."

To be honest, I really was afraid of all fowl, including the mean rooster that ruled the henhouse where I had to gather up the eggs from underneath the sitting hens.

> Most folks who care about you don't want to put you in harm's way.

More than once I dropped the bucket of eggs running from those roosters. That resulted in my usually calm mother fixing scrambled eggs for breakfast. However, Mom was not always as calm as Dad. She believed in physical punishments. And when she asked you to do some chore or run an errand, she meant NOW.

I loved to read as a youngster, and sometimes I guess I got lost in a book. I remember one of those books (a comic book as I recall) being torn out of my hands. I looked up from the couch and knew I had not done something Mom had asked me to do, at least not in a timely manner.

"Go cut me a switch off of the weeping willow tree in the back-yard. NOW."

Well, I did it, and she used it. I guess it must have worked, because I don't recall going to that willow tree much after that.

At the age of 33, Mom was diagnosed with a brain tumor. It was the big "C." She suffered through several surgeries, but the medical technology back then did not allow the surgeons to remove all the tumors each time they operated. Mom had worked in a hosiery mill in town after she could no longer work in the fields with Dad and the hired hands. She wanted so badly to continue to support her family financially. But that eventually became impossible.

When I wasn't in school or having to work with Dad in the fields, I had the job of sitting with and caring for her. She had lost some of her ability to speak and was prone to seizures. One of the great stresses this caused was her inability to recall words for well-known objects, including people's names. She could look right into my face and not be able to say my name. Sometimes this stress resulted in emotional outbursts and epileptic seizures that were quite frightening for me, as a young boy, to observe.

There was one time when we were both sitting on the couch in the bedroom, and Dad was in the fields somewhere. I had been trained that when Mom had a seizure, I was to take an "ahh stick" and place it between her teeth to prevent her from accidentally biting her tongue, creating a serious bleeding problem. As usual, I was focused on reading a book when I felt the couch shaking. I turned to Mom, and she was having a seemingly serious seizure. I grabbed the ahh stick but could not force it between her teeth, even with her tongue already there and starting to bleed. I had also been trained to run to the neighbors for help in such an emergency. The closest neighbors owned and managed a little country store, just down the hill from our house. It was probably about 300 or 400 yards away. The store was rented by a couple of very heavy middle-aged ladies. In fact, "seriously obese" would be a better description.

I went screaming into the store, "Mom's having an epileptic! She is bleeding badly, and I can't get the ahh stick between her teeth. Help me!"

Picture this: Two really obese ladies trying to run 400 yards up a hill in a panic, being led by a 10-year-old little boy. But we all made it in time to force her teeth apart and stop any serious damage. Much later, Mom told me that she had been totally aware of all that was happening. She thanked me for being a "man" and actually had quite a laugh about my failed efforts to insert the "ahh stick."

One Sunday, Dad and I drove to the First Baptist Church in town. I had been studying the Bible and the Sunday school books that were used to teach us morality, character, and ethics. After Sunday school this particular morning, I told Dad that I wanted to join the church. I was only 11 years old, pretty young for a big decision like that, so Dad suggested we stop by the pastor's office before "preaching." The night before this meeting, I had a very spiritual dream—one that I felt was a calling to join the church.

The pastor didn't hold back and went straight in, asking, "Do you think God will forgive your sins?"

"I don't think I've committed any that were so bad that he wouldn't," I replied.

The preacher told me that all sins were the same, neither too big nor too small.

"Max, if you will try to live your life, pretending you have a compass on you at all times, you will find life a lot easier and happier. Now, that compass is not a magnetic one pointing to North, but a moral one. It needs to always point to God's teachings for you to follow. Believe that right is always right and wrong is always wrong, but when you feel you are in troubled waters, and not real sure if you are doing what's right, think of that compass and where it points. You'll make the right decisions, I promise." That was and still is a great lesson for my personal and my business life.

So, when the call to join the church came at the end of the preaching hour, Dad and I went up front, and I joined up. However, when we got home, my ill Mom was upset, for two reasons. One, she was not able to be there, and two, she felt that I was too young to make such a decision. Dad supported me, but the argument stuck with me for years, creating some doubts in my mind as to whether or not I had created the problem by not discussing my decision with both parents first. I don't remember that the argument lasted very long, nor resulted in any long-term problems, but I do remember how calmly my dad responded.

That was another lesson on how to handle extreme stress. Stay calm, stay focused on the result you need to accomplish.

Mom died a few years later at the age of 35. Much too young. The visitation was in our living room, where Mom lay in an open coffin. The funeral was in the church where Dad also wanted an open coffin. Walking by that was hard for a 13-year-old. Afterwards, Dad and I got into the car designated for the family to ride to the graveyard service. It was the only time I ever saw my dad cry. He had sacrificed so much for her.

> That was another lesson on how to handle extreme stress. Stay calm, stay focused on the result you need to accomplish.

How he did it seems miraculous to me. The hospital where Mom had all of her surgeries was about 70 miles away in Memphis, and the journey there took several hours, traveling over rough gravel roads in his old pickup truck. That was, of course, on top of his responsibilities on the farm and taking care of me. But somehow, he did it.

I am embarrassed to admit that it took me a long time to fully realize the sacrifices my dad made for me and the efforts he went to in order to give me my shot at a great childhood and one much different than his.

***

BY THE TIME my mother passed away, Dad had acquired an additional small adjacent farm. He had also acquired a really nice country farmhouse. It was a one-story white building sitting up on a small hill. It had a very attractive living room with a brick fireplace—the room that I remember most vividly.

We had a porch with a green cane swing that would seat two, where Dad could sit and look out from the hillside over his farm. He spent many Sunday afternoons there, gazing out over the large front yard and the green lawn to the Tennessee trees, his crops, and the pastures. This was the second place I recall Dad taking a deep breath and saying, "Wonder what the poor folks are doing." It just didn't take wealth to give my dad contentment.

Now, imagine this beautiful pastoral scene with you sitting in that swing on a late summer afternoon. Inside the adjacent living room, your wife is in a coffin, and your neighbors and friends are coming by to pay their respects and offer their condolences.

Just a few weeks later, as a newly widowed parent, you give it all up for the benefit of your teenage son. You move away from that life defined by sitting in that swing on a beautiful Sunday afternoon, away from all that you had built and bought with hard work and the proverbial "sweat of your brow" to a two-bedroom rental in town—the spare rooms of an elderly couple who agree to rent to you and your son.

That rental has one room up the rickety stairs to a small area with a double bed, which you will share with your son. It has a freestanding metal rod for a closet. Down the stairs is a tiny kitchen with a gas burner stove, a half refrigerator, a metal sink, and a metal shower for bathing. Next to the kitchen is a very small "sitting room," which is large enough for a two-person couch.

Every morning, you get up early, dress in your farm work clothes and head down to the little kitchen to prepare a breakfast meal for your son. Not really knowing how to cook (in the old days, that was a "woman's work"), you do the best you can with eggs and bacon and maybe a piece of toast. Some days, it's a bowl of cereal and a glass of apple cider. You make sure your son gets up, gets dressed in whatever he wants to wear, and gets out the door on time to walk to school.

Now, much later than you normally go to the fields and the crops, you drive your truck out to the farm and start your workday. As you go about all the hard work to make the farm somehow produce a profit, you look up on the hillside to the white house sitting there, empty of your beloved wife and no longer home to you and your son. Try as you might to swallow that lump in your throat, manage the hurt in your heart, and keep yourself from weeping, the tears mix with the dust on your cheeks. But somehow you just "keep on keeping on," making a life for your son and for yourself. You somehow know that giving up that home and moving to town was the right thing to do, the right thing for your son, and actually for both of you.

Are you still imagining yourself sitting in that swing, or do you see the empty swing, swaying with the breezes coming off the land?

Even through the grief, my dad always made it to my basketball games and track meets; he was a "band parent," and in his truck he hauled all our band instruments to the football games; he even drove me and two other All-State Band members to Nashville to perform with the All-State Band at the Grand Ole Opry. He built a full basketball court in a pasture so I could practice, and he built a tennis court in the dirt in one of the fields for me and my country friends to learn how to play the "in-town sport." That dirt tennis court eventually led to me and a classmate winning the town's men's tennis doubles tournament!

***

BEING A GREAT horseman, Dad taught me the responsibility and skills necessary to control and care for animals, especially the horses he bought for me. I learned to ride in farm rodeos and parades in a few different towns.

He was also very serious that I learn how to discipline and control horses. I rode many miles alone to visit my country cousins, often filling my saddlebags with books—mostly comic books from the grocery store. We traded those comic books with each other like other kids traded and collected baseball cards. I was even allowed to ride the horses to school in the summers.

Learning independence was always on Dad's agenda for me. One Saturday, I saddled up my new horse and told Dad I was going up the road to my cousins' house to trade some comic books. I wouldn't be gone too long, maybe an hour or so. Dad thought that was a great idea as it was only a couple of miles' ride.

Along the way on the gravel road, I needed to cross an old bridge across a creek that ran through our farm. When I got to the bridge, the horse just stopped and balked... *badly*. I couldn't force the animal to cross the bridge no matter how hard I tried. I even tried leading it across by foot! And, frankly, it became a bit scary as the fear that the horse was experiencing became worse. So, I gave up.

When I rode back into the front yard of our home, Dad happened to be there. "That was pretty quick," he said. "Weren't your cousins at home?"

*Oh no, what should I do?* I thought I didn't want to lie, but he would be really upset if I let him know that the horse defeated me. My male genes won the internal argument.

"Oh, I decided not to go after all. I'm not sure they have been to the grocery store and bought any new comics."

I was never able to fool my dad.

"You didn't go, did you? What happened?"

*Crap, now I not only have to 'fess up to telling him a fib, but I have to admit that I was unable to control my horse.*

"I couldn't get this new horse to walk across that old bridge. Seems like he was really frightened by it. I tried several times, but he just always balked. Got kinda dangerous."

The next thing I knew, he grabbed me by the waist as I sat in the saddle, smoothly swung up onto the horse right behind me, and spurred the horse hard with the heels of his plow shoes. Off we went at a hard gallop. I didn't know if he was going to throw me in the creek, leap into the creek on the horse and swim across, or what! As we approached the creek at a full gallop, the horse reared back, sliding on all four hooves to a dead stop.

Dad said, "Now ride this horse across that bridge!"

But the same thing happened. The horse wouldn't cross. Dad kicked the heels of his plow shoes into the horse's withers. The horse bucked violently, almost throwing us both off and onto the gravel.

"Get off! I got it."

Man oh man was I glad to dismount.

Then he said, "Hand me that big dead tree limb lying on the ground at the bottom that oak tree over there."

This was not looking good for Dad, the horse, and maybe me. I was sure hoping the tree limb that I picked up wasn't going to be used on me. And as it turned out, it wasn't. But the horse was not so lucky.

Dad rode the horse up to the start of the bridge, and again, the horse balked and reared. Dad swung that limb perfectly, and it landed precisely between the ears of the horse's head. The young horse trembled nervously, stumbled a bit, and Dad reined it again to the start of the bridge. When the horse hesitated, Dad repeated the tree limb maneuver.

This time the horse shook badly as it walked right across the bridge. Dad turned the horse around, and without hesitation, the horse crossed the bridge. I could see the wild eyes of the horse trying to look up toward its ears.

Once back on my side of the bridge, Dad swung off the horse in one smooth motion, called me, and said, "Get on this horse—NOW!" I don't know who was shaking in the knees more, me or the horse. But up I went onto the saddle. Dad handed me the tree limb and said, "Now ride this animal across that bridge. And if he balks at all, one little bit, do as I did, and do as I say: Rap him hard on the head between the ears."

So, off the horse and I went, walking awkwardly toward the bridge. One thing I knew I didn't want to do was attempt to hit the horse between the ears. I was absolutely sure that the horse knew that he had defeated me before, that it was not my dad sitting in the saddle, and that he had a shot of winning again. Therefore, I made sure that the big old tree limb was visible to the horse as we approached the bridge. Good news! The horse did not hesitate going across *or* coming back. What a relief!

But what would Dad say? Or maybe worse, what would Dad do?

Well, he again just made that smooth gliding motion, grabbing my waist and swinging up onto the horse, right behind me and the saddle. All he said was, "Let's go home."

When we rode into the front yard, he swung off the horse and looked up at me and said, "I guess you'll be going on over to your cousins' house now. Do you have any questions?"

With a bit of a tremble in my voice, I said, "No, Sir." I reined the horse back onto the gravel road, heading for the bridge once again. When we approached the bridge, I was sweating profusely. And you know why. What the blue blazes would I do if I couldn't get the horse to cross the bridge? Would I go home and tell Dad I had failed once again? Would I cook up some hare-brained story as to where I had been?

The horse—looking warily at the tree limb I had in my hand, swinging alongside his neck and head—wound up doing me a huge favor. We marched right across that rickety old bridge without hesitation. As I rode into my cousins' front yard, one of them yelled out, "Where the hell you been? We been awaiting on ya for what seems like an eternity!"

My reply was quick and accurate. "Dad was teaching me something about horsemanship."

Now, while that was an absolute truth, Dad had taught me a lot more than horsemanship. Sometimes to complete the journey you're on, you must apply a little pressure on your opponent. Hopefully it won't necessarily be physical, but you may need to do *something* to help them see that removing the obstacles to your progress is a jointly beneficial move.

When I was riding that same horse into town to late summer band rehearsals, one of the problems I ran into was where to put the horse. Much to the chagrin of the football coach, I turned my horse loose on the football field. After all, the field was totally fenced in, which was necessary to keep people from sneaking into the games.

But that didn't last too many seasons. I turned 15 and was able to get a motorbike license. Dad

> Sometimes to complete the journey you're on, you must apply a little pressure on your opponent.

bought me a moped (a motorized bicycle) which I rode to school during winter basketball season. Thanks to my having to use the farm "tractor gasoline," the thing only ran consistently about two-thirds of the time. That meant that I had to pedal it home. Tennessee winters can be cold, especially after taking a hot shower following late basketball practices. Pedaling that moped the five miles home on that lonesome gravel road is something I won't soon forget. But hey, I made the team!

When faced with serious adversity, my dad just did what was necessary to get through it. It might have been a family illness, bad weather destroying a year's crops and income, and so much more. Yet he persevered. What a great mentor to learn from. And as you have read, he was obviously a fantastic parent.

I also learned about the importance of family taking care of family. I spent a lot of time staying with my grandparents who had a farm nearby, as well as with my uncle and aunt at their home on their adjoining farm.

And here is another great lesson: You cannot make it through this life and career without help, very often from family and friends.

*** 

WHEN WORLD WAR II ended, Dad reluctantly needed to leave Mom and me on the farm so that he could go to Detroit to find work in the auto industry. There were just not sufficient farming income opportunities for him at home. That was not a great move for him, and so he came back to Tennessee and became a share-cropper on my grandfather's land. Eventually, as you have read, he borrowed money from the government and bought a small farm, added land to it over the years, and finally ended up with about a 500-acre row crop farm next to his twin brother's.

> Managing debt is a great skill to acquire.

That was about the only money he ever borrowed. I am quite sure he thought interest was a sin. He never owned a credit card. And that is a lesson that would have saved me many a tough time if I had listened to him early on! Managing debt is a great skill to acquire. Positive leverage is a wonderful growth concept, while too much debt can bury you quickly when even a slight downturn in your expectations rears its ugly head.

In fact, I eventually became so drawn to what I then called "positive leverage"—borrowing money cheaply and investing it at a return rate greater than the interest rate on the borrowed money— that a good friend of mine said, "Max, you are so leveraged on your assets, you probably don't even own your underwear free and clear of debt." I don't recall just how I answered him, but I know what thought went through my head. He was right! I had put the purchase of my "skivvies" on a credit card!

Later, that leverage attitude would cost me dearly. You see, I am sure it was Dad's entrepreneurial attitude that gave me my first taste of risk-taking. The farm was certainly an entrepreneurial venture. Not even the old *Farmer's Almanac* could accurately predict the weather. Would the spring planting fail because of a late winter freeze or maybe flooding? Would insects show up and ruin the crops, e.g., locust or boll weevils? Would the cattle become infected with disease? Would it rain on the cut hay in the field, or would it be taken into the barn too early, heat up, and cause the barn to catch on fire? I believe you had to be an entrepreneur to take on the risks of being a farmer, hoping for something like a good cotton crop to pay back the bank loan which was taken out to buy the cotton seed for the next year's planting.

A now deceased friend of mine, Dr. Robert Schuller of the famous *Hour of Power* television program from the Crystal Cathedral, once told this story about his growing up on a farm. A terrible disaster hit his father's corn crop, and instead of having a great number of wagonloads of corn to sell to market, he was only able to harvest one wagonload. However, he didn't sell it, but instead said a prayer to God, thanking him for the one load of corn seed, which would be sufficient to plant next year's crop.

*That* is an entrepreneur's optimism.

# Chapter 3

## THE GREATEST GIFT FROM GOD

I REMEMBER OTHER times when Dad, without seeming to be lecturing me or even advising me, taught me so much. Things that led me to become a serial entrepreneur.

I think of the time I offered him a chance to invest a little money in one of my ventures. Being the most financially conservative person I have yet to meet, he said wisely, "No, I don't think so. You know, Son, you're not always right." Man oh man, did that turn out to be prophetic!

Dad actually retired from farming when he was in his 50s. He took advantage of a government program called the "Soil Bank." Sometimes the government initiates programs that astound me, and unless you conscientiously or politically object, most often, you would be remiss in not taking advantage of what is offered. Such was the Soil Bank program. Because the government wanted to keep the prices of certain farm crop products at a certain elevated level to protect the farmers from creating an oversupply in the marketplace, this program was established.

The government would pay the farmer NOT to grow a crop. Thus, the supply was being controlled artificially. The pay was roughly equivalent to what the farmers would have profited if they grew the crops and took them to market, and the advantages were obvious. There was no risk of flooding, droughts, insect invasions, or a drop in market demand. Secondly, the most obvious was the farmer didn't have to work! *Well, not exactly.*

As I remember, there was a requirement not to let the weeds overrun the fields or some such. So, what was one of the biggest immediate problems?

What the hell were the farmers going to do with their time? They certainly were not accustomed to sitting on their rumps. So, some, like my dad, sought to find other jobs. That happened after selling off most of the farm equipment such as tractors, plows, combine machinery, and trucks. Which, of course, was another incentive to enter the program because it meant additional cash up-front! My entrepreneurial dad's plan was to take advantage of having the farm as an asset which would continue to produce cash, while he turned another asset—his time and talents—into another source of continuing cash income, e.g., a job! He also made sure there was an exit strategy, which was another extremely important entrepreneurial lesson at the time. The Soil Bank program that he chose was for a period of 10 years, at which time one could restart the farming operations.

Sounds good, right? It was. Well, at least it was for 10 years. But by then, a lot of things had changed. The cost of farm equipment had risen dramatically, prohibiting some of the farmers, including Dad, from starting over. And a lot of progress and improvements had been made in the technical side of farming, as well as the parts of farming involving the entire agribusiness scene. Very large industrial farming companies had been formed and bought up many farms in the Soil Bank program. Those corporate entities had the investment capital to relaunch the farming operations, and they had "economies of scale" that the small-acreage farmer did not have.

Dad chose not to restart farming operations. He was not the same physical specimen that he had been in the late 50s and mid-60s. He had a good job (or so it seemed). But damned if he was going to let the big corporate raiders have the farm that he had acquired in parts and pieces and had lived on for so many decades! So, he sold it to his twin brother, who owned the adjacent farms, and was prepared to do battle with the "big boys."

The lesson for me was (and is) that even though it is very difficult to look very far out into the future, you best have a plan B in case the future doesn't turn out like you and the majority of "experts" think it will. Remember, "Sometimes failure just ain't your fault."

So, Dad had a plan B. First, he had another job lined up (and another one if the first one failed). Second, he could now draw Social Security monthly payments. Third, he had a solid bank account resulting from the sale of the farm. And fourth, he had one additional asset: a small stock investment in the Tennessee Farm Bureau from which he never touched the dividends (but rather reinvested all of them every year back into the company). He also made sure to not sell any of the stock as it continued to appreciate in value. And a big fifth, he had no debt!

I was a different story, though. I didn't always live my personal or professional life within those parameters of being careful about too much leverage. Still, when I first started my entrepreneurial career path, I truly understood two things.

1. The phenomenal benefit of compound interest: At 10% interest, capital and reinvested interest income will double in 7 years, and at 7% interest, capital and reinvested interest income will double in 10 years.

2. If you can borrow at an interest rate less than an investment return rate (ROI), you are making money on your borrowings.

There are some risks with the latter, of course. The ratios can switch, i.e., the interest costs can sometimes be higher than the ROI (ouch). And it can also result in your having a 0-percent return on your investment, which may also have become worthless. Yet, you still owe the loan principal and the unpaid interest. Being the overly competent risk-taker that I was, the latter certainly wasn't going to happen to me.

But of course, it did, and more than once. Therefore, I learned to seek out and listen closely to my corporate tax lawyer and my tax accountant *before* creating the investment entity.

During the Soil Bank years, Dad didn't retire. At first, he secured the job of utilities manager, reporting directly to the mayor of our little town of Humboldt, TN. He was able to obtain that position because he had always protected his reputation. He was known for his honesty, his impeccable character, and his integrity in all his business dealings with the merchants in our town. (Thanks for the role modeling, Dad.) Nevertheless, it was a position controlled by politics. When an election came around and the mayor was defeated, Dad was replaced.

That led to Plan C. In his 60s, he actually drove an old oiler truck for a highway construction company. That meant driving his car for a couple of hours to get to the actual highway construction site, then driving that non-air-conditioned truck all day long in the hot, humid summer days. The roads he traveled were not the main interstate or state highways, as his boss/owner required routes which later were determined to be ones on which the state and federal highway truck inspection stations were NOT located. At the end of the day, which started at sunup and ended at sundown, he would drive hours to get back home to have some late-night supper, clean up, grab a few hours of sleep, then get up and do it again. Yep, he was the epitome of "when the going gets tough, the tough get going."

Even though Dad only had a 10$^{th}$-grade education, he was extremely wise. And being born a "Depression-era baby," he was also extremely financially conservative.

Once, when he was in his mid-80s, we were talking about travel, which he had done very little of in his life. Much to my surprise, Dad said to me, "Son, if there is something you really want to do, you ought to go ahead and do it."

That was just not in character for my tightfisted, penny-pinching dad, who some joked still had the first dollar he'd ever made. So, I was certainly taken aback by this advice to let loose and spend some travel money.

"That doesn't sound like you to suggest my now spending money, even on travel," I replied.

His reply echoes loudly even in my head today: "As you get older, it won't be because you won't be able to travel and do other things. It'll be because you won't want to."

*Wow!* As I am now in my senior years, I recognize how true that is. I have been blessed with financial success and could travel just about anywhere at any time I want. Yet there are so many oppor-tunities that I just don't care to take. Age changes your priorities and desires. Thanks to Dad, it also changed the timing on when I *did* take his advice. I traveled at a young age and purchased "stuff" that wasn't necessary but that I still enjoyed.

The lesson here is to enjoy the journey. That seems to be more important than the destination. My goal was always to achieve financial independence. It was an elusive goal, mainly because of my poor investment savings efforts. I have also never really been "risk-averse."

But there must come a time when the level of risk that an old, tired, worn-out, beat-up entrepreneur takes must be reduced.

I have always said I would never retire, that I couldn't imagine what it would be like. I tried to change my mind and give retire-ment a shot. I even announced it to my family and friends. Maybe some who are reading this will be able to successfully cross that barrier. So far, I have not been able to do so, thus this book (among many other things).

***

OKAY, BACK TO Dad. I have asked him other questions that I knew he would answer wisely, or at least with great humor. An example happened once when I was visiting him after he had moved into an independent senior living facility. He was single after having tried remarrying a couple of times. I said to him, "Dad, you've just got to quit getting married. Enough! You don't stay happy in your relationships, nor do these marriages last very long. And besides, where are you meeting all these ladies anyway?"

His answer was classic. "At funerals."

"What?!?"

"My friends are dying, and when I show up at their funerals, there are all these nice, well-dressed and friendly widowed women. Next thing I know, we're dating, and sometimes we get married."

I'm sure you've heard of or seen the movie, *Wedding Crashers*. Well, my Dad was the original Funeral Crasher.

After Dad's second divorce, he had moved into a small brick house in a really nice community. And, yet again, he met a lady at a funeral that he had gone to school with at a little country schoolhouse near his dad's farm. Her husband had died, and Dad decided to date her. She lived in a different town and had done quite well financially for herself, holding an executive job for a very large U.S. government agency. On the surface, it sounded like it just might turn out to be a good match. Dad told her he was not going to move away from where he lived, so she would have to sell her house and move into his house. Pretty bold, I thought.

However, in true Dad fashion (having been burned before), he told her that she would have to buy a half-interest in his house when she moved in... and she did! (What charm, Dad!) When they did eventually divorce, Dad bought back her half-interest in the house (at no more than what she paid him for that half, of course). Depression-era baby financial conservative.

I had enjoyed a recent success about that time, so I wanted to do something special for my father. I remember during all those tough years on the farm, he had always said that when he "got rich," he was "gonna buy him one of those gold Cadillacs."

One month, with that thought in mind, I rented a car in Memphis and drove it up to Dad's home to visit for a few days. The first morning, I told Dad I needed to take my rental car downtown to see someone and that I would be back in an hour or so.

Instead, I went to a neighboring and much larger town that had a Cadillac dealership. I drove my rental Lincoln onto the car lot, and out came a car salesman.

"Good day, Sir! Can I help you find yourself a new Cadillac? We sure 'nough got ourselves a whole bunch of 'em lined up for you to look at."

"Yes and no," I said. "I'm interested in buying a new car for my dad over in Humboldt, and I want to surprise him."

"Are you serious? Are you for real? Man, every father ought to have a boy like that. Damn, that is mighty fine. So why don't we go into the office, and we can get all the loan papers filled out to get you qualified."

"Actually, that won't be necessary. I'll just write you a check."

His eyes lit up, and the smile stretched the skin around his mouth almost up to his ears. He could feel that commission already crawling into his wallet.

"Well, all right then! Let's just pick out the Caddy you want, and we'll get the license and registration papers all filled out."

"Excuse me, Sir, what I'd like to do is leave my Lincoln rental car here with you and take one of your new cars over to Humboldt to surprise him."

"Now, let me see. You want to just take a new car off the lot without paying for it or anything and drive it on over to Humboldt?"

"Yes, Sir, that's sorta what I had in mind."

Now, what I was thinking was that they would want to hold a check or send one of their managers with me or something to secure the vehicle. But nope. Much to my surprise, he said, "I think that'll be just dandy. You just go ahead and pick out what you think your old dad would like and head on back over there to Humboldt."

So, I found one that was gold, took the keys, and drove off the lot in a new Cadillac, having given them no security except leaving behind a rented Lincoln that belonged to Avis!

I pulled into the short driveway behind the carport where Dad had parked his old Chevy. I went inside and said, "Dad, I need you to go back downtown with me. There are a couple of legal papers that I need you to witness before a Notary."

"Okay, let me get my coat on."

As we walked out of the carport to the Cadillac with Dad heading for the passenger side door, I asked, "Dad would you mind driving? I need to look over these papers on the way downtown."

"Sure," he said, and I tossed him the keys.

As he walked back around the front of the car and toward the driver's door, he paused and said, "This isn't the car you drove up here in, is it?"

"No, Sir, it isn't."

"Well, whose car is it?"

"It's yours, Dad! I want you to have it."

He began to shake a bit as he opened the door, got in, and started looking around. All I can remember him saying is, "This is one beautiful automobile."

"So, Dad, start it up, back out of the driveway, and let's head back over to the Cadillac dealership to finalize everything."

We drove a short distance, maybe a couple of blocks, to get onto the main highway to drive back to the Cadillac dealer's facility. The speed limit on that highway was 65, but Dad was driving about 25! And his shaking was getting worse.

*Oh my goodness. His palsy is really bad this morning*, I thought. But of course, that wasn't it.

"Dad, you need to speed up. You're going to get us killed driving so slow!"

"Okay, I'll give her a little gas." Within about 15 minutes of driving down the highway, he looked over at me with tears in his eyes, and he said, "I can't take this car. I just don't need it."

And then he spoke these words which brought the tears to my eyes: "Son, you have accomplished everything you wanted to by offering me this car. So, don't you feel bad or disappointed that I'm not going to take it. There is nothing more you could have done to make me more happy or proud of you."

> Sometimes the dream is more important than what's real.

"Dad, are you sure? You've always dreamed of owning a gold Cadillac. And now you can have one."

"Yeah, I'm sure. That was then, and it *was* my dream. But sometimes the dream is more important than what's real."

We both were silent for a few minutes.

"Dad, you know what the problem is now? We've got to go tell that salesman that you don't want the car."

"Reckon he's not likely to be very happy with me. But he'll get over it."

"I'm not so sure he will, certainly not very quickly, and probably not very soon!"

We pulled into the dealership car lot, and there he was. As soon as Dad opened the door and got out, the salesman starts off.

"Mr. James, Mr. James. It shore 'nough is your lucky day. Ain't that a fine automobile you a 'bout to own? One of the damnedest best ones we have on the lot. Course your son there says you can have any one of 'em you want. What do ya think? Want that one, or want me to show you some others?"

"Well, Sir, you sure are right, alright. It is one fine automobile." There was a long pause, and then he continued. "But Sir, I'm not gonna take it."

"Mister James, I don't think I heard you right. Did you say you don't want this Cadillac?"

"Yes, Sir, I did say that. It's truly a wonderful car, but I just don't need it. My old Chevy back there in the carport will do me just fine."

And then, almost from the top of his lungs, that salesman shouted, "Mister James, you're a damn fool!"

"Well, yes, Sir. I've been called that more than once. And I thank you for letting my son bring the car over to my house, but I believe we'll just take the Avis rental car and head on back over to Humboldt."

"Well, I'll be damned if that don't beat anything I ever seen. A full-grown man turning down a free Cadillac! My boss ain't gonna believe me. Hell, wait'll I tell my wife. She fer sure is a'gonna think I somehow screwed up this deal.

"'Don't you lie to me,' she's gonna say. 'What in Jesus' name did you do?'

"Mr. James, you got yourself a good 'en in that youngin' of yours. I wish he had offered me a free Cadillac. For damn sure, I would've taken him up on it 'fore the last words came out of his mouth."

And with that, Dad and I took the Avis and headed back home. I asked him a couple of times if he was positive that he really did not want the Cadillac. He was sure and said that it would have just been a waste of money.

"But Dad, surely there is something that I can do for you, to give you something that you maybe really still could enjoy."

He said that he understood and would give it some thought. Later that day, he told me that he might like to have a bigger house so that he could have all the family over like his family used to do out in the country.

*Great*, I thought! I had offered a car, and now I need to find a house? But if I could swing it, I would. I called up a former high school classmate who was now a realtor. He offered to help and said he would pick me up at my dad's house; that he had a house in the same general neighborhood that was not on the market, but he knew it could be bought. The house was only a couple of blocks from where Dad lived.

Talk about an upgrade! The house was on about a full acre, maybe more. It had a huge front yard with a circle driveway. Beautiful old oak trees were dotted throughout the front and in the back. In addition to all the beautiful trees out back, there were a tennis court and a swimming pool. Yikes and holy cow! What was my friend thinking? If Dad wouldn't take a car, why in the world would he move into something as luxurious as this? Turns out the house was owned by one of the principal owners of the highway construction company that Dad had driven that old asphalt oiler truck for.

Dad said he thought a move there was okay. Really! Surprising, but at that point, nothing should have surprised me. I guess to move into that prestigious place was an ego booster that Dad felt could represent the cumulation of decades of struggling, saving, and sacrificing. So, I bought it, and Dad moved in.

Right away, he had a party for all the relatives. His five brothers and their wives and children (and grandchildren) all showed up. Dozens of pictures were taken. I bought the inexpensive wine, the Jack Daniels bourbon (or was it Early Times), and a joyous sit-down dinner was enjoyed. Dad's chest was all puffed up, head held high, and he wore a smile like he had entered the gates of Heaven. It truly was the apex of his living there.

Soon after the party, I got a call from Dad exclaiming, "Do you know how much it cost to have this yard mowed?!"

"Yes, Dad. I have your nephew mowing it and cleaning up all the yard, front and back. Please don't worry about it. I'm paying him. It isn't costing you a penny."

And a few days later. "I just saw the gas bill for heating this pool. Why does it have to be heated? The river and the cow ponds you swam in on the farm weren't heated, and I don't remember you not wanting to go swimming there."

"Dad, please stop worrying about the expenses. I'm paying them. I want to do it, and I can afford it."

"But do you know how long it takes to sweep the leaves and grass off that tennis court? And who the hell that I know knows anything about tennis anyway?"

Eventually, my brother and his wife moved in to help Dad out with all these "chores." They were in college in a neighboring city. What we had on our hands was a case where "one plus one should have equaled three."

But Dad's constant worrying about the pool heat, the cost of air conditioning the house, the yard mowing, and a host of other things that were not easily accepted resulted in my brother calling and saying that he would rather swim in an apartment pool than listen to our dad rave on about the costs. So that left Dad in a big house with his swimming pool (which was now cold) and his tennis court with leaves blowing across it (and him out there with a broom constantly sweeping it off so it would look good to folks driving by).

And then it happened. I got a call from Dad.

"You know *that* house you bought?"

"What house are you referring to? What is *that* house?"

"You know, the one you bought for me to live in."

"Yeah, what about *that* house?"

"Son, you need to sell it."

"Why, Dad? What happened?"

"I moved."

"You did what?!"

"Yeah, I bought another house back in the neighborhood where I used to live. So, you need to call your friend and have him sell it. I've already moved."

"What?!"

"Yeah, that place was just too big and way too expensive for me to live in. So, as I said, you need to sell it."

Shock! Anger! Tears of anger and laughter! Yes, laughter!

He did it again. No Cadillac and no big house with a tennis court and a pool. Just a little brick house in the old neighborhood. He was pleased that he could stand on the floor furnace in the hall and see into every room in the whole house. And the yard was so small, he probably talked a neighbor into cutting it while he was cutting his own yard. Oh, I'm sure he paid the neighbor something for his troubles, probably a small can of gasoline for the mower—at least enough to mow both yards.

I called my high school classmate and told him to put the house back on the market. I also said that I thought that he could handle that without a commission since I had just very recently paid him a full commission, not to mention that he had not had to spend any marketing money to sell the house to me in the first place.

"Well, Max. You know, I have lots of expenses down at the office. Things are a bit slow, and God only knows how long it will take to sell that big house. This little town doesn't have a lot of potential buyers who want a costly swimming pool, much less a tennis court, for goodness sakes." *(You mean suckers like me?)*

Nevertheless, the house was listed, and months later, it was sold for considerably less than I paid for it, not to mention I had paid two 6% commissions and two sets of closing costs. But you know what? Dad had enjoyed it for a short while, entertaining the family and boasting about his son who had bought it for him. And after the good kinda wore off, he found that little brick house where he stood on that old floor furnace looking into all the rooms.

Hey, entrepreneurs! What lessons did my mentor dad teach me? About materialism vs. comfort? Yes, that, and more for me and each of us.

\*\*\*

LATER ON, DAD had cut his hand and wrist pretty badly while trying to fix that now-infamous floor furnace. Seems like the whole house smelled of raw gas. The heating company came over on more than one occasion but couldn't seem to satisfy Dad, so he thought he would give it a go himself. That, of course, was not a very good idea, and he ended up at the hospital with a hand full of stitches.

When our family and I found out, it was time to talk with him about not living alone (and for goodness sakes, the solution was not to go to more funerals where he was the "Funeral Crasher"). He eventually and reluctantly agreed, giving up his morning coffee with his old, retired farmer friends at the local McDonalds where they gave them all free coffee. He left his old hometown of Humboldt, and I moved him to Memphis into a midrise independent living facility.

Thankfully, he adjusted much quicker than I expected. There were some advantages. His other son, a doctor, lived in Memphis with his wife and Dad's two grandsons. Also living close by in Memphis, which turned out to be a real plus, was an ex-wife (a geriatric specialist licensed nurse whom Dad had married after my mother died when I was 13). And I guess the other thing that helped with his adjustment to the new facility was the ratio of women to men, about 80-20. They sure kept him busy.

I was able to lease a two-bedroom unit so that when I visited him in Memphis, I could stay with him and enjoy time together. Dad continued to mentor me through his actions and words without being pushy or domineering. One of the things I could see was that establishing a routine in your life, both personal and business, was particularly important.

First thing he did when he woke up each morning was to make the bed and not haphazardly. Then he would put on his robe, come into the kitchen dining room area, and fix his own breakfast. He did this until about his 91$^{st}$ birthday. While eating, he would begin reading the newspaper. Then he would wash his dishes, return to his room, shower and shave, get dressed in a newly starched long-sleeved shirt and nice pair of pants, and then shine his shoes to a high gloss. Reminds me of the Naval Admiral that is out on the speaking tour these days with a simple message: "If you want to be a big success, make your bed every morning!" Point well taken.

As I mentioned, the ratio of women to men was favorable to Dad. He had always been a handsome fellow, dressed well, had a true southern gentleman's demeanor, and looked much younger than his true age. The ladies often seemed to knock on his door and bring him pot roasts, cakes, cookies, pies, meatloaf, and stew. One day, we were sitting in the living room area, and there was a knock on his door. He got up, opened the door, and there stood a nice lady with something on a dish which was covered with a cloth.

"Here, Rupert, I brought you something good to eat."

Dad took the plate and, without saying anything, promptly closed the door! I was horrified. Here was this sweet elderly lady who had prepared some food for Dad and even brought it to his door, and he just accepted the plate and closed the door in her face!

"Dad! That was really rude of you. It wasn't like you at all. What in the world came over you? Not even to thank her for the offering?"

He growled a bit and said, "I was nice to her because you were here."

"What! And what do you usually do when I'm not here?"

"I take the dish, and as I close the door, I tell 'em, 'You're too late, I can't help you anymore!'"

I honestly thought I would die laughing. I'm sure I must have wet my pants a bit. Yep, they were after my nice, old, gentlemanly, handsome dad.

At about the age of 92, Dad woke up on his bathroom floor, having failed to yank the emergency bathroom "help cord" before he passed out. It was a tough decision, but it had to be made. It was time to move him into an assisted living facility. We found a two-and-a-half-room unit that he seemed to be okay with. Nice facility, but as is so often true of seniors at this stage in their lives, everybody is old but them!

Because he didn't have the best of hearing, he would talk very loudly, especially in the big dining room.

He'd say something like, "See that old woman over there? She drools and spills her food at every meal, and that one sitting with her, I think she must be losing her mind."

"Dad, that's not a very nice thing for her to hear."

"Don't worry; she can't hear a damn thing anyway."

As Dad continued toward his time to leave the planet, he gave me more and more good information and guidance about becoming a senior. His courage was amazing. His refusal to take on too much medical attention told me that he was in full control. He grew too weak to walk all the way to the dining hall, but that didn't stop him. He would say, "Come on, I'm hungry. Let's go eat; I don't want to be late."

And off we'd go. But he couldn't make it all the way because he'd run out of breath and sufficient energy. And, you guessed it, he still wouldn't ask for help. "Just let me sit here on this hallway bench for a minute." Then up and on we would go.

Finally, he could not make that trek any longer, so full-time hospice was necessary. Oh boy, did he complain about the cost.

"They make more in an hour sitting around here in the kitchen than your mother and I did picking cotton all day long for 50 cents. And your mother could pick more in a full day down on her hands and knees than any woman or man in the fields with her!"

Tough to the end. Frugal to the end. And in as much control as he was allowed.

Dad was just two months shy of his 95th birthday when I got that call that we all fear, dread, and regret. "Your dad is really sick. I don't think he can last much longer. You'd better fly back here as soon as you can."

I arrived there late one morning and went directly to his living quarters. He was in bed, awake but now obviously very weak. He had been having trouble clearing the phlegm from his throat. He asked me to bend down and put my ear close to his mouth so I could hear what he wanted to say.

"Hi, Son. I'm glad you're here. I just want you to know I'm really proud of you."

And then he said without fear, "I'm gonna die this afternoon."

The pain in my heart was matched only by that in my gut. With tears cascading down my face and a choking-sized lump in my throat, I eked out, "Dad, it's okay. If you're ready to go, I'm alright with it. You have had a great life, loved and respected by us all. Dad, if you want to go, just let go, relax. We will take away your pain. I love you."

With that, I sat down next to his bed and held his frail hand in mine until many hours later, he passed.

What a life, and what a blessing to have had such an amazing, devoted, loving, wise, and talented man in my life.

And as appeared elsewhere in this book:

**The greatest gift I ever had,
Came from God, I called him Dad.**

# Chapter 4

## THE COTTON WAS GETTING TALLER

HOW DID I get to the Air Force Academy, and more importantly, "Why?"

I guess you could label it "When preparation meets luck and opportunity."

Some might judge that in high school, I might have been labeled as a BMOC (Big Man on Campus). That designation did not necessarily suggest a big ego, nor a person with a head swelled so big you couldn't fit it into a gym. However, it *did* refer to someone who had numerous accomplishments as a student. Those could include athletics, scholastics, and extracurricular activities. With a strong blessing from Above, added to a very strict mom and dad who wanted me to have a better life than they, I was fortunate to attend good small-town schools. There, the teachers were friends of the family and dedicated to helping us become good citizens who contributed to our community. We were proud of our school, and we worked to keep its reputation strong.

I started playing trumpet in the 3rd grade. I choose the trumpet because one of my cousins, who was six years older than me, was a trumpet player. He made great sounds come out of that horn, plus he got to go to all the football games with the marching band, wearing a beautiful red-and-gray band uniform. For a good old country boy, that, too, looked like "tall cotton." I remember practicing outside the house on the farm, serenading all my adjacent farm friends and the farm animals. The band director's requirement was a minimum of 30 minutes of practice a day. That must have worked okay for me because I was awarded a blue ribbon to wear on my band uniform. But that ribbon came with a condition. I could wear it if, in an additional four years or more, I was qualified to be in the "high school band" even though I would still be in middle school/junior high school.

Somehow, that happened early for me. I got my first uniform when I was in the 7th grade. My dad was so proud that he immediately joined the Band Parents Club and volunteered to drive his old truck, hauling all the big band instruments to the "away" football games. Our band director was also a strict disciplinarian, requiring not only that you could play the music well but that your uniform was perfect for performances. Shoes shined, pants pressed with a sharp crease, instruments polished and in good working order. Little did I know then that this would be good training for the Air Force Academy.

My junior year (11th grade) in high school was my best year. I seemed to peak that year. I was a member of the debate team, and my partner and I won the State Regional debate contest. I was also chosen to play the lead in our annual speech club play of *Meet Me in St. Louis*. I lettered in basketball and track, was the student conductor of the orchestra, played in a Dixie Land band at events around our county, was elected president of the Student Council, and president of the Band, was the editor of the school yearbook, went to Boys' State and ran for governor, and made the Tennessee All-State Band with a performance at the Grand Ole Opry original concert facility (the Ryman Theater) in Nashville.

As the Frank Sinatra ballad goes, "When I Was Seventeen, It Was a Very Good Year."

I guess all of those activities I sought to participate in were also an "*entrepreneur searching for a good deal for himself while sharing the results and rewards with others in those organizations.*" It also was a great chance for me to begin learning the two critically important fundamentals of leadership:

First, learn to follow while being a teammate whom others could rely on.

Second, all that experience boosts your chances of becoming a better leader.

But the last year started off slowly… and not so successfully. I ran into a problem with my basketball coach. One afternoon after school, I was scheduled to have my picture taken with the other band members, as well as individual shots for the class yearbook. The professional photographer was only there for that afternoon. Since I had been selected as "Most Likely to Succeed" and a couple of other designations, it was important to the schoolteacher in charge of the yearbook (and me as editor) that I not miss the appointments. So, I went as instructed.

However, that made me late for basketball practice. When I walked into the gym to get dressed for practice, the coach came charging over to me, demanding an answer as to why I was late for practice. When I told BoJack where I had been, he became furious. He told me to never mind getting dressed for practice.

"You are benched for the next two games!"

As he stormed off back to the team, who was standing around with mouths open, I asked if I could practice on my own. As I recall, he said, "I don't give a damn what you do."

So, I practiced on my own, and I still dressed out for the next two games even though I sat on the bench. We didn't have such a great game in one of those two contests (I am quite sure it was *not* because I was benched), but what a great feeling I experienced when during one of the down quarters, the cheering section of my fellow students started chanting, "We want Max, we want Max." But I must tell you that did *not* make the coach any happier. Nor did it change his mind about me continuing to "warm the bench."

Then, during a later practice, I had a couple of teeth knocked out by a flying elbow. Not only did it really hurt when those two teeth came through my bottom lip, requiring several stitches, but there went my trumpet playing. I just could not press the horn's mouthpiece up against that sore, swollen, stitched lip. This resulted in my not earning "first chair trumpet" in the band, nor was I able to even try out for All-State Band again.

And, of course, it interfered with my teenage social life. Think about it!

On top of all that, I fell while running the low hurdles in the Regional Finals Track Meet, which ended my participation for the rest of the season. I still have the black cinders in my knee where I hit the track, knees first as my trailing leg caught the hurdle.

My grades, however, continued to be good. But I didn't have a great idea of what I wanted to study in college. And, well, that assumed that I would *go* to college. I really was remiss in not doing any serious planning for attending college. I guess I just assumed that I would go to UT (University of Tennessee), but I didn't even apply for scholarships! Not sure why no one pushed me or, worse yet, why I didn't pursue financial aid myself.

All in all, not a great year as a senior. But then a local politician arranged for my dad and me to meet my local congressional representative, Congressman Robert A. "Fats" Everett. Fats told me that he had read all the articles about me that had appeared in the local newspaper and the Memphis papers. He congratulated me and suggested that he might consider my coming to Washington, D.C., to work for him as his administrative assistant. From time to time, he would select outstanding young men from his district to come to Washington to be pages, for the experience. But he wanted me to come as his admin. My dad eventually agreed that I could go, and I was elated.

The cotton was getting taller!

It was the first time on an airplane for me, but off I went with my little suitcase in hand. At first, Fats wanted me to stay in an apartment house with many of the pages that were there for their congressmen. I didn't like it. Probably because I wasn't "worldly" enough.

Instead, I found a private residence that rented out their upstairs bedroom, and they took me in. It was quite a long way from the Capitol building and the congressmen's offices. But I was willing to get up very early to take a local transit bus from the Rock Creek area to Pennsylvania Avenue. There, I would get off the bus, grab some breakfast at a small diner, and then use my ticket transfer to hop on another transit bus up Pennsylvania Avenue to the Capitol.

All this was quite an adventure for a 17-year-old country boy who had very little travel experience.

Fats put me to work right away. My "chores," as he called them, were many. They ranged from the mundane, like running the "addressograph machine" for all his mailings to the district constituents to chauffeuring dignitaries that would come up from Tennessee. Those guests included the governor of Tennessee and his family, and once, I even chauffeured the Honorable Senator Estes Kefauver. *Wow! Can the cotton get any taller?!* I would also escort these visitors around the Capitol and host them in the Senate Beanery. Fats also made sure that I had the time, often accompanied by him, to visit other historical facilities.

One of the "chores" I had was to write a regular newspaper column for the folks back home in his district. It was a "what's going on in Washington" or a "young man's view of Washington, D.C.'s political happenings." The column was published in all the local town newspapers throughout his congressional district. When I eventually returned to my hometown, I was frequently invited to speak to various cities' social and business organizations, e.g., Chamber of Commerce, Rotary Club, Women's Voter League, Jaycees, and Parent-Teacher Association about my adventures in Washington, as well as an insider's view of a congressman's office.

The work in Washington was not only educational but also immensely enjoyable. But that wasn't all! I had some exciting social opportunities as well. One evening, I was watching a local television show, which was a "dance party" type where teenagers in a TV studio were being telecast while dancing to the rock & roll hits. On these television shows, there would often be a celebrity performer. This particular evening, the host announced that Paul Anka (a very successful young Canadian singer) would be visiting soon. The big deal was that the TV station was sponsoring a contest for a young man and woman from the viewing audience to be on the show with Paul Anka and have dinner with him at the nightclub and restaurant where he was performing. *Hmmm, sounded like that would be fun.* I wrote a letter explaining why I should be selected and hoped for a shot.

Here I was, "a young man far away from home, way down there on the farm in Tennessee, up here in the big metropolis of Washington without any local friends to share time with." I also made a big deal about my being a trumpet player like Paul Anka and thus would be able to identify and converse with him no problem.

Doggone if I didn't win the contest! There was also a very attractive young lady who was selected. So, off to the TV studios we went! We met Paul Anka, appeared on the TV show with him, and then attended his performance at the nightclub/restaurant. I kept lots of his autographs on the pictures that were taken with him (as well as the dancing girls who were part of this show).

This was a great example, even as a young man, of always looking for opportunities you can take advantage of. Give it a shot. Who knows, you just might win!

And I guess I did okay with supporting my congressman. He asked me if I wanted to have his job someday when he retired (he normally received more than 90% of the votes in the elections back home). Politics, and the power therein, was something that I had tasted and loved and was probably addicted to even after such a short time and limited exposure. So, of course, I said, "Yes."

"Okay," he said. "We have a lot of squares to fill and boxes to check off for you to be qualified and acceptable to the voters. First, you need to go back home and finish high school."

"Really, Sir? After being up here and doing this work, I would prefer not to go back to high school. Is that absolutely necessary?"

"Okay, tell you what. You can do it by correspondence."

"Sir, I'm sure you know this, but small Humboldt High School doesn't have a correspondence course program."

"Listen up. Here is your first lesson in becoming a congressman. For a congressman, they *do,* or they *will.*"

So, he picked up the phone, called the chairman of the Humboldt school board (a banker, as I remember), and said something to this effect:

"Hello, Howard. How y'all doin' down home there in Humboldt today? Listen, Howard. I got one of your youngins' up here with me. Doin' a damn fine job he is, too. I'd like to keep him up here for a spell longer, but I need you to do me a favor. Would you call up the superintendent of the school and tell him to have Max's teachers send him his schoolbooks and all his assignments? I'll see to it that he does all the schoolboy work, and we'll send his homework back to 'em. Oh, and have 'em send up the tests also. I'll monitor his taking all those exams. Okay, Howard, I'm much obliged to ya. Oh, and by the by, I'll send him back down there to take his final exams."

And that is just what happened. Once we got the ball rolling on that new "chore," Fats said we needed to look at the other boxes that had to be checked off.

"Okay, Max. Next on the list is you need to go on off to college and get your degree."

"Actually, Sir, I haven't done much about going to college. Our family doesn't have a lot of money, and I haven't received any scholarships or financial aid offers, so I'm not sure I'm going to be able to do that until I make some money, or maybe I can go part time."

"Nope. That won't be necessary. So, here is lesson two in becoming a congressman. The government will pay for darn near anything. As a congressman, I have the right to appoint young men to go to the military academies. We need to get you ready to take all those qualifying physical and academic exams and fill out the applications to West Point, Annapolis, Air Force Academy, and Coast Guard Academy. Which one you think you would prefer if you could qualify?

"And by the way, that would also begin the process of filling another square toward becoming a congressman. The folks back home just love military folks. You put on that uniform with the medals and your having served and defended your country! That's a great record for the folks to consider when they step into that voting booth. Yep, I like where we're headed with all this!"

# Chapter 5

## AND SO IT BEGAN

MILITARY! WHAT DID I know about the military? Not much. I knew my dad had served during WWII. He was in the Calvary, riding mules to spread communication cables and wires. Mostly he trained horses, especially the Army officers' polo ponies. I'm pretty sure they don't have those jobs around anymore. Not a lot of polo ponies assigned to Army officers these days.

But come to think of it, that Air Force Academy was brand-new. I had read the article in *Life* magazine about the first class to graduate in 1959. Those pictures looked mighty enticing: a totally futuristic-looking architecture of all glass and aluminum; cadets dressed like Steve Canyon (the patriotic comic book fighter pilot hero) with their Eisenhower jackets, yellow sashes around the waist with a silver saber, hanging there, and patented leather brims on those beautiful hats. And maybe best of all, they were walking down those spiral staircases in the social center with beautiful ladies on their arms, into a gorgeous social hall. They were all getting ready to go to pilot training to become a "jet jockey."

*Wow, now that is something I might go for*, I thought.

Man oh man, did I have my priorities screwed up. Actually, I had the priorities "backasswards." One should go to the Air Force Academy first to become an officer in the U.S. Air Force. Second, to get one of the best educations available in the world. And third and last, because of the honor of being selected to attend. Not to mention the fact that they paid you to go there rather than you paying some university to attend.

But my final decision was not in that alignment. First, my ego was enormous to think that I might be selected to go to the Air Force Academy. Only one person in my immediate family had ever gone to college, nor had anyone from my part of Tennessee ever gone to an academy. Actually, I think maybe there was one man who went to West Point for a short period of time.

Second, I *did* want a great education, mainly so I could get a great job and hopefully have a great career. Doing what? I had not a clue. Maybe an optical physicist, whatever that was.

And third, maybe I would really like being an officer and flying airplanes. Sounded exciting and adventurous. I had only flown once, and that was in the back of a commercial airline on my way from Memphis to Washington.

Still, off I went to take the physical exams, and I began to study some material to help me pass the entrance exams. But Fats did not just choose one candidate to submit to each academy. He chose 10 applicants, and they competed against each other for that slot. It certainly was a smart political move, giving that many voters back home the chance to have their young relatives compete for the honor.

And guess how that turned out. Out of the 10, I was not selected by the Academy. Instead, one of Fats' 10 applicants was an excellent baseball player that the Academy wanted to recruit into their athletic program to compete on the intercollegiate baseball team. And he was selected.

However, I believe that very often, luck meets preparation.

As it turns out, not all of the final selectees chose to go to the Academy. There were other universities that wanted them and offered athletic scholarships to play on higher-ranked teams, and many universities wanted the scholars to join them. And at the ages of the candidates, there certainly was the choice between fraternity life and freedom, or no freedom and a summer of hazing and basic military physical and mental training. Additionally, Doolies (first-year students) were not allowed to go home for the first 13 months. Therefore, the Academy had a number of slots that went unfilled with the first choices. A pool of those who did qualify for entrance, but were not selected in this first round, for some of the reasons mentioned earlier, were put into the classification of "qualified alternates."

What a great day it was when I received that letter from the Academy admissions office informing me that I had been selected as a qualified alternate! Luck had met preparation. My ego was so overblown you couldn't have squeezed it into a gymnasium. My family and friends celebrated for weeks.

Then, off I went to start my university studies, my preparation to become an officer in the United States Air Force, and hopefully a "Leader of Character."

By the way: My local competitor, who was chosen over me because of his baseball athletic skills, broke his leg during his senior year of high school baseball spring training. The Academy wanted him badly enough that they made an exception and allowed him to come to the summer program anyway, even on crutches. Of course, he had the same treatment as the rest of us when it came to all the mental and emotional pressures, but because of the crutches, there were no physical punishments, physical training, nor any of the other drills that required total mobility.

The result was that he was able to observe what was happening to his "classmates." That was enough to persuade him that Vanderbilt University's baseball team and that campus in Nashville looked far more attractive than a full year of being a Doolie! He resigned before the summer had hardly begun. As I recall, the letter that he sent me later that summer included a picture of him on campus at Vanderbilt,

> Some Days the
> Dragon Wins!

arm around some good-looking young coed, and a beer in the other hand. The note said, "Wish you were here. Good luck."

I have a cartoon that shows an old knight who has obviously just been in a fight with a dragon. His helmet is all askew and pretty beaten up. His armor is bent badly, and his long thrusting spear is broken into several pieces. The caption says:

"Some Days the Dragon Wins!"

That is so true of many of my battles with the "dragons" that opposed me as I learned how to deal with many different pressures that the Air Force Academy brought to bear on my four-year journey to becoming an Air Force officer and pilot.

The first-class year at the Academy is known as the "Doolie" year, and the freshman cadets are known as "fourth-class Doolies." The origin of the word "doolie" is uncertain. The Greek word *doulos* means "slave" or "one who does menial tasks." But in the dictionary, its first definition is "a first-year cadet in the U.S. Air Force Academy."

The battles with the dragons (upperclassmen) started the minute you arrived for your first summer of basic training. Most of us arrived in summer civilian clothes, maybe Bermuda shorts and a nice golf shirt. When we got off the buses at the induction point below one of the dormitories, it was suddenly another world. We were told to stand at attention, chest up, chin in, eyes focused only straight ahead, shoulders back, hands held rigidly to your sides, heels together!

*Hey, wait a second. I just got here. I haven't even had a chance to look around or tour the campus. And who the hell are you guys in uniform anyway?*

Thoughts and questions were erased almost immediately. And any actions that did not fully comply with those instructions were met with additional commands, specifically:

"Drop to the ground, smack. Give me 25 pushups."

That lasted for about 30 minutes, as I recall. And then it was off to the barbershop to have your head shaved, the second step in the theory of basic summer. The program was designed to transfer a young man from the culture of his past civilian life and totally break his ego, stripping him of his character and his self-perceived hero image of the BMOC (Big Man On Campus) attitude. Then they'd start all over and build him back up mentally and physically to what was needed to survive the Academy and become an effective leader and officer in the United States Air Force.

The first year was tough. Very few Doolies, if any, would tell you differently, even those who had gone to military high schools or military prep schools. I was in awe of many of my classmates, both those who were in unbelievable condition with great physical skills and those who were scholars with intellectual levels that I had never seen. And that admiration continued throughout the four years and still exists to this day.

My thoughts were, "Where did you guys come from? Are there many like you on this planet!!!" But I wanted to compete, so I did the best I could do and somehow made it through the summer. There are always times when things get tough, and you really need someone to help you through, and I remember one point during that summer when I thought, *This is just crazy! I could be either on a scholarship to the University of Tennessee, Vanderbilt, or maybe even Ole Miss. Or maybe back in Washington with my Congressman!* I was so down that I wrote a letter home to my dad, saying that I was seriously thinking about calling it quits and heading home. I don't remember what reasons—excuses really—that I gave him other than I hated the hazing.

A week or so later, still hanging on, I received a reply letter from Dad. My stepmother had typed it on one of those old Royal portable typewriters, and there were many cross-outs and whiteouts, which meant to me that she and Dad had struggled with the right words.

"Son, you can come on home if that is what you are sure you want to do. You do need to think about what you are leaving behind, but equally important, think about this. As you walk down the sidewalks on Main Street in our little town of Humboldt, you'll meet lots of people that you know and even more that know you, are proud of your accomplishments, and know you're representing them at the Air Force Academy. They know that the military academies are really hard, that they are tough on you, especially the first year. They know that someone from Humboldt several years before you went off to West Point but didn't make it. He came home."

And then he said something that struck me deeply: motivational words that made me hold up my head.

"When you look them in the eyes and speak to them on Main Street, you will know that they are thinking, 'He couldn't make it. He wasn't tough enough to stay and finish. He gave up.' Will you be okay with that? Can you handle it?"

There was no way I was going to let my dad down because I knew he was thinking about his walking down Main Street, too. He knew exactly how I would have felt when I walked through what would have been a gauntlet of local folks. I still have Dad's letter. It is a prized possession and always a constant motivation, knowing that there are others there to help when you really need them. And that is never a good substitute for family when the going gets really tough.

**Thanks, Dad. I stayed.**

# *Chapter 6*

## ENTREPRENEURIAL LESSONS FROM THE U.S. AIR FORCE ACADEMY

ONE OF THE great aspects of the Academy is that you are immersed in leadership training. To learn to lead, you must first learn to follow. That was what the Doolie year was mostly about in the military training curriculum. From there, as you moved through the years, you were given more leadership opportunities and thus more chance to "practice" what you thought were the best leadership skills. And there was always an upperclassman to correct you when those skills were misapplied. During your last year, the senior year of being first classmen, there were officers who were there to observe and correct.

> To learn to lead, you must first learn to follow.

In addition to the "cadet chain of command" being a learning experience, there were other opportunities, including athletics. If you were qualified for an intercollegiate team or teams, you learned early on that you needed to follow, support your teammates, and lead when given the call. The same was also true for everyone else because participating in an intramural sports team was required every semester. They ranged from football, soccer, boxing, lacrosse, and my favorite, rugby.

I had many successes as a cadet at the Academy, but many of those came with some hard lessons. One of the reasons to consider involvement in intercollegiate athletics was to be assigned to the athletic training tables in the dining hall. The amount of hazing of Doolies underwent was considerably less there than on the regular dining tables. At the regular tables, Doolies were required to sit at attention and respond to questions such as "What are the performance characteristics of the F-100 Super Sabre" or "Spout off the third verse of the Star-Spangled Banner" or maybe "Give me General MacArthur's speech to West Point starting with 'On the fields of friendly strife are sown the seeds that on other days...'"

Often, I had left those tables and watched the waiters dump my barely touched plate into the waste bin. The athletic tables weren't easy either, but it was understood that the "jocks" that were Doolies needed to eat in order to compete at their maximum best.

Since I had lettered in basketball and track in high school, I was fairly certain that I could make one of the intercollegiate athletic teams as a "walk on," even though I had not been recruited. But it became obvious very quickly that competition was stiff, and it left me wondering where these jocks even came from!

Even though I had made the first team in basketball in my hometown, making even the JV team here seemed like a tough option. At 5'10" and not able to jump competitively with these guys, much less dunk the ball, it was apparent that this was going to be almost impossible. Yep! I didn't get past the first cut.

Next, I headed over to the fencing tryouts. No, I had never fenced before. Well, actually, I had, but it was barbed wire and fence posts on the farm. How many first-year cadets could possibly be going out for the fencing team? I had no idea what the differences were between an epee, a sabre, or a foil. But it turned out that several Doolies certainly did, as they had been on fencing teams or in clubs back home. But anyway, I gave it my best. I vividly remember the coach whacking away on my mask and shoulders with his sabre. Not only was my best not good enough, but repeatably making those lunges toward an opponent was a "stretch" on the groin muscles that I found unacceptable for one reason in particular. I suspect you well know what I mean.

*Pass on fencing. Now what's next?*

Having won the tennis doubles tournament in my small hometown, I decided that was the next team I would try out for. Seems the tryouts consisted of a singles match against one of your classmates. The singles champion from some region of Kentucky stared at me across the net. How good could he be? How about 6-0, 6-0, 6-0? Back to the squadron dining table and more Doolie knowledge and very little food.

But hang on a second. I had another athletic success in my background. I had won the 4-H Club summer camp diving contest around the age of 10. That was right after I had learned to swim. How tough could the diving competition be? And besides, I was running out of time *and* sports!

Hard to believe, I know, but I made the team (and it had nothing to do with winning a 1-meter diving contest at the age of 10 against a bunch of country boys who spent most of their youthful swimming experiences dog paddling in the dirty old cow ponds on their farms).

I really enjoyed this sport. I was taught that the way to enter the water perfectly vertical, making minimal splash on entry, was to take each dive to the very bottom of the pool. Since we had a 10-meter diving platform, the pool was very deep, leading to a lot of water pressure against the ears and into the nostrils when you went to and pushed from the bottom of the pool. But the platform was not for me. Spinning around rapidly from a height of 30-plus feet and hitting the water in all sorts of unusual positions was not something that appealed to me. So, I stayed at 1 and 3 meters.

It is hard to forget what learning some of those dives involved. From the 1-meter, I somehow mastered the one-and-a-half forward in a pike position. With eyes closed tightly, I managed the one-and-a-half inward dive without banging my forehead on the diving board. Now up to the 3-meter board. From that height, with the body spinning rapidly, if the body hits the surface of the water in a mostly flat position, it's like hitting concrete. Well, maybe not quite that bad, but it can badly blister the skin or worse.

As I was learning the two-and-a-half forward tuck, I would get lost in the spin and not know when to open up from the tuck to enter the water vertically. The coach had the answer. He said that he would call me out of the tuck position at just the right time, and I would rotate out of the tuck spin in time to enter properly. Sounded good. So, out to the end of the board I would go, take as big a spring off the board as I could, and go into a really tight, rapidly spinning tuck. Then the coach would yell, "Pop!" At that moment, I would untuck from spinning two-and-a-half times, and, sure enough, there was the water with me heading in headfirst and perfectly vertical with very little splash. Well, almost. It wasn't great, but it was okay.

"Okay, you got it. You now know the timing as to when to open up," the coach said, matter-of-factly.

"I'm not so sure, Coach. Call me out again, so I get the handle on this timing."

He agreed, and out to the end of the 3-meter I went, sprang as high as I could, tucked tightly, and spun rapidly. As soon as I heard the "pop," I opened up to a really nice entry into the water. Coach said that I looked fine, and for me to go at it again quickly while the timing was fresh in my mind. Muscle memory and all that. Standing on the approach end of the board, I yelled down to the coach and pleaded for just one more "assist" with a properly timed "pop." He was hard to convince, but finally, he agreed for the third and last time.

It felt good to finally know that I was close to mastering this skill. With a smile at the coach and my teammates, I hit the end of the board perfectly, sprang really high off the board (at least another meter), and entered the spin. Toward what should have been the end of the spinning, my doubts panicked me. *He is not going to yell. He thinks I have the timing down without him. I KNOW it is time to pop! Now!*

Right *AFTER* I made that decision and had opened up, I heard him yell. But I had already popped... too early! The impact of falling from more than four meters, combined with the speed of two-and-a-half rotations fully face forward was brutal. In fact, it momentarily knocked me out. Next thing I knew, the coach was in the pool pulling me out. The blisters and redness were immediately visible and damned painful.

Lesson learned. Trust your coach when advice is given. In fact, depend on it. The alternative option is to debate/discuss the advice and agree or modify BEFORE you act.

For several weeks after that, I was restricted to learning the timing of a two-and-a-half forward tuck from 1 meter, not 3.

But I also learned something else. Sometimes in life, you are given options, none of which are something you would choose if you had a choice. But if you do have that choice, consider at least a third option: *Don't do it!*

Taking those dives to the bottom of the pool not only created pressure on the ears, but also forced water through my nose into my sinuses. Eventually, I began to have serious sinus issues like headaches and difficulty breathing through my nose while sleeping as well as performing the strenuous and rigorous requirements for Doolies during the first 10 months. When I went to the doctor (flight surgeon) to have the sinus problems treated, he

> Sometimes in life, you are given options, none of which are something you would choose if you had a choice.

made it clear that I had two options. I could continue on the diving team, OR I could plan on going to pilot training in the Air Force. But the sinus issue could worsen, possibly permanently damaging my sinuses and preventing me from passing the qualifying medical exams to become a pilot.

Yes, Sir! Back to the regular tables in the dining hall and off the training tables. But my athletic endeavors, in addition to intramural sports, were not over. I eventually made the all-star rugby team. It was a great sport that I have enjoyed for many years, though not so many as a participant. I even went to the World Cup in New Zealand and watched the All Blacks win the championship over Ireland. What a game!

During an intra-squad practice match, one of the football players that switched to rugby for the spring was on the opposition squad for this practice. He was a starting lineman on the varsity football team, and at the time, I recall I weighed about 160 pounds, stood 5'10," *AND GAVE UP CLOSE TO 100 POUNDS AND 5 INCHES TO HIM.* Somehow, he got loose from our defense and was headed for the goal line with a huge head of steam.

The only thing left was for him to just get around me. I leaned forward, weight on my toes, ready to move left or right as he tried to maneuver around me. Problem was, he did not zig or zag in either direction; he just steamrolled over me. I woke up in the ambulance on the way to the hospital. Turns out, I got myself a serious concussion!

In comes the same flight surgeon that had advised me to drop from the diving team.

"Now what's the problem, Max?"

"Just a little rugby bang-up with a fellow teammate who was somewhat larger than me," I said.

"No more rugby for you, or you will be making your way toward becoming a 'ground pounder' and not a pilot."

"But Sir! I have finally found my sport. Don't ground me from playing now, please."

Finally, after what felt like ages and what appeared to be some deep thought, he said, "Okay. But on one condition."

*Great*, I think. "What is the condition?"

"You can only play one position."

*Okay, but what position on a rugby team is a safe haven for avoiding concussions?*

"And what position will you allow me to play?"

"Coach. That's your only option."

And that answer ended my rugby days.

Another lesson learned. When a medical professional gives you good advice, you had best take it. Even though these dedicated doctors are not always right, they more often than not advise the more conservative solution, looking out for the good long-term benefits.

And, in addition to lessons learned from the "chain of command" and athletics, there were many other opportunities in which I learned to lead as well as enjoy the extracurricular activities. And since I had been often labeled as a "jack of all trades and master of none," I sought out numerous other adventures. The Air Force Academy student magazine was called *The Talon*. I was chosen to work on that magazine, first as layout editor, and eventually as the editor. This leadership role led to my being elected as the vice president of the Intercollegiate Press Association (and some fantastic "boondoggle trips" across the nation).

Some of the greatest extracurricular activities came with being chosen as the resident of the Cadet Officers' Club for my first-class year. This was really a hoot! Our club was given the right to use the downstairs area of the Antlers Hotel in downtown Colorado Springs. This facility was next to the outdoor swimming pool and

> When a medical professional gives you good advice, you had best take it.

had plenty of room for dancing, music, and lots of beer kegs for our Saturday night functions. All great leadership experiences, of course.

When you are part of something great, and it ends abruptly, that doesn't mean the effort ended in failure. One of my roommates (we changed roommates each semester) was a great guitarist. He had studied guitar with the famous folk singer, Joan Baez, and he could pick the strings magnificently. He would pull out his guitar, and we would sing some of the folk songs that were popular in the late 50s and early 60s, songs by the The New Christy Minstrels, Joan Collins, The Kingston Trio, Peter, Paul and Mary, The Irish Rovers, and many others.

So, I bought a Sears Silvertone guitar from an upperclassman for $10. My roommate taught me the chords and how to accompany him, and once I learned, he picked while I mostly strummed. Our classmates would hear us singing in the room, and since restrictions were so rigid about what you could do and where you could go during "Call to Quarters" (CQ, a.k.a. study time), we soon ended up going to the shower room. The shower room wasn't considered a restricted area during CQ… and it also had nice acoustics.

One of the gentlemen who joined us had a beautiful tenor voice, AND he wrote home to have his grandfather's banjo sent out to him. It was a beautiful, old, ivory-inlaid banjo. Next, a classmate joined us who had a wonderful baritone voice and played accompanying instruments from the tambourine to bongo to bass fiddle.

We were finally able to mix it up pretty good and quickly became known as "The Pikesmen." We were invited to a ton of private parties that the cadets' dates would host at their homes. We loved it: free booze, lots of ladies, and great music. It often sounded like we were having a real "hootenanny"!

Well, the Academy eventually found out about us—the shower group singing and the "wild parties." We were called to meet with an officer in the Academy's Headquarters Building (the Head Shed).

*Now what! We have not busted any regulations. Or have we? How can they ding us for playing music in the shower room?*

Turns out the officer we were scheduled to meet was the Information Officer, or as we feather merchants called him, the Director of PR (public relations) for the Academy. He wanted to buy us blue Air Force Academy blazers then book us for shows at the Academy and community events around Colorado! His purpose was to attempt to create a softer image for the Academy from the public's perspective. Our first booking? The beautiful resort in Colorado Springs, The Broadmoor Hotel. We performed before the National Music Underwriters Association's national convention. And we were informed that one of the attendees at the convention wanted to sign us to record an album!

**"The Harder You Fall, The Higher You Bounce!"**

But the big bounce didn't last too long this time. While the military JAG department was going through all the negotiations, our lead guitarist was dismissed from the Academy. That left us as a trio. *Okay, so what! Big deal!* The Kingston Trio did just fine, as did The Chad Mitchell Trio and Peter, Paul and Mary.

But truth be known, we just were not as good without our professional guitarist and his beautiful voice. We still made some parties, but no community appearances—and certainly no album contract. Later, we lost our banjo player. That left us as a duet. Imagine a strumming-only amateur guitar player and bongo/bass fiddle/tambourine player. Needless to say, the days of "The Pikesmen" were over.

Sometimes, when you have climbed the mountain and reached what you thought was the pinnacle of success, in order to climb the next mountain to even *greater* success, you first must go down into the valley. Reaching the top is always joyful and exciting, a time for celebrating the journey and enjoying the rewards. And most often, the slide down into the valley is terribly painful, depressing, and financially costly. That is why a strong entrepreneur must want success badly. And a serial entrepreneur knows that there are always mountains to climb, and the valley is where you start a new journey.

Another really interesting leadership lesson was learned through my last year at the Academy. A second-class cadet (junior year) in my squadron and I were good friends. He was an outstanding cadet. His high school sweetheart and he had become engaged, and she had moved into the Colorado Springs area to be near him. Only first-class cadets were allowed to have cars at the Academy, which I did, but this particular friend of mine was not yet allowed to have a car. He would often knock on my dormitory door and ask if he and his fiancée could double date with me in my car. I don't remember ever telling him no.

That year, the cadet wing was called upon to go to Washington, D.C., to march in the parade honoring the death of John F. Kennedy. So, we were piled into planes and flown over. The weather was so bad (freezing cold, snow, and sleet) that some of the planes with the cadets never made it into the area. Those of us who did, however, suffered mightily. But my double-dating friend's father (General Ryan) just happened to be the Commander of the Strategic Air Command and the future Chief of Staff of the

Air Force, and we were invited over to his home. *Wow! What an opportunity—to meet the chief warrior in the Air Force.*

As we sat in his living room, enjoying a couple of "adult beverages," this tough, gruff four-star general got around to asking me what I was going to do when I graduated next year. He wanted to know if I had been given my first assignment as a newly commissioned second lieutenant. And of course, he said, "I assume you are headed for pilot training."

Four Stars were telling me that the only course of action to become a success in the Air Force was for me to get my pilot's wings.

"Yes, Sir, I am going to go to pilot training right after graduation and commissioning. There is a new pilot training program, and I have signed up for that. I assume, Sir, that you are familiar with that new program?"

"Actually, I have not been briefed. Why don't you fill me in?"

"Yes, Sir. Well, instead of going to the normal pilot training programs, we will go to fixed-wing basic training at Randolph AFB. We will fly the T-28's. Following Basic there, we move to Stead AFB in Reno to transition into helicopters. After finishing that class, we will receive our wings as Air Force pilots and be assigned to an operational squadron that has missions that require helicopters. I am really looking forward to it."

I thought the general was going to choke and spit his drink all over the room. I'll omit the salty language that came out of his mouth, but it went something like this:

"What? You are going to go into choppers? You have just ruined your entire career as an officer in my United States Air Force! Helicopters?! What the bloody hell were you thinking? You will never make it past the rank of captain. You need to learn to fly all the jets and bombers, just like I did. Or maybe transports and refuelers. For God's sake, Mister, what have you done? You will never make it up the ranks of AF officers who have the experience required to be promoted to field grad and general officers. Egads, and my son said you were super sharp. Son, fix me another drink!"

Well, what would you think? The number-one officer in the Air Force has just told me my Air Force career was already over, ruined before I was even an officer? Ouch!

As I shrunk down into my chair and gulped down the rest of the Scotch I was drinking, I guess I felt like crawling into a hole. But instead, I reminded my friend that maybe we needed to rejoin our squadron mates at the barracks at the AF base where we were staying. Here I was, a lowly cadet and not even a lieutenant yet, and the chief of staff on the United States Air Force had just told me in a lot of four-letter words that my career is already over.

So, this is what I said to myself: *Not all the advice given by those who have succeeded greatly is good advice for all. And I will buckle down and prove to that four-star general that he could be wrong.*

> Not all advice that you receive is perfectly suitable for you.

I think I did. As did some of my helicopter classmates. Two of us were selected as Distinguished Graduates later in our careers, and one became not only a fixed-wing test pilot but had three missions into space as an astronaut, including commanding two of the missions. Others went on to successful military careers as well as distinguished professional careers in civilian life.

I did not take the chief's advice but instead went through the new program and learned to fly helicopters. I have zero regrets. As you will continue to read, the experiences and contributions to the Air Force all worked out well and are something that I take great pride in. To be chosen for

> I will not doubt my dreams,
> but rather will doubt
> my doubts.

that singular honor of the 2010 Distinguished Graduate is the top highlight of my extremely diverse career accomplishments.

The lesson, I suppose, is that not all advice that you receive, even from those whose careers are historically notable, is perfectly suitable for you. I was perhaps listening to that different drummer.

You alone can choose what direction you go. Maybe there's somewhere down deep in you that's saying, "Here is the path I will follow, and I *will* achieve my dreams. **I will not doubt my dreams, but rather will doubt my doubts.**"

I have always remembered that when I receive advice, especially that which I have not sought, I will weigh it carefully. It just may not be what I need.

And now, I say the same to you.

# Chapter 7

## IT WAS CADET BONEHEAD

THERE WERE LOTS of lessons learned at the Academy. But the one that has served me best came with a heavy load of emotional grief.

My last semester at the Academy, I was the Squadron Commander for "Fightin' Fourth Squadron." Each of the 24 squadrons had an officer that was responsible for monitoring and assisting the leadership in each squadron. Their title was Air Office Commander (AOC). Unfortunately, the AOC assigned to our squadron was a Marine aviator with the rank of major. He did not want to be at the Air Force Academy. He was sure it was a very bad blotch on his career progression in the Marine Corp. He didn't like nor appreciate the Air Force organization, including the squadron that I commanded. He chose to show off his preferred Marine Corps training and insist that we learn his Marine ways.

One morning after reveille, with everyone reporting "present" in the hallways, I went back into my quarters to get dressed for assembly and leading the squadron in marching to breakfast. I was standing at the sink and had just lathered up for shaving. There was a pounding knock at my door, and when I opened it, there stood the Marine, fully uniformed in his spit-and-polish appearance.

He yelled to me, "Mr. James, do you know what is going on in this squadron?!"

Not happy to see him there while I was rushing to make assembly and lead my squadron to breakfast, I replied in a much-too-sarcastic manner.

"Yes, Sir. The three S's." (For the unwashed, that means showering, shaving, and… well, you can guess the third.)

"Follow me. Now!"

I wiped the shaving cream off my face with a towel, threw on my uniform bathrobe and slippers, and marched down the hallway behind him.

Standing in an alcove in front of one of the cadet rooms was one of the Doolies in my squadron, dressed in full, Class-A blue uniform. He was standing at attention with his rifle at "present arms" position and sweating like he had just had a sauna.

The Marine AOC asked him, "Mr. Cadet, what have you been doing here at this position?"

"Sir, I have been doing rifle pushups!"

Now, let me clarify here: A rifle pushup is a physical punishment that was not allowed. After several pushups, when the arms might begin to tremble, it was likely that the hands on top of the rifle, which was lying on its vertical edge, would become unbalanced and roll over, smashing the fingers and knuckles. That was strike one! Rifle punishments would result in the upperclassman who gave them out receiving a major "write-up" that came with walking tours and being restricted to quarters.

Strike two was the fact that physical punishments were not allowed to be given during the period starting 30 minutes before a meal.

"And who instructed you to do these rifle pushups?"

"Sir, it was Cadet Third-Class (a sophomore) Bonehead." (Of course, that was *my* name for the third classman.)

"And where is Cadet Bonehead?"

"Sir, I do not know!"

At this point, the AOC reached over and gently opened the door to the third classman's room. And there was "Bonehead" lying in his bed, taking a snooze.

Strike three! All physical punishments had to be monitored and supervised by an upperclassman.

The marine turned to me, and with a big ugly grin on his face, said, "Well, Mr. James, I suspect we will be seeing you a little later in the day. You can post back to your room now."

So, I went back to my quarters, finished shaving, and got dressed. I marched the squadron to breakfast, came back to my room, and headed off to my first class.

I knew it was going to be a rotten day.

There I was, sitting in an advanced math class of some sort, with my mind a million miles away. I couldn't help wondering when the next shoe was going to drop and how heavy it might be. Maybe it would be a "class-two" punishment, which would entail the loss of a couple days off base leave and privileges, and perhaps even walking a few tours. Marching tours, dressed in full uniform, carrying a combat rifle, back and forth in the same line for an hour had to be the biggest waste of time one can imagine—*especially* when you only have a few hours of rest, entertainment, or maybe catching up on some classwork.

*Surely*, I thought, *it would not possibly result in a "class-three" punishment!* That would entail hours and hours of tours, plus being confined to your room for weeks... or even months. Naw! It really wasn't my fault that Cadet Bonehead broke two or three little old regulations. Hell, I wasn't even there. I was simply doing what was required of me, e.g., preparing to be fully in uniform and on time for my duties to lead my squadron as we marched to breakfast.

And then it started. There was a knock on the classroom door by a Chief Warrant Officer (CWO), who was an aide to the Commandant of Cadets, a one-star Brigadier General who was responsible for all cadet activities and military training.

"Excuse me, Sir, but is there a Cadet James in your class?" The CWO asked the captain who was conducting the class.

"Let's see. Yes, I believe there is. Cadet James?"

"Here, Sir."

At that point, the CWO said, "Sir, the Commandant is requesting Mr. James to join him in his office."

Now at this point I'm beginning to panic. *The Commandant? No, not him!* He was a former hard-ass troubleshooter from the Strategic Air Command with a reputation of "take no prisoners." He thought the only way to train future lieutenants in the Air Force was to grind 'em down 24/7. And to add insult to injury, I had already had an unpleasant experience with him. This Brigadier General already had me in his sights for the next shoot down.

You see, I had been on the staff of the cadet magazine, *The Talon*, for three years. And in my senior year (first-class year), I was the editor. *The Talon* was very popular among the cadets, as it featured articles about our intercollegiate teams, star athletes, and other outstanding men; cartoons drawn by cadets depicting the humor of living at the often-called "Rocky Mountain Monastery" or the "Blue Zoo"; cadet-authored short stories, and a series on "Squadron Sweethearts," which were pictures of cadet girlfriends and/or fiancées competitively selected by each squadron and submitted to *The Talon* for publishing. But the most popular section of the magazine was the center section, which contained two pages of jokes.

Back in the days of 1963 and 1964, risqué jokes were far less offensive than today. The best source of jokes that were perhaps a bit "off-color" were the other university magazines, particularly those from the Texas Aggies. While I was vice-president of the Rocky Mountain Collegiate Press Association, I had met some of their staff, who encouraged me to reprint any of their humor that I chose.

*The Talon* had a total circulation of over 5,000. Parents of cadets were always hungry for any information about what was happening at their sons' school, especially the Doolies' parents since they were not allowed to go home from the Academy for the first 13 months. I never had a single complaint from anyone inside or outside of the Academy.

That is, until one day, the publisher of *The Talon* called me to tell me that the Commandant had wandered down to the loading dock which handled the inbound shipment of the magazines, and he had pulled an "early" copy for himself. That resulted in his calling the publisher and giving them holy hell about the "dirty filthy jokes" in the latest edition. He also ordered them to come pick up the 5,000-plus magazines. I had worked with this publisher for three years and had an excellent relationship with him.

"So Max, what do you want to do? I can't reprint 5,000 magazines, and you don't have the money in your budget anyway! I think if we try to tear out the two center pages, that will reduce the magazine by four facing pages, meaning that you will lose whatever is printed in front of and behind the joke pages, so that won't work. And, of course, you are going to catch hundreds of angry letters from your subscribers. Good thing you don't have a phone!"

"Crap! Let me mull it over for a day or so. I'll call you back. In the meantime, try to do nothing. And leave the magazines on the loading dock."

I sneaked a copy of the magazine from the loading dock and must have stared at those jokes for hours. What was so wrong with the three jokes that the Commandant was so irate about? Nothing that I could find that would justify trashing the full magazine.

Then I had an epiphany. *What if I could somehow just make those three jokes disappear?* Obviously, I couldn't erase them, nor can I get the whole *Talon* staff together, scissors in hand, and carefully cut them out, since that would cut out what was on the back pages behind the jokes. I tried that. And there was no tool I had in order to blacken them out. It either punched through the page or just didn't hide the written words.

But what if I taped over them? *With what, though?* Scotch Tape wouldn't work. But how about rolls of thick black tape? Sometimes creative and innovative solutions do immediately appear… but they may require a radical change of plans or even modifying the product.

So, all *The Talon* staff gathered together with their scissors. The exact size of the—shall we dignify the objection by the Commandant and call them "offensive" jokes—was templated, all three in separate sections or on separate pages of the magazine. Then we took rolls and rolls of this black tape, cut little pieces to match the size of the jokes, and pasted them over each of the three jokes in over 5,000 magazines.

Without a second review by the Commandant, we distributed *The Talon* to the full list of cadets and subscribers. And, of course, the first thing the cadets throughout the Wing (that includes all squadrons, which back then would amount to a little over 2,000 cadets) did was grab some form of steamer, e.g., an iron, and steam the black tape off the page in an attempt to see what was so offensive, funny, or risqué that it had to be covered.

*Whoops.*

So, for the next issue of *The Talon*, I printed black blotches in the shapes of jokes with the caption, "Let's see you steam these off."

Interestingly enough, I did not hear from the Commandant about this little creative maneuver around his instructions to the publisher and, thereby, to me.

Well, at least not until that day I was "invited" up to his office to discuss Cadet Bonehead's putting the Doolie through unauthorized, poorly timed, unsupervised physical punishments. I was wondering if he would happen to remember that I was the editor of *The Talon* and gotten away with a bit of skullduggery trickery, and—in my mind at least—outmaneuvered him.

The CWO was accompanying me down the hallway when he asked me to stop.

"Max, the Com is really angry today. I'm doing my best to stay out of his way, so when you get there, I plan on shutting his door and leaving you two alone. But before you go up to the 'Head Shed' (the building where the Commandant's office was located), the Group Air Officer Commander for your squadron (a Lt. colonel who reported directly to the Commandant), wants you to stop by his office."

This day was just getting worse and worse. This was the officer that the Marine AOC directly reported to. There was no doubt that he had gotten a full report from the Marine.

Lt. Col. Ashmore greeted me with a returned salute and asked me to take a seat. He looked like he was deeply contemplating something— maybe my being in terrible trouble was impacting him negatively. What he told me was that the CWO was correct, and the general was indeed in a foul mood. He said I should just imagine I was back three-plus years as a Doolie, stand fully at attention, run my chin in, and try to just answer "Yes, Sir" and "No, Sir" and "No excuse, Sir." He also instructed me to come back to his office when the general had finished with me. And with a serious grin, he said, "Good luck!"

As I posted into the Commandant's office and gave the best salute I knew how (after all, I had practiced that salute for four years), he began to talk. Actually, I don't think anyone would have characterized it as "talk." Screaming is probably too drastic a description also, but I suppose yelling is accurate!

"Mr. James, you have obviously lost control of your squadron! One of your men committed three punishable offenses against another cadet. That cadet who broke these regulations put that Doolie in harm's way. And that cadet is your personal responsibility. He is under your chain of command. As the Squadron Commander, it is your job to ensure that all of your men are protected. You have a chain of command under your leadership who are all responsible for those under their command."

And then his voice became even louder as he hollered, "Do you understand me?!"

I did, and I replied appropriately with the only answer acceptable: "Yes, Sir!" But I was not very loud.

"What did you say, James? I'm not sure I understood you!"

"Yes, Sir," I again replied, but this time somewhere just below a yell.

"In your position as a Squadron Commander, you have broken several regulations yourself. And that demands that you pay for your incompetence." The general then yelled for his "assistant"—the CWO who had escorted me from the classroom—to get into his office and look through the Cadet Regulations Manual to find the appropriate regulations and punishments that applied to my situation. The CWO began to leaf quickly through the pages but had no luck finding the regulations the Commandant was needing.

With very little patience, something that this Commandant had never been known for, he began yelling at the CWO.

"What is your problem? Give me the damn manual!"

He also had no success in finding regulations that applied to my situation. The reason is, there were none! Failure in a cadet command position, except in illegal situations, was punishable by reduction in rank. With his anger increasing with every page he turned, unsuccessfully finding what he wanted, he finally threw the manual back at the CWO and said, "Never mind! Here are your punishments!"

"As a start, you are hereby reduced from the rank of Cadet Lt. Colonel to Cadet First Class. Furthermore, you are stripped of all 'privileges and rewards' you have earned by your having received the designations of Dean's List, Commandant's List, and Superintendent's List. That means you are now restricted to your cadet quarters, and I want you to immediately move out of your room in the squadron area. In fact, find an area that is isolated from the entire cadet wing and move there. No roommate!

"You will not leave that room except for required academic and athletic classes and events, meals, and other wing formations. In fact, you will now not only not march as the Squadron Commander at the head of your squadron, but you will march as the last man at the very back of your squadron. And you will turn in your Cadet First-Class sabre and be issued a rifle like all the lower classes of cadets carry for all marching events. And this reduction in rank and command will be announced to the entire cadet wing at this evening's meal formation in the dining hall. Now, Cadet James, are we clear?"

"Yes, Sir."

And with that I offered a rather sorry salute, did an about-face, and left his office. My uniform was soaking wet, and my hair was starting to curl. And now I had to face the music again in the AOC's office, as ordered. *Would this day ever end?*

As I returned to the Group AOC's office and was escorted in, I saluted him and, at his request, took a seat.

"Well, Max, how did it go? Not too well, I would assume?"

So, I filled him in on the session with the Commandant, relaying as best I could remember all of the verbal punishments that had been laid upon me.

"Pretty rough," he said. "I want to share a personal story of one of my experiences when I was a Squadron Commander, as you were, in World War II."

"When I was in the China-Burma-India Theater in WWII, I was a Squadron Commander of a fighter squadron. Two new wet-behind-the-ears lieutenants, fresh out of pilot training, were assigned to my squadron. After one of their early missions, instead of immediately landing (preserving scarce fuel and maintenance supplies), they decided to practice a few aerial combat maneuvers, a friendly dogfight. When they landed, I called them on the carpet and chewed them up one side and down the other. But a few missions later, they repeated their air combat antics. They flew into each other, a midair crash, destroying two critically important fighter aircraft and ending the lives of two important warriors.

"As a result of that happening in my squadron, I was recalled from the war zone to the Pentagon, never to experience aerial combat again. And that is the reason that I have this silver leaf on my shoulder and not something of higher rank." And then he gave me this leadership principle: You

> You can delegate authority, but you cannot delegate responsibility.

can delegate authority, but you cannot delegate responsibility.

That is the most important lesson I learned at the Academy in all of my four years there. And I have used that principle in all of my companies and other leadership positions I have had. Sometimes the lessons we learn are painful ones. It was humiliating to have my demotion and punishments read to all of the cadet wing. However, that pain was well worth the rewards that this principle has brought me throughout my career.

Oh, and by the way, Lt. Col Ashmore was able to reinstate all my privileges as a First Classman on the various achievement lists. My only responsibilities for the rest of the second semester were to pass academics and take my privileges earned by achieving the requirements to be recognized on the Dean's List, the Commandant's List (isn't that ironic!), and the Superintendent's List.

This great mentor also reinstated me to Cadet Lieutenant Colonel for all the June Week graduation ceremonies and placed me back on the First Group Staff.

That reinstatement also allowed me to receive the "Eagle and Fledglings" award as a Distinguished Graduate at the Graduation Award Ceremony.

# Chapter 8

## START 'ER UP

FROM THE TIME I left the Air Force Academy until the time I volunteered to serve in Vietnam, there were great lessons to be learned, many that would serve me later in my civilian life as a corporate employee and especially as an entrepreneur.

After a 30-day vacation (and honeymoon), I reported to Randolph AFB in San Antonio, TX, for basic pilot training. It was another program where a lot of really hard studying was necessary, and you couldn't procrastinate. The day after studying, you were likely to need to know that information in order to answer questions from your flight instructor in his preflight briefing. And, of course, it was critical to continue learning how to successfully keep the aircraft in the air!

I prepared diligently, which often required burning the midnight oil. Serious preparation is always necessary if the operation is to succeed. I learned that early on in pilot training.

I was the first to fly solo in my class. Great reward. But I was also the first to flunk a flight-check ride, given to me not by my flight instructor, but by the squadron commander! I wasn't properly prepared, probably because I was playing basketball on one of the base teams. Even worse, I later broke my ankle playing basketball and had a cast up to my mid-shin. It's impossible to fly with a cast molded around your ankle and leg, so I got myself behind by not focusing on the major task, which was learning to fly the plane. However, with extra hard work and focus, I was still able to catch up and graduate from basic pilot training.

My next assignment was to finish up my pilot training in helicopters at Stead AFB in Reno, NV. The training that I had finished in fixed-wing aircraft qualified me to obtain my civilian pilot's license. I just needed to take (and pass) the written exam at an FAA office.

I had some vacation leave built up, so I headed to my hometown of Humboldt, TN, with plans to go to the FAA offices in Memphis, pass the exam, pick up my pilot license, and spend a couple of weeks flying a small private plane around the Humboldt area where I had grown up on the farm.

Well, there was one small problem: I flunked the ground school written exam! I couldn't believe it. After all the flying and military flight school classes, how could I flunk?! The instructor graded my exam and explained that I had missed two too many questions, showing me the ones I missed (and the right answers). *Hmmm. If I could just take the test again, now that I know the correct answers to just those two questions, I would have my license.*

"When can I take the exam again?" I asked.

"You have to wait 30 days before retesting, or earlier if you go to an approved ground school."

Problem was, I didn't have 30 days before my vacation leave expired, and I had to be in Reno.

"Where is there one of the ground schools that teach the information?"

"Actually, we have one right here at this location."

"How long do these schools last in order to finish and qualify for retaking the exam?"

"There are two options," he said. "You can sit through classes that are taught by qualified instructors, or you can go through the material by a workbook and slides. It would take several hours to go through the course by slides."

"In how many hours could one quickly go through all the material?"

"Best case, probably five hours."

"What time do you close?"

"About six hours from now."

"Good. Where can I enroll and get started?"

I went into a small classroom with the slide projector and workbook. I didn't feel like I really needed to review every single slide and page. After all, I just wanted to have someone sign off that I had taken the course. I only needed to take the exam again, answer those two questions I missed, pick up my license, and head back home.

I filled out all the necessary stuff in the workbook, looked at every single slide, and about four hours later, took the exam again. *This should be a snap. Answer all the questions just as I had before, except correct the two answers I missed.*

They gave me the fresh exam, and with a headache that was on the side of nausea, I removed the security tape on the exam book, opened it up, and... *No! This can't be! A totally different exam!*

The headache quickly spread to my gut.

But somehow, I passed this one with "room to spare" on the passing margins!

I got in the car, rushed to a pharmacy, bought a bottle of very strong over-the-counter painkillers, and slowly and carefully drove a couple of hours back to Humboldt. I don't think I felt the joy of being a licensed commercial single-engine pilot until the next morning!

Next, it was time to get checked out in one of the small planes at the little airport in Humboldt. Looking forward to some "civilian" flying without the constant sharp supervision of the military instructor pilots, I headed out to start flying.

I parked the car and walked over to the Quonset hut-type hangar, where it looked like the available planes for rent were parked. There was a man dressed in an old straw farmer's hat, standing next to a Piper plane, seemingly working on the engine. He was dressed in a wrinkled khaki shirt and trousers, holding a greasy rag in one hand and a wrench in the other.

I walked up to him, and as he turned around, I noticed that he only had one eye. Now, I don't mean he was just blind in one eye; I mean there was only one eye in his head. Where the second eye should have been, there was only an empty socket; no false eye in place. I probably looked a bit uneasy—if not totally shocked.

I recovered my composure and asked, "Is there a licensed instructor pilot here today? I am an Air Force pilot that just received my wings. I also just passed the ground school and received my commercial pilot's license. I grew up here in Humboldt, and I would like to get checked out in a small plane so I can fly around the countryside and take some of my friends and relatives up for a few rides."

"That's not a problem," he said. "This plane that I am working on right here is ready to fly and available for renting."

"Great!" I replied. "How can I get in touch with an IP (Instructor Pilot)?"

"That's not a problem either. I'll be your instructor."

*What? Are you kidding me? A one-eyed instructor, wearing a farmer's straw hat and greasy khakis? This guy is going to teach me to fly an airplane I've never been in?*

"When do ya wanna get checked out?" he asked.

With what I recall was a very nervous answer, I stuttered, "I guess as soon as possible."

"Okay, help me roll this Piper out of the hangar, and we'll crank 'er up and get you in the air."

"You mean right now?"

"Yep, just let me just wash off this grease."

After we rolled the little Piper out onto the concrete, he walked around the plane looking for God knows what, and he said to me, "Okay, get in and let's go."

*Wait a minute! What about a real preflight, walk-around checklist? And don't I need to be taught what is important to check before we get in the plane?*

Apparently, he didn't think so. Okay well, he was the licensed instructor pilot, so I got in.

"Okay, Max, so start 'er up."

Being used to a multipage interior cockpit preflight checklist, I had no idea what was really next but certainly didn't expect "Start 'er up." Problem was a simple one: I didn't know how to start the engine. I looked at the dash but didn't see anything that I thought was useful for starting the plane. He reached over, pointed to a key in the ignition, and said, "Just turn the key clockwise, you know, like you do in your car."

I gotta tell you, that was an embarrassing moment. Really? That simple?

So I did as he said. And just like that, the motor started, and the propeller began turning. Oh yeah, and the wheels also started moving. My second instruction on "flying" the plane came next.

"Put your feet on the brakes. You know, like you do in your car."

That's it? That's all we need to do to start this plane and taxi out to the runway?

Just before I managed to taxi this new "bird" onto the runway, he told me to stop and check the mag (magnetometer). Fantastic! I was finally going to be able to do something that I knew how to do in the cockpit of an airplane.

After checking the mag, I was instructed to "take the runway." Since there was no control tower, there was no one to ask permission to take the "active runway" to check whether or not there were other aircraft in the pattern or anything else. Just "take the runway, Max."

I managed to taxi this little Piper onto the runway, centered it up in the right direction, and put on the brakes again.

"Okay, let's go," he said. Having been shown how to "rev up" the engine, I throttled it up to the maximum.

"Now, take your feet off the brakes. C'mon, let's get airborne!"

Down the runway we went. I had both hands on the yoke, and it began to push back at me as we picked up speed. This didn't seem just right, so I yelled over the sound of the engine, "What is the takeoff speed?" (The ground speed at which the aircraft can safely lift off the runway.) With a frustrated look on his face, he said, "It was about 20 knots ago! Are we going to fly or just taxi down the runway? Quit pushing on the yoke. Let's get airborne!"

Amazing what I didn't know about this plane, and yet suddenly, we were flying.

"Okay, Max, there are just a couple of things we need to accomplish before you can go solo. We need to practice recovering from a stall." (This is when the airspeed slows so that the plane is no longer able to fly, as there is insufficient lift over the wings.)

This I knew how to do, and as he slowed the plane down into the stall stage, I demonstrated that I knew how to maneuver into a full recovery.

The next thing that I had to do was to demonstrate that I could safely land the plane. He made the first landing, talking me through the various important factors to "get 'er down on the ground."

Next, it was my turn, and apparently, I satisfied him (and me).

"Okay, legally, you have to make four more of these, and then the plane is yours to fly solo. You have enough fuel to fly for about two hours. So, let's get these four landings out of the way."

*That's it? That's all I have to do to fly solo?* The second and third landings went fine. The fourth landing also seemed to be fine, except suddenly, as the plane touched down, there was a pretty loud boom, and the aircraft made a hard right turn. I was able to control the runout and stopped the plane on the runway.

"Damn, I was afraid that was gonna happen! That right tire's been gettin' awfully bare."

*You thought that was going to happen? And you were going to send me solo? This may not be as great a summer as I had hoped.*

"Taxi it over into the grass there and shut 'er down. I'll have to call Sears and Roebuck over in Memphis and order a new tire. I don't keep spare tires in stock here. They'll put it on a Greyhound bus, and it oughta be here by about 4 o'clock this afternoon. So, come on back then, and we'll get that last landing in, and off ya can go."

And that's just what happened. Late afternoon, we got in the plane with its new tire. I started it up, taxied it out, revved 'er up, sped down the runway, and circled around to line up for my fifth landing. This one was satisfactory with the one new tire (I had a good look at the other tire before we took off). My instructor said to pull over and stop at the other end of the runway and let him out. I did so, and he said, "Okay, she's all yours. Have a great time."

Wow! It had taken me many weeks to get qualified to go solo in a fixed-wing AF plane, and here I was now, taking to the sky after a very few hours of very limited instruction in a new plane. But I did one of the things he had told me extremely well: I had a GREAT TIME!

My grandfather, who was about 85 at the time, had never flown. He showed up at the airport, gave me $5 for gas, and said, "Max, how 'bout you fly me over my farms and all the areas where I grew up?" What a thrill that was for me—and apparently for him! We flew for over an hour at a high altitude that allowed him to see all the areas that he had only known from the ground, as well as altitudes that were very low so he could closely see his home and those of some of his sons and friends. In fact, he enjoyed it so much, we went up more than once!

Then came my direct family: my parents and my young brother and sister. My dad particularly enjoyed being able to see all the lands where he had lived as a boy and built his farms and homes. What a great feeling when he said, "Son, I'm proud of you."

I must admit that I enjoyed taking up my old high school buddies and "showing off," even giving them a few unexpected and surprising thrills.

But summer ended, and it was time to get to my next assignment: helicopter training. Off I went to Stead AFB in Reno, NV.

What an experience it was to move from fixed-wing flying to rotary-wing flying. Some have described hovering in place in a helicopter as being like balancing a pogo stick on top of a basketball. Every time you move one of the controls, all of the others must be moved to maintain position. At least, that's the way it was in my first assigned helicopter, the H-19. This was a reciprocal or piston engine that was housed directly behind and above the cockpit. The noise level was practically deafening. In fact, many of those who flew the H-19 have suffered hearing loss and other hearing ailments such as tinnitus, which I deal with to this day. It is a constant ringing and hissing in both ears.

> Hovering in place in a helicopter as being like balancing a pogo stick on top of a basketball.

After becoming fully checked out in this chopper, my next training was in the H-43. This is a smaller helicopter with counterrotating blades. It is used mostly for rescue directly around the airbase. It's not a long-range chopper, but the downdraft from the blades when positioning the chopper at a burning object—say a plane that has crashed and is on fire—pushes the fire away from the chopper, allowing a rescue firefighter or pararescue man to go to the burning plane to assist pilots and crew in the plane, and allows the fire team to extinguish the flames.

It was a really exciting flight to learn to fight fires with the helicopter. The night training missions were the most thrilling, taking off in the night environment, flying to the burning aircraft (an old mockup), and maneuvering the helicopter right up close to the blazing bird.

The camaraderie that develops among those flying helicopters in the Air Force is tremendous. You become a team whose primary mission is that of the official mission statement of the Air Rescue Service: **"That Others May Live."**

I still belong to several social media groups ranging from Vietnam Chopper Pilots to Air Rescue. And my IP, Instructor Pilot, in that old H-19, and I have stayed close friends for over 55 years. We meet in Newport Beach, CA, every year for some golf and war stories—lots of war stories to share about the close calls when flying helicopters, especially with student pilots.

> That Others
> May Live.

After finishing helicopter training, my first assignment was a great reward. I was fortunate to go into the newest helicopter in service at that time, the CH-3. It was a two-jet engine amphibious helicopter that could fly at about 175 mph, carry 25 combat troops, and had a range of 780 miles and could climb to 21,000 feet. The crew consisted of a pilot, copilot, flight engineer/gunner, and a pararescue man or flight surgeon. It was designed to penetrate deep into enemy territory to rescue downed pilots during the Vietnam War.

But before heading off to the jungles of Nam, my first assignment after leaving helicopter training was to the wonderful East Coast of Florida—Cocoa Beach, to be exact. That was the location of Patrick AFB, which served as a support facility for NASA as well as an alert station of fighter aircraft to protect our East Coast. The astronaut program was just beginning to come into full swing. What an exciting time to work directly with the astronauts, assisting them in their training for rescue in the event something went wrong during the early stages of their flights.

As a new CH-3 pilot, I was most often the copilot on our missions. I flew in "Chopper Gold." The mission was to be airborne and ready to affect a rescue of the astronauts prior to liftoff, during liftoff, and for a few minutes afterward as the rockets took them southeasterly downrange and into orbit. We had to be flying directly at the launchpad and be within one mile at liftoff.

The astronauts could climb out of the capsule prior to actual liftoff, and if the launch tower was damaged, they could hook onto a cable and slide down it for about a half-mile to the ground, where we would pick them up, execute emergency medical assistance if necessary, and fly them to a safe location at the hospital.

The astronauts could also eject the capsule from the rockets. Then our job was to get to the capsule as quickly as possible. If necessary, the onboard team would assist in getting astronauts out and onboard the chopper.

The most frightening for all was if the launch failed or if the mission was aborted right after launch. This would put the capsule and the astronauts in the water just off the beach at Cape Canaveral. We would fly to their locations, hover over the capsule and/or the astronauts, put a rescue team in the water, and lift them into the chopper to be rapidly flown back to receive medical attention. All the things needed to complete a mission successfully depended on being properly trained, including practicing, being flexible and able to adjust the mission to meet the exacting conditions necessary for rescue, and having courage sufficient to move into dangerous conditions to complete the rescue mission. That type of training was a great experience not only for my time in Vietnam and Laos but also as an entrepreneur in the business world.

There was also a great balance between these critical missions and enjoying life. There was a bar and restaurant grill in Cocoa Beach called Shirley's Pillow Talk. The interior design was just what you might expect from the name; there were huge pillows on the floor, sorta like beanbags, where you sat. The waitresses were also appropriately dressed to match the theme. We would sometimes meet with some of the astronauts and some of the folks from NASA Houston Space Center after a day of training. It was great fun to get to know all of these people on an informal basis.

One evening, we were sitting on the pillows, imbibing in an adult cocktail or three. The pillows were arranged in pretty much of a circle so we could all talk and listen to each other. One of the folks in our group that evening was a very famous television journalist who covered the astronaut launches live on his network. As we were laughing and chatting, a very large man stumbled up to our group, tapped the TV anchor on the shoulder, and began to berate him, telling him he was the worst anchor on all of television, mostly using four-letter language.

The journalist slowly stood up, and with no warning whatsoever, cold-cocked this jerk with one blow. The fist to the face was not telegraphed in advance at all. The bar management came over and dragged the unconscious man out the side door. The journalist casually sat back down on his pillow and said, "Now, where were we?" He was quite a man's man. Tough like the astronauts that enjoyed their adventurous lives.

Another mission we had was to take the choppers down to many of the Caribbean islands. We had a team of scientists and communication engineers on board who would check out the communication booster facilities, making sure that the signals from downrange tracking stations would be clearly transmitted back to Florida and Houston. These islands were often small and uninhabited. One I remember had no clearing that would allow the helicopter to land. Even though our chopper was amphibious, it was not a good idea to land in saltwater unless absolutely necessary because of rust issues. So, on this particular island, we were able to land with the wheels on large rocks just off the beach. My pilot had tremendous flying skills. Of course, we kept the blades turning while the engineers went ashore to check all the instrumentation at the repeater site.

Other times, we would land on these remote islands so the pararescue men could do some of their water training. One time, they convinced me to go with them on an underwater navigation training swim. So, I suited up in all the appropriate gear: wetsuit, flippers, oxygen tanks, masks, and a huge knife strapped to my leg.

I asked the PJ, "Do I really need to carry this heavy knife on a training swim?"

"Yes, Sir, you do. These waters are full of sharks, so you might well need it."

"Sharks! Why have you got me on a supposedly fun swim, dealing with sharks? And how am I supposed to handle a shark with what now seems to be a not-so-big weapon?"

The answer from this tough PJ was not really acceptable. "Don't try to cut the shark. That would probably just bring other sharks into the area... and onto you."

"What the hell good is the knife then?"

"Use the butt of the knife handle and just hit the shark on the nose!"

"What!!! Are you joking?"

Well, I went on this navigation run anyway, but I don't think I swam with both arms, as one hand was down my side, close to the knife.

A year later, I was back on duty at our rescue facilities at Patrick AFB. We had visitors, as two pilots were back from Vietnam on a short mission to do some training on the CH-3s. They were from a unit nicknamed the "Jolly Greens."

I listened closely to their stories about the war they were fighting in Vietnam and Laos. They were dedicated to doing their part in performing their specific assignments in this air war. That assignment was to rescue fighter pilots who were shot down in combat in North Vietnam and often in Laos. It all sounded like a mission that I had prepared for throughout my helicopter pilot experiences and training, as well as the purpose of my military training at the Air Force Academy.

I was married and the proud father of a daughter, so that had to be a part of my decision. After very frank conversations with my wife, I decided to volunteer for Combat Air Rescue. I wanted to serve my country, my fellow warriors who flew fighter jets, and join with my helicopter pilots as a member of the Jolly Greens. The mission rang a bell in my mind, one that I am proud to still honor as being one of the greatest accomplishments in my lifetime.

**"That Others May Live."**

# Chapter 9

## FAILURE IS NEVER FINAL

ONE CAN (AND should) spend a lot of time preparing for what may happen in their professional life—or personal life, for that matter. I had the privilege and honor of doing just that. I spent those four years at the United States Air Force Academy preparing to become a "Leader of Character." That included being prepared to make the *ultimate* sacrifice if necessary, but it also meant being prepared to handle really tough situations that wouldn't necessarily lead to the loss of my life.

Leadership starts with being able to lead YOURSELF through tough times. I love the expression, "Tough times never last, but tough people do." When those times inevitably come, how will you respond? With confidence? Without fear? Going on "autopilot" because you are well-trained and educated and experienced? Or will you freeze?

> Leadership starts with being able to lead YOURSELF through tough times.

Will you take the easy path and do little or nothing,

turn tail and run, accept likely failure, or panic? Or will you get up, dust yourself off and go at it again, and again and again? Can you accept failure, especially when you have given it your best?

I don't think I'm much different from most veterans in our reluctance to discuss the personal tragedies of war. But, of course, we like to tell "war stories" like this one:

"There I was at 10,000 feet when two MIGS came out of the clouds at my 6 o'clock. With superior skill and cunning, I inverted my rescue chopper and dove for the jungle below. With the rotor blades over-speeding, the jet engine warning lights all flashing bright red, the fighter pilots calling out, 'Bandits, bandits, bandits. Get the hell out of there, Jolly Green!'"

Well, you get the idea.

So, it is with that veterans' reluctance that I use my experiences in the Vietnam War to continue with the theme of "bouncing back."

My class at the Academy had really bad or really good timing, depending on your attitude. We graduated in 1964, went to pilot training, and almost immediately went to war. It was what we had prepared for, and hopefully were mentally and emotionally ready for as well. War is always tragic, and our class was certainly no different. We paid the price in terms of casualties in air combat and POWs (Prisoners of War). And, no doubt, many suffered permanent physical and emotional scars that remain with us today. In fact, in some senses, maybe we all do.

My first mission might have been the most damaging to me personally. My home base was in Thailand, but we sat "alert status" in Laos (before the United States was officially engaged in the "Secret War" in Laos). Our mission was to go into the hot areas of the war zones when a combat pilot was shot down, whether

Air Force, Navy, CIA, or Air America. So, we sat alert just about 75 miles from Hanoi in Laos. Our FOB (forward operating base) consisted of either a canvas tent or a plywood structure, depending on whether or not the North Vietnamese regular army had overrun the FOB from the last time we were there.

In fact, I can clearly recall one launch from that base because of the enemy troops coming in. We went airborne, circled around the area watching the action, and then landed after it was all over, nailed up some more plywood walls, hung new Playboy centerfolds on those walls, and waited for the next scramble alert.

Since the fighters were obviously far faster than a rescue helicopter (even with our two jet engines turning those blades), we were based close to the North Vietnam targets so that when the fighters launched from Thailand, and we launched from the FOB, we could meet up with them or be on airborne alert as they crossed into North Vietnam on their bombing or reconnaissance missions.

And it happened on my first mission as the pilot of a Jolly Green rescue helicopter. In order to save time, and time saved lives when a pilot was shot down, we went airborne and positioned ourselves on the Laotian-North Vietnam border, waiting for the call to join our escort airplanes and head to the rescue position where a fighter jock had been shot down and hopefully was still alive on the ground. We joined up with two airplanes that had the mission of escorting us to the location and giving us fire cover as we attempted the rescue. These cover birds (call sign "Sandy") were the old A1Es from another war era. They were propeller-driven and very vulnerable because of their very slow speed. The guys that flew those missions were some of the bravest to ever strap on a fighter aircraft. I owe my life many times over to their courage and skill.

The downed pilot popped a smoke flare, which allowed us to locate him through the jungle trees' canopy. He was in a really hot enemy area with the bad guys chasing him, trying to kill or capture him before we could yank him out of there.

Thankfully, we made radio contact with him. The loud, chaotic noise over the radios during one of these missions was amazing. You had the radio talk amongst the high-altitude jet cover, coordinating their bombing and strafing runs to protect the downed pilot, as well as keeping the enemy away from our efforts to go into a stable hover and pick up the pilot on the ground. You also had the low-flying Sandys talking with each other (and with us) to give protection from the ground fire and their coordinated strike runs as they attempted to drive the enemy troops away from the pilot. Yet it was incredibly important that all transmissions be carefully monitored and *crucial* that those critical to our part of the rescue be clearly understood.

The pilot was identified by responding on his radio with that day's secret code identification. As calmly as I could, I asked him, "Are you mobile? Do you have injuries?"

He had survived his fighter being hit directly by ground fire or a SAM missile, as well as serious injury from the aircraft ejection and his parachute landing through the thick jungle canopy.

"I'm not seriously hurt. I can get to the pickup point!"

"Do you need the PJ (pararescue man) to come down and assist you onto the cable and jungle penetrator?" (That was the device that we would lower to him through the trees.)

He radioed back, "Negative. I can make it on my own. But the bad guys are closing in rapidly. I've moved from my first position."

"Can you pop another smoke?" (This was a smoke flare, usually pink, that would give us his exact position over which to hover.)

"Affirmative!"

He popped his smoke, which immediately came up through the trees. That allowed us to now attempt to come in for a hover down at treetop level and drop the rescue cable directly down to him.

I did a high-speed pass at about 150 knots right over the smoke, then rolled the helicopter over onto its side and made a tight, 180-degree turn, then pulled the helicopter quickly into a dead-still hover. Immediately, we took heavy automatic weapons fire from the ground as we sat there like a sitting duck.

"Sandy 1, Jolly Green 56 is taking heavy ground fire."

"Roger, Jolly, we are rolling in again, hot and loaded. Can you hold your position?"

"Giving it all we got."

The Sandys really shot up the area surrounding us as the survivor's flare smoke billowed up through the trees.

Heavy ground fire continued, and suddenly, the Sandy lead yelled, "Get the hell out of there, Jolly Green. We need to call in some heavier air power. The ground fire is too damned intense for your chopper to survive."

We pulled off the target as quickly as we could, went to a relatively safe altitude and position, and circled until the faster fighter jets could come in with their heavy munitions and drive off as many of the bad guys as possible. The Sandys then went back in to check out the situation.

The downed pilot was still alive and had not been captured. Now, the tough decision had to be made. Do I risk the crew of four onboard (and the chopper) to get the one downed pilot?

The crew enthusiastically responded, "Let's go get him!"

So, we went back in to try again. As we pulled into that second hover attempt, the ground fire was still intense. The North Vietnamese soldiers had begun utilizing their "wait and kill all" strategy which meant "cease firing until the rescue chopper is in a hover, maybe even with the downed pilot and a PJ coming up on the cable." Then they would open up with all the firepower they had.

With the Sandys doing all they could to circle us and fire everything they had on board at the enemy, again we were ordered, "Get the hell out of there, Jolly Green, while you are still able!"

During that last attempt, we lost contact with the pilot on the ground. I never found out whether he was listed as MIA or KIA. But to this day, I well remember his last name. It is seared into my conscience. It will never leave my memory. Even now, there is a lump in my throat and eyes that begin to water… because I failed! Resulting in a very "hard fall"!

There were other times that our Jolly Green helicopters were unable to retrieve a downed pilot, and there were too many times when the failure was because the Jolly Green was also shot down during the rescue attempts.

The good news is that we were far more successful than not. My crews and I were blessed to pick up 10 downed pilots during my tour in Vietnam.

I certainly consider that an example of "the harder you fall, the higher you can bounce!" Ten pilots came home when, without our continuing efforts, their alternatives would have been death or the "Hanoi Hilton."

**Failure is never final.**

\*\*\*

I WAS SHOT out of the sky twice during my tour of duty in Vietnam and obviously survived them both. One of those is possibly a story worth telling.

The coast of North Vietnam was so heavily fortified with anti-aircraft weapons that both Navy and Air Force fighter pilots said it was like flying through a solid wall of metal flak. One Navy pilot found out the hard way how dangerous that wall was. His aircraft was hit and virtually exploded under him as he ejected over North Vietnam. Being in Laos, we were closer to his downed position than the Navy rescue helicopter forces code-named "Big Mother." So, we busted through the "wall of metal" over the Laotian/North Vietnam border with our escort fighters.

The downed pilot was located on the side of a steep mountainside karst. He was in relatively good shape, and we were able to communicate with him clearly. It was an extremely hot summer day, and the altitude where he had landed was very high. As we and our support fighters checked out the area for ground fire, it didn't seem to be very intense, so we went in up against the mountainside for the pickup.

The Jolly Green chopper was fully fueled, including the tip tanks. Note: A helicopter has less ability to hold in a hover if the temperature is high and the air is thin because of the altitude. Simply put, at certain weights, temperatures, and altitudes, the chopper will "fall through" when attempting a hover. Every time we attempted to hover over the downed pilot's position, we "fell through" and could not hover. We just didn't have enough power to stay airborne.

The pilot, having survived being shot down, ejecting from his exploding aircraft, and now being chased by the enemy on the ground, was exhausted from executing escape and evasion tactics since he dropped out of the sky into the jungle environment. Imagine now hearing from your rescue forces, which you can see flying overhead. You can talk to them on your survival radio, but the rescue effort has failed, night is falling, and the rescue forces must leave.

"Pilot Alpha Charlie, this is Jolly Green 56. We are unable to hover over you. You're going to have to do the best you can to survive for the next 9 or 10 hours. Godspeed on evading the enemy during the night. But the entire rescue force will be back at morning's first light to pull you out of there. We can do it with less fuel onboard and the cooler predawn temperatures. We *will* bring you home!"

And that's what happened. However, when we returned to our very remote FOB in Laos after dark, we faced our own survival issues. The little area where we were hunkered down was not an airfield with runways. In fact, the landing was made by having the Laotians on the ground pour jet fuel into four barrels, then place them on four corners of an area on the ground that would make up a square large enough for a helicopter to land within. And they had to be ready to use flashlights to guide the landed taxiing chopper out of the square to a safe area so that the second chopper could land in the lighted square. Thank God, it worked.

During that evening, we defueled the choppers to the minimum amount we calculated it would take to fly back to the downed pilot's position, recover him, and return to Laos. We took off the fuel tip tanks, removed all possible extra weight, including the small amount of armor (a one-inch slab of titanium under the bucket seats positioned under our butts) we had for our protection from ground fire. We didn't get much shuteye that night.

Before first light, we were again airborne and crossing the border back into North Vietnam. Thank the Lord above; the pilot had survived the night without being wounded or captured. He had run and hidden all night, successfully avoiding being found by the numerous enemy troops looking all over the mountainside for him.

We were able to make radio contact, and he directed us to an approximate position where we could reach him quickly after he risked popping smoke, possibly showing the enemy forces his exact location.

The cooler temperature and lightened load made the difference, and the hover was solid. As we took a lot of ground fire, we put the survival cable down through the jungle canopy, and he jumped on. As soon as he had cleared the tree branches (maybe a little before, actually), and with him still dangling on the cable, we pulled out backward and turned our bird away from and down the steep karst mountainside. After pulling him off the cable and into the chopper, the pararescue man checked him over carefully. The recovered pilot was in reasonably good shape with only minor wounds and injuries but was totally exhausted and dehydrated.

A few minutes later, everyone on board and all the additional support rescue forces were finally able to take a deep breath. Only the Sandys were still with us as we crossed the border heading back into Laos. The PJ was attending to the injuries of the Navy pilot while my crew chief onboard was checking the battle damage to the chopper.

That's when everything started to unravel.

"Captain James, we have a problem back here."

"What's up? Pilot okay?"

"For now, Sir. But we have an oil leak."

Now, there are two kinds of oil leaks that can occur on a helicopter: Either one of the two jet engines had an oil leak, or the transmission was leaking.

An engine leak is not necessarily a terminal event. First, it may be a small leak that will not require that the engine be shut down immediately. And second, there is not just the one engine, but two engines powering the rotor blades.

However, the transmission is another matter. If the transmission loses its oil, it will freeze up and quit turning and powering the helicopter blades. When that big "overhead fan" quits turning, the aircraft has the glide ratio of a rock. The aircraft engineering manual says that without any oil in the transmission, the helicopter may have rotors for only a few minutes to a few seconds.

"Chief, please tell me it's an engine oil leak!"

"Sorry, Captain, it's the transmission!"

"How bad is the leak?"

"It's pouring out pretty damn fast!"

At that moment, my stomach tried to crawl up my throat. It felt like it was closing up, and for a second, I was having trouble even breathing.

My first instruction was, "Chief, tell the PJ to put a parachute on that pilot. He may have to bail out again… along with you guys."

The PJ came on the intercom. "Captain James, the pilot has just gone into shock."

Now, I want you to put yourself in that poor pilot's position. Shot out of the sky by ground fire or a surface-to-air missile (SAM), parachuted into the side of a mountain through thick jungle trees and their thick canopy, and endured a failed rescue attempt. Then, he was chased all night long by enemy soldiers, having to survive and evade before being successfully rescued by a Jolly Green at first light the next morning, survived the ground fire coming at him during his ride up the cable and into the chopper, celebrating on board with the crew, and then told that he might have to parachute into enemy territory again!

And now it should become clear why the PJ had decided to pour some whiskey into him. I concurred, of course. We always carried such a "tonic" onboard to help calm down a recovered pilot from the emotional trauma he suffered. I can't think of a time when it was needed more!

I needed to put the Jolly Green down immediately, but we were over unknown territory, possibly held by enemy forces. And I saw no clearing in which to land. I called SAR Headquarters (Search and Recovery) with my "mayday."

"Mayday, mayday, mayday. This is Jolly Green 56 with a serious transmission oil leak. I need to know if there is any safe area around here so I can put this thing down quickly!"

And then this frustrating response: "Ah, roger, Jolly 56. Understand emergency oil leak and need immediate info on probable safe landing site. Stand by."

"Stand by? Are you kidding me! I don't have time to STAND BY!"

"Chief, how are we doing back there?" I asked desperately.

"It's getting worse, Sir."

And then over the radio comes, "Jolly Green 56, this is SAR. The following are map coordinates for a village that is about 30 miles from your present position. We think it might be safe to land there."

"What! You THINK it might be safe?"

"Yes, Sir. That is the best we have for you."

"Roger, I have the coordinates."

Continuing to fly with reduced engine speed and power and decreased rotor blade and transmission torque, we descended slowly toward the coordinates.

Saigon called again with additional information: "Jolly Green 56, be prepared that the landing site is a village. We still have reason to believe that it is probably occupied by friendly Laotians."

As we neared the site, it was in fact a village with huts on each side of a dirt "street" running about 75 yards in length. That was the clearing we needed for the landing. I knew that it had to be a rough touchdown, hopefully with a short rollout. Pulling in power to the transmission could cause it to freeze up and lock up. That would cause the aircraft to rotate sharply with little control and a possible rollover. The resulting landing on "Main Street" was pretty much a "fly it into the dirt" naval-air-carrier-style controlled crash. But it worked. Damaged the landing gear and tires, but as they say, "Any landing that you can walk away from is a good one."

*So far, so good. No one is shooting at us from the village structures.* In fact, the village seemed almost deserted. We shut down the engines, stopped the blades from turning, and prepared for the worst. Is this a possible ambush?

I told the PJ to prepare his only weapon (an M-16) for immediate action. I unbuckled from the cockpit, unholstered my 45-pistol, and stepped into the cabin of the chopper. The PJ and I carefully moved out of the chopper to the front end, looking down the dirt street between the structures.

I swear it seemed like something out of a bad old Western movie. Two "cowboy" guys facing down the dirt street, waiting for the bad guys to meet us to "slap leather" and see the fastest survive.

And out from one of the structures at the far end of the dirt street came two people. Both were dressed in white garments, with one carrying something in his hands and arms underneath a big, blanket-like wrap. *What the hell is he carrying?* They made no gestures and simply began walking slowly and directly toward us.

With sweat rolling down my forehead into my eyes, I made no fast movements. I told the PJ that it didn't look good, that when they reached a distance from us of about 25 yards without some kind of friendly signal, we had to "drop 'em." I couldn't let them blow up the chopper, the wounded downed pilot, the crew chief, and of course, the PJ and me.

At about 40 to 50 yards, the two of them stopped. It was now apparent that one of them was a man, and the person carrying something underneath the wrap was a female. With the hairs standing up on the back of my neck and sweat now running freely out of every pore, I watched as the man reached over to grab the wrap. Oh crap! The moment of truth. He (not so gently) pulled the wrap up and off.

There in a large vessel was… hot tea!

I don't know how long it had been since I had taken a breath, but that first deep inhale had to be one of the sweetest of my entire life.

Honestly, what came next could have been Scene 2 in this bad movie, though no longer in a Western setting. The village was sitting high up on a relatively flat mountain plateau, almost like a mesa. Suddenly, up from seemingly nowhere popped a white Huey helicopter. It quickly landed right in front of Jolly Green 56, blowing dirt and dust everywhere. A "civilian" pilot jumped out and came trotting over to us. He was dressed in combat-style, elephant-skin boots, Bermuda shorts, a short-sleeved sport shirt, and a baseball cap. He had two gun belts around his waist with two holsters holding some model of serious pistols.

"Welcome to our village!" he said. "I see that you've already met the chief. Good guy. Tough. Fearless. Glad we were able to help the folks down in Saigon find you a safe spot to land that monster you fly. If you haven't heard yet, they're sending up another Jolly Green to take you and your passenger back to Udorn, Thailand. And they are also bringing in a test pilot and maintenance team to see if they can fix up the mess those North Vietnamese made to your bird and then take her home. So, looks like you're all set. Enjoy the tea. I gotta go. There is a rumor that there is a war to win. See ya!"

Here we were, in the middle of an undeclared war in the jungles of Northern Laos—not too far from not only North Vietnam, but also China—drinking tea with a Laotian village chief, sitting in the shade of a shot-down Jolly Green rescue helicopter, drinking whiskey with a downed Navy pilot, and waiting for a ride home. As they say, "You just can't make this stuff up."

***

LAOS WAS FULL of personnel who worked for Air America, the CIA, and folks like us. We were not allowed to wear military insignia while we were on the ground in Laos. Remember, there was no acknowledged U.S. involvement in Laos at that time. But one morning, I was grabbing a little snooze nap in our staging base compound in Laos. It was raining so hard it would have been like flying in the bottom of a swimming pool, so we were grounded.

The crew chief came into the sleeping area, roused me, and said, "Captain James, we have a visitor. You need to get out here."

A visitor? Who could possibly be "visiting" this miserable place? As I walked in, a tall, imposing man dressed in fatigues stuck out his hand and said, "Hi. I'm Stuart Symington. Just wanted to say thank you to you and your crew. Not many folks back home know you're here or what risks you're taking for your country. But I need you to know that a bunch of us do, and we appreciate what you are doing. It's important to your fellow fighter pilots and all those American warriors on the ground. Wish I had more time to spend with you, but I have to meet with the Laotian General to lay out a new strategy. Thanks again, guys. Stay safe. See ya back home."

Symington was a former Secretary of the Air Force and was then a Senator from Missouri. He once said that the "Secret War in Laos" was "a sensible way to fight a war."

Remember to always give your "troops/employees/partners" a pat on the back, showing your appreciation for their efforts and successes.

One of my "extra-duty assignments" during my tour was to brief all fighter pilots when they first came into the war zone and were assigned to a Thailand base on the most current rescue techniques if they were shot down. Clearly, they needed to know the most important things they had to do if they

> Give your "troops/employees/
> partners" a pat on the back,
> showing your appreciation for
> their efforts and successes.

were on the ground in enemy territory after being shot down. I wanted not only for them to know how to best participate in a successful rescue recovery, but I also wanted them to know how not to foul things up so that my crew and I would also survive!

One such time was when I went to the Ubon airbase in Thailand, where many fighters were stationed. One of the outfits there was the 8th Tactical Fighter Wing, commanded by then Colonel Robin Olds (later to become the Brigadier General Commandant of the Air Force Academy). He was a legendary fighter pilot.

We landed at Ubon, taxied in our little fixed-wing, prop-driven airplane to a parking area, and shut down the engine. Before we could complete the checklist and get out of the plane, there was a long red carpet rolled out for us. As we exited the plane and began walking down that beautiful red carpet, standing at the far end of the carpet was Col. Robin Olds.

We saluted him. He returned the salute and stuck out his hand to welcome us to his

> If one son of a bitch on this base lets you buy your own drink, I want his name!

command. And then he said something that made it clear to us that our mission to rescue his pilots that were shot down was important and very much appreciated by him and his warriors.

"If one son of a bitch on this base lets you buy your own drink, I want his name!"

And with that, he saluted, did a proper "about face," and marched off.

That was certainly humorous, one of the many forms of appreciation that I received from so many fellow warriors. One pilot that we picked up sent me a case of Scotch every Christmas for several years. One of my most rewarding pickups was one of my classmates from the Academy, Class of 1964.

Here's another incident that even now seems hard to believe. After I resigned from the Air Force, I went to Stanford Graduate School of Business to earn an MBA. While standing in line to receive my books and other materials on the first day, I started to chat with the man standing behind me in line, Chip Fowler. Chip was also a helicopter pilot and had resigned his commission in the Army after having served his time in Vietnam.

While we were talking, another man standing in line behind Chip stepped out and approached us. He looked at me and said, "Did I hear correctly? Is your name Max James?"

He did not look overly friendly at that moment, plus it was a time on campus when there was significant opposition to the war, especially by undergraduate students in many of the colleges, including Stanford.

I thought, *How in the hell did I get singled out for this opposition? But here we go. I guess all those rumors of campus violence are true, and I am about to find out just how violent.*

So, I took a defensive stance, ready to combat whatever was coming.

He quickly approached me, stuck out his hand for me to shake, and said, "You picked me up in North Vietnam after I was shot down. I was wounded pretty badly, so as soon as you got me back to an operating base, the medical folks rushed me off for treatment at the hospital. I never got a chance to thank you. So, thank you for what you did!"

Now, that is one hell of a small world story, right? But man, to be singled out and thanked years after the rescue mission was so appreciated.

As an entrepreneur, I have tons of stories about being greatly rewarded by past employees and partners coming back to me years later to express their appreciation and thanks for what we were able to accomplish together.

As they say, **"It just doesn't get much better than that!"**

The bestselling book of all time, published in more languages than any other says, "When you give to others, it comes back tenfold." In another place in that book, it says "one hundredfold." I believe it because I have lived it. I have always made sure that those who worked with me in my companies knew it was important that we give back. And often, we were rewarded in many ways for doing so.

Take the time to stay in contact with your spiritual guide. Pause, pray, meditate, or whatever you choose. But many have been able to "keep on keeping on," experiencing this more often than not: "There are no atheists in foxholes."

# *Chapter 10*

## THE ONE LESS TRAVELED

IF YOU LOOK up the definitions of "warrior" and "feather merchant," you will quickly discover the differences.

"Feather Merchant" has several definitions according to Wiktionary (the free dictionary), but the one most used by the military is "slang for civilians, often those with a cushy job, someone who does not do worthwhile work."

"Warrior," on the other hand, is defined by Dictionary.com as "a soldier who shows or has shown great vigor, courage, or aggressiveness."

I did not want to give up being an air warrior, but stuff happens.

While I was in Vietnam, I was selected by the Air Force to go back to graduate school and to go into the field that I had hoped for: management. That meant obtaining an MBA.

My ego was so big you couldn't fit my head in a gymnasium. That year, only 29 pilots were chosen to go back to graduate school (there was a war going on, after all). And only one helicopter pilot was selected. We were critically short of chopper pilots in 1966 to start with, and the enemy kept reducing the numbers that we did have. In fact, the cross-training of pilots from fixed-wing aircraft into helicopters became a major program but wasn't too popular among fixed-wing pilots. My officer rank during most of the war was lieutenant, but I was sometimes outranked by my copilots. I frequently had a B-52 lieutenant colonel as my copilot.

When I returned from the combat zone to my station at Sheppard AFB in Wichita Falls, TX, I flew down to Randolph AFB in San Antonio, TX, to meet with the person in charge of placing selected grad school applicants into the various universities. He was a chief master sergeant.

"Well, Captain James. Congratulations! You should be proud of your selection, and to be chosen in your preferred field, even better. I suppose you are anxious to find out which university we are planning on you attending?"

"But I thought I would be able to choose the graduate school that I wanted to attend, assuming I could qualify and be accepted?"

"Well, probably not. That is, unless we agree on the same one. So what school were you hoping for?"

"I have three on the top of my wish list, and a fourth alternative if I can't qualify for the first three."

"Really? You've picked out three or four, have you?"

"Right, Sgt. I've picked Stanford, Harvard, and Wharton. Pretty sure I can get into at least one, but if not, then I would like to select Vanderbilt."

"Captain, I don't think you are going to like this, but we've had trouble getting some of our officers into those schools, and in a couple of cases, a few of those that did make it in had trouble finishing the program. We've looked at your Academy academic record, and we don't think you would be a good candidate for attempting to get into those three."

"Wait just a damn minute, Sergeant! What academic issues do you think you found? I was on the Dean's List every semester but one, including the summer classes! That is eight semesters plus three summers. Seven out of eight is a pretty damn good academic record, especially at a university that's ranked as highly as the Air Force Academy."

"Be that as it may, we have scheduled you to attend the university in Dayton, OH."

In a bit of shock and quite frustrated, I'm thinking, *What university is in Dayton? Not the University of Ohio.*

"And what university have you selected for me in Dayton?"

"Captain, you are going to Wright Patterson AFB, the Air Force School of Logistics Management."

"What! Supply officer school? I'm a pilot, not a damn supply officer. I am *not* satisfied with going to that school. I plan on going to one of the others that I've chosen."

"I doubt seriously that will happen, Captain. Your orders will be cut and dispatched to you for your move to Dayton, OH, this summer—just in time to begin the fall semester at the logistics school. Our university there is fully accredited, and besides, it is tougher than those other schools anyway."

"I don't doubt that for a minute, but the result is to become a supply officer, not to obtain a graduate degree and an MBA from a prestigious university."

"Captain. You just need to go on back up to Sheppard AFB. Start packing your household goods. The Air Force has made its decision! You are going to move to Ohio!"

*Whoa*! What the hell is going on here!

I flew back to Wichita Falls and immediately started applying to the other four schools. I was not going to supply officer "university." In fact, I decided that I would go to one of the schools that had a joint MBA-JD program, where you could attain both degrees in four years instead of the normal two plus three.

And the good news came.

I was accepted by each of those schools. In fact, Vanderbilt offered me a full fellowship if I would attend their law school for three years. However, they didn't have a joint program.

So, I settled on Stanford.

With this new information in hand, off I went, flying back to Randolph AFB to meet with the sergeant. I walked into his office and said, "Congratulations, Sgt! I have some good news for you. So, let's review the bidding: I was one of a few pilots chosen to go back to graduate school. I was the only helicopter pilot chosen, *and* I was chosen in the field where the Air Force needs me and the field that I wanted, management. You have programs with the Stanford Graduate School of Business but have had issues getting applicants accepted. Well, here's the good news. Look at this letter. I made it in!"

With not even the flicker of a grin, he looked up at me from his desk and said, "Captain, I briefed you fully when you were last here: You are going to Wright Patterson AFB's School of Logistic Management. Period, paragraph, end of conversation!"

"No, Sarge, that is not the end of the conversation. *Here* is the last word: Come September, I am going to Stanford. I will either be wearing my Air Force *blue* uniform, or I will be wearing *blue* jeans! And right now, I don't give a tinker's damn which one!"

And with that, I left his office.

I'm sure you can guess what happened next. You can't bluff the Air Force.

So, 10 days before registration at the GSB at Stanford, I resigned my commission, moved my family to the San Francisco Bay area, and enrolled in fall classes to start my journey to the Stanford Graduate School of Business's MBA program.

I truly loved the Air Force. I loved flying, and I loved the structure of the entire organization. Plus, I was having a fantastically good time. Maybe it was because that time of my life had real purpose. I was a combat instructor pilot teaching pilots headed to war everything I knew from my experience about how to stay alive.

In our wartime culture for decades past, as well as at that time, an old saying was being played out in reality: "Eat, drink and be merry, for tomorrow you may die!" And party we did—with each class after they graduated from our program and before they left the good old U.S. of A en route to WAR.

There are numerous entrepreneurial lessons in the events above—the verbal exchange with the Air Force and resultant decision and action. All entrepreneurs will face such decisions and make tough choices as to what paths are necessary to meet their personal goals. Sometimes these choices are painful and really tough. But not making them to suit *your* personal preferences will be more painful and tougher, and you will quickly proceed down the *wrong* path. Trust me. When I have taken the easy road, more often than not, I've regretted it later.

When you come to a fork in the road, Yogi Berra said it best: "Take it!"

While I have often laughed at that advice, it is my experience that most serious and successful entrepreneurs will instead take *this* advice from the poem "The Road Not Taken" by Robert Frost, a part of which says:

**"And I shall be telling this with a sigh,
Somewhere ages and ages hence,
Two roads diverged in a road and I
I took the one less traveled by,
And that has made all the difference."**

There is one more interesting story that occurred before I put on my blue jeans and headed to Stanford.

Early one morning, before I got out of bed, the telephone on the nightstand rang. I answered it to hear the voice of the Dean of the Stanford Law School.

"Mr. James? This is Dean Bayless Manning from the Stanford Law School. Do you have a minute to talk with me?"

"Absolutely. Good morning, Sir."

"I wanted to call you personally to congratulate you on being accepted into the Graduate School of Business here. Great program. I'm sure you are going to enjoy it and benefit from everything they have to offer."

"Thank you, Sir. I am looking forward to getting out there and going to work."

"And a second congratulations on your remarkable scores on the LSAT (Law School Admission Test). You certainly are qualified to attend our school here at Stanford."

"Sir, thank you again. That is fantastic news!"

"Mr. James, I do have an important question for you. Our joint Business School/Law School combined program is unique and very much sought after. We only have a limited number of spots for applicants to this joint degree program. So, let me ask you this. Is it your plan to be a businessman who knows a lot about the law, or a lawyer who knows a lot about business?"

"Sir, I'm not positive how things will turn out, but right now, I would have to say my preference would be the former; to be a businessman with a Stanford MBA who is well-educated in the law by the Stanford Law School."

"Thank you for your forthrightness, Mr. James. I would have hoped you would have chosen the legal field as your preference. But since you did not, we will be awarding another applicant this spot in our joint program, a person who prefers the law as his first choice for a career. May I wish you much success in your chosen field of business management? Good day, Mr. James."

*What the blue blazes just happened?!* I blurted out a choice that not even I was sure about. And the result was that I just blew my chances, for the time being, of having options as to my chosen career field.

Not too hard to see the lesson there. Do not "cut off your nose to spite your face." I'm not even sure that I fully understood that expression at that moment, but I felt I had done just that. What a stupid mistake.

The expression is actually described as a needlessly self-destructive overreaction to a problem, like sawing off the branch you are sitting on.

Anyways.

*Goodbye, Texas. California, here I come.*

The campus at Stanford is indeed beautiful. Certainly not like the glass and aluminum architecture at the Air Force Academy. My first experience reminded me of the comedy act of Tommy and Dicky Smothers. They were discussing their educational experiences in college, and the question came up from Tommy as to why it took Dicky five years to graduate instead of the normal (back then) of four years. His response was, "Four years of classes and one year of trying to find a place to park!" Early on, I spent many hours trying to find a place to park my little MG sports car.

It was during this period in the '60s that there was tremendous objection to the Vietnam war on campuses across the nation (with the exception of the military academies, and some even within those hallowed halls). The "industrial/military complex" was the subject of much dissension; thus, the business school was often the object of this derision. As veterans of the war—there were many of us in my class—we were also the target of students opposed to the war. The GSB facility was hit with bricks and worse. Often there would be demonstrations in front of and sometimes within the building.

Finally, we more senior vets had had enough of the disruptions to our attempting to reenter civilian life by gaining a new level of education.

One morning, there was a large crowd of students that had gathered in front of the GSB building. They were chanting their disagreements with the businesses that were in some manner supporting the military and their actions in Vietnam.

A few of us, veterans all, walked out onto the steps in front of the building and faced the "disruptors."

Our message went something like this: "We are here at Stanford to get a further education. That is our sole purpose in being here.

We choose not to participate in your actions against the policy of the U.S. government. We were asked to serve our country, and we did so with honor. We have been trained in warfare, including hand-to-hand combat, to overcome the physical aggression of those who would attempt to keep us from our goals.

"Please, let us not move to that point in your actions to disrupt our attaining our goal simply to gain an education at Stanford."

They dispersed, thankfully. And we never saw another broken window through which a brick had been thrown.

"Peace and love!"

There are times when an entrepreneur feels like he is flying solo with thunderclouds all around. One has to remember that he possesses strengths that can and must be displayed to "stay airborne"—to "keep on keeping on." Many will doubt you, choose not to support you, or even encourage you. They will attempt to step on your dreams. It is then that the successful entrepreneurs will take the path less traveled, and "they will mount up on wings like eagles" (Isaiah 40:31).

> There are times when an entrepreneur feels like he is flying solo with thunderclouds all around.

# Chapter 11

## TRAVELING WITH THE WORLD'S RICHEST MAN

WHEN I WAS a student at the Stanford Graduate School of Business (GSB), most of us grinders sought (and needed) a summer job between the first and second years of study. I had decided to concentrate my studies in real estate, and I was hoping for a summer apprenticeship in that field.

One evening, while reading a local newspaper, I saw that a very successful businessman in the high technology industry had decided to diversify into real estate. The article announced that he was forming a new real estate investment and commercial brokerage company to serve the Silicon Valley market. (Not sure we called the Palo Alto area "Silicon Valley" way back there in 1969, but I digress.) Since I had not had any luck landing a summer job, I thought, *What the hell, I'll try to call him.*

Surprise, surprise! His number was listed, and he actually answered the phone! And even more surprising, he told me that he had just hired a president of this new company, and he would give him a call and tell him that I would be calling about a summer job. He suggested that if the interview went well, he would see that the job was mine.

So, I called this fellow, and he invited me to come into his office for an interview. It went well. Actually, maybe not quite so well. That is to say, I got the job... but the pay was zero! Unless I actually ended up making a sale as a real estate agent and thus earning a commission, I would gain all this fantastic real estate experience but no money.

Oh yeah, and there was another small problem: I didn't have a California Real Estate License. But innovative thinking almost always finds a solution. So, during the day, I went to graduate school at Stanford, continuing to work on my master's, and at night, I went to a local community college to take the necessary undergraduate college courses required to take the Real Estate Brokers' License exam. Somehow, I managed to successfully get through both courses of study without flunking out of either.

While I didn't make a single commission all summer long, I did learn a lot AND met several successful individual investors.

Following that summer internship, and during the first semester of my second year at Stanford, I received a call from an attorney that I had met during the previous apprentice summer. He asked me if the students in the GSB program were required to write a business plan for any of our classes. I told him he was correct, that it was a requirement.

"I think I have an opportunity for you to write such a plan for a new venture one of my clients wishes to begin. If you are interested, I would like you to come to my office, and I will fill you in on the details. What do you think?" Clearly, he was looking for a free consultant onto whom he could shovel some of his workload.

But I remembered that one of this attorney's clients was an international "merchant prince" named Adnan Khashoggi, who was being labeled as the "Richest Man in the World," notably in a biography by Ronald Kessler. In fact, Harold Robins, a highly successful fiction writer during that time, had written a novel about the life of just such a merchant prince, *The Pirate*, using Adnan as the model for his main character. It even hit *The New York Times* Best Seller list! Of course, my first thought was, *what if this proposed project to write a new business plan involved Adnan?! Wow!* So, off I rushed to the meeting.

The project was, in fact, for one of Adnan's ventures. I was given the task of creating a business plan to set up an offshore REIT (real estate investment trust) domiciled in Luxembourg. It was a great assignment, and somehow, I managed to pull an "A" in one of the classes that required the creation of a business plan.

But far more importantly, that classroom assignment led to one of those life-changing moments: I was hired by the attorney to work for several of Adnan's companies, concentrating initially on real estate analysis and purchases. Sooner than I had anticipated, I was on an airplane heading to the Middle East, specifically to Beirut and Riyadh.

In addition to the REIT project, I was asked to research how we might take the technology that existed in the United States' field of agriculture and utilize it in the deserts of the Middle East, specifically Saudi Arabia. We chose a company, Arizona Land and Cattle Company, to help with this project.

Secondly, we wanted to thoroughly research how best to participate in the real estate markets in the United States, looking at being able to present properties to potential Adnan contacts in the Middle East.

And lastly, since the U.S. banking industry was viewed by our potential offshore investors as one of the safest, most highly regulated industries in the world, it seemed probable that some of these potential investors would be attracted to investments in that industry. Other members on our team sought out opportunities that we could present for investments in banking.

The final presentation to Adnan and his team of analysts was scheduled to be made on his yacht while it was docked in Malaga. There were three groups that would represent these opportunities: the founder and major shareholder of a small regional bank in Walnut Creek, CA; the owner of a large area of land in Arizona that was already working with the Arizona Land and Cattle Company (several of his major innovations included irrigating arid lands with cattle waste treated with radioisotopes and distributed through irrigation pumps that would irrigate several acres from a single pump); and lastly, a successful owner of a real estate company who had numerous investment opportunities for consideration.

I was in Beirut prior to this planned meeting, and Adnan asked me to fly with him on his Boeing 737 to Malaga. But first, we had to stop in Milano for a meeting with Fiat, which Adnan represented in Saudi Arabia. We landed late that evening, and upon arriving at a five-star hotel, discovered that while there were no problems with Adnan's suite reservation, somehow, the hotel had not held enough room reservation for our little entourage! Given Adnan's influence, the hotel quickly arranged rooms for the rest of us at another lodging facility, not too far from the hotel where Adnan would be staying. I was one of those who needed to relocate.

Before we departed to the alternate hotel, Adnan sincerely expressed his apologies to me for the mistake and turned to his assistant to ask for some "cash" to give to me for any and all expenses I might encounter as a result of having to relocate. The assistant pulled a roll of bills out of his briefcase that would choke a horse. Tempting though it was to take the money, we had a standing rule in the company that we would never take any gifts or extra compensation from Adnan or his personal team. We were professionals and paid well (at least the one who wrote that rule decided we were), and thus, it would not be appropriate or ethical to accept "favors."

So off I went with two others to the alternate hotel. The "two others" were two of Adnan's bodyguards. Guess he was worried about my safety. When we attempted to check in, we were told that there was only one room available for the three of us! Egads! And it was only a small, one-bedroom suite. As I remember, his two bodyguards were Korean martial arts experts. Clearly, I was not going to disagree with them about who slept where, so they took the bedroom, and I took the couch. Oh yeah, and the luggage never made it to our hotel. So, during the Fiat meeting the next day, I was noticeably absent. Well, maybe *unnoticeably* absent." After all, what did I know about Fiats!

But after landing the next morning in Malaga, the entourage split up; Adnan and his personal staff headed for the yacht while I headed into the city to my hotel. My early assignment was to greet and host the three groups that would be making presentations to Adnan about potential investment ventures. Our dinner plans quickly changed, as it was announced that we were to have dinner on the yacht. And what a dinner and party that turned out to be! One of the best.

The next morning, I was deep in recovery mode from the party when there was a knock on my hotel room door. It was a steward from the yacht who told me that Adnan wanted me there right away. I said I would join him just as soon as I bathed, dressed, and packed my suitcase.

"No, that is not acceptable. Just put on some clothes and get moving," the steward said, saying he would pack my things and follow me on board later.

Adnan asked me how the three groups responded to his dinner and party, and if there was any feedback that he should know about that I might have picked up from informal conversations following the presentations. I gave him my input, which was all favorable. He stood up and said to enjoy the day as we were heading out to sea for a day or so. Now, mind you, the "we" going to sea were Adnan, a celebrity guest and her mother, and a ship's crew of 21… plus little ol' me.

It was a great voyage filled with helicopter skiing, food, sun, and suds. On the day we headed back into the port of Malaga, apart from most of the crew and me, everyone else was down below taking naps or packing. So, I took the opportunity to climb up on the very top part of the yacht's decks, up where all the radio and radar antennas are located. It was also where the seagulls gather. I called it the "poop deck."

As we slipped into the port, the setting sun was a magnificent sight. There were many tourists out in the bay, pumping away on those little paddle boats, dressed in typical tourist attire of Bermuda shorts, loud, colorful madras shirts and blouses, and straw hats. As the yacht passed by them, they would wave at me up on the poop deck, and I would salute back to each of the paddle boats, to my left and right and forward. It felt as though I was not just the captain of the yacht, but that I *owned* it.

And then it happened. I had an epiphany! *I had lost my perspective!* I truly was living in that "tall cotton" like I was the plantation owner, when, in fact, it cost more per day to operate that yacht than I was being paid in a year. I was little more than a hired hand, surely nothing more than the boss's cotton-pickin' foreman. It was time to make a serious directional change. Time to get back to earth, put my ego in my pocket, and get working on securing my family's future while being at home with them in the good ol' U.S. of A.

> I truly was living in that "tall cotton" like I was the plantation owner, when, in fact, it cost more per day to operate that yacht than I was being paid in a year.

On the flight back to Beirut on that beautifully appointed private 737, Adnan came out of his sleeping quarters, sat down on the couch beside me, and once again wanted to fully discuss the three alternative investment categories we were examining. To this day, I suspect that he had already made up his mind and was using me as a sounding board. Although my ego probably rationalized that some of what I had to offer was useful.

In any event, he told me that he had decided that the safest investment was the one he was going to go after for his investors—at least initially. And that was the banking investment. I was surprised (and a little disappointed) since that was the one of the three I had not been involved with. Plus, I came from the farm/agriculture, and my so-called field of expertise was also real estate.

When we landed in Beirut, Adnan said that he wanted me to go to the Vendome Hotel, where the attorney who had hired me and I were staying. I was to let the attorney know of the decision. I really did not want to do that, as I knew the attorney would be furious. He had seriously wanted the agricultural deal to win the day. He truly felt that there would be simpatico with the so-called "desert investors." The idea of bringing Saudi wealth, much of which had moved into the Middle East during the Arab Oil Embargo, back into the United States while exporting U.S. agricultural technology to Saudi Arabia to make the deserts highly productive with food production was a dream of his and met his financial objectives for the future of Adnan's organizations.

I strongly suggested to Adnan that he should be the one to tell the attorney. Guess who won that debate! But there was still a compromise. If I would deliver the "bad news" to the attorney, then I was to get right back to the airport and head for Venezuela! *WHAT! Why would I want to go there?* Seems that Onassis had an island, so Adnan wanted one—and had found an available one off the coast of Venezuela. But there was more. If I would do this, then I should go on to Acapulco, check on the various villas that we had purchased at Las Brisas, and invite my wife to join me there. Now *that* was a sales offer that I bought into, so off I went.

Eventually, I took the actions to back up the change I needed and flew to a Board of Directors' meeting in Salt Lake City. I was the chairman of the Board of the Salt Lake International Center, a 1,000-acre industrial park we were developing near the airport. I resigned from the board, and 30 days later, I was living in Sacramento.

There I was, with my family and no job, but with my dream of becoming a real estate entrepreneur. In Sacramento, perhaps I could be a "bigger fish in a smaller pond"—a much better option than competing with the extraordinary talent that existed in the San Francisco Bay area and Silicon Valley.

During my time with Adnan, there were many adventures and experiences from which I learned not only business principles, but life lessons as well. Maybe you will spot some of them in the following stories.

***

THE ADNAN TEAM (Triad Companies) was located in Los Altos, CA. We had been working especially hard on a wide variety of investments, looking at everything from agriculture, office buildings, ranches, movies, banking, golf resorts, industrial properties, and probably much more that I don't remember. Las Vegas was booming, and Adnan really enjoyed his visits there. As a "high roller," he was obviously welcomed to visit. Kirk Kerkorian knew Adnan well, so we were invited to the groundbreaking of the new MGM Hotel and Casino (now named Bally's and the scene of one of the most horrible hotel fire disasters in history).

What a night. As I recall, MGM movie celebrities such as Janet Leigh, Rock Hudson, Dean Martin, and Wayne Newton were all in attendance. Adnan decided to invite all his executive staff and their spouses from California to come as well. A huge tent was erected on the site, and all of us received a memorial miniature golden shovel commemorating the event. It was a wonderful party with drinks flowing freely.

The next day, we dragged our bodies out to the pool at the Sands (where Adnan was staying in luxurious private bungalows, located in an area around the huge pool). Sometime around noon, we decided that we were sufficiently recovered from the previous night's overindulgences and that we could handle some lunch. We ordered a poolside luncheon for all the executive staff and friends. Just as we finished gorging ourselves on the food (and drink), Adnan sent his personal assistant out to the pool to let us know that he had set up a special luncheon for us in his bungalow.

*Oh no! The last thing we needed was more food and drink.* However, he was footing the bill for our entire trip (airline transportation, hotel rooms, and all expenses—excluding gambling, of course). So, we gathered up our gear and headed over to his accommodations. Thinking he would "do it up right," he had hired "hostesses" to greet us. The "us" included our wives. The "hostesses" greeted us dressed in their "teeny weeny little bikinis," served all of us cocktails, and joined us for lunch.

The suddenly suspicious wives, eyebrows raised, started asking if this was how it always was when we traveled with Adnan, particularly the "hostesses." *OUCH! Who screwed up that decision to have "hostesses" greet our wives?* Our guys gave lots of really weak explanations and excuses to their wives for months following that trip.

Here was a tough lesson to learn: Always preview in detail just what the setup is for any and all meetings and events that you plan on attending.

***

I HAVE ALWAYS referred to this next story as "Sitting in the Outer Tent." Some of Adnan's investment teams were in New York City, waiting on him to arrive to review some investment ventures we were considering. Since his arrival was delayed, and since the

Roosevelt Suite at the Waldorf Hotel had already been reserved for him in his absence, we decided to enjoy his fabulous accommodations for a day. Again, this ol' country boy was in tall cotton.

But after the reprieve, we headed back to meetings with our boss, the attorney. Adnan was very intent on our finding a way to provide affordable housing building methods that could be utilized in the desert climate of Saudi Arabia. There was a system that had been developed by a scientist in Boston called Componoform. I can't begin to give it proper architectural merit, but it was a solution to the corners of concrete joints in concrete structures.

*Whoops!* Somehow, the presentation material had not been sent to the Waldorf. So, I was instructed to get my butt to the airport, take the airport shuttle from NY to Boston, see Mr. (or maybe it was Dr.) Egon AliOglu, who was the inventor, and pick up the package. Then I was to jump on the earliest shuttle back to NY for the meetings. So off I went, grabbed a seat on the plane, and flew to Boston. When I walked into the offices of AliOglu, I asked the secretary if I could see him to pick up the package. She said to take a seat and she would go into his office to get the presentation material for me. After she was finally able to interrupt him and enter his office, she came back out and told me that the package was not yet ready and would not be that day. Bad news, no doubt.

So, I jumped on the next shuttle back to New York, took a cab back to the Waldorf, and reported to the attorney that the package was not available. He was furious and suggested if I wanted to remain in good graces (meaning not being fired) that I get my butt (my word, not his) back to the airport and back to Boston.

"Damn it, James, you sit in that office until Egon AliOglu personally puts that package in your hands, and I don't give a damn how long it takes or if you're back today or late tonight!"

*Ouch!* But that is just what I did. The secretary was somewhat ticked off, of course, at my insistence that I would be in her domain, even if it meant napping on the office couch. Somehow, AliOglu was able to put together everything we needed sometime very late that evening and handed it to me so that I could grab yet another flight back to New York.

Mission accomplished.

Much later, after everything had settled down (and everyone had calmed down), the attorney told me this story. In the olden days in Saudi Arabia, the king would gather up a large contingency of his staff to travel throughout the kingdom, personally meeting with his tribes and listening to their needs and plans, making sure that the kingdom was in good shape. There would be a very large royal tent set up for the king in which he would hold court. If you wanted to see the king, you would sit in a second large outer tent that was in front of the king's royal tent. There was no queue or order of priority as to who would be invited into the king's royal tent first (or next), so you simply sat in the outer tent until you were admitted.

> Many times in your business career, you are going to have trouble getting in to see those that are important to you.

The point of the attorney telling me this story was pretty straightforward. Many times in your business career, you are going to have trouble getting in to see those that are important to you, especially if you are there to get an answer, present your proposal, or "make a deal." Seems there is almost always a "gatekeeper" that must be dealt with, or maybe the person you are hoping to see is just plain old reluctant to deal with you. Therefore, what you need to do is "sit in the outer tent." This is something that I have done dozens of times in my career and have insisted that many who have worked with me also learn and remember.

***

IN MEETING WITH companies and individuals that had real estate properties that they wished us (who had the real estate responsibilities) to analyze, the pressure was on both sides to make a great first impression. I was given the task of going to Dallas to meet with the owners of a major resort property located in Scottsdale, AZ. I was fully prepared with all of my analytic financial charts and numbers, dressed in proper business attire, and with all my travel plans confirmed. But there was one major problem: *I missed the plane!* All these Texas big-shot businessmen were scheduled for this meeting in their corporate headquarters, and my only excuse was, "Sorry, I missed my flight." *Surely, I would lose my job over this one.*

I called the attorney who, not so calmly told me once again to get my butt on the next plane, call these important fellows, and make excuses. All of which I did. In those days, the stress would sometimes lead to migraine headaches. This was one of those times, and it was a doozy. By the time I arrived in their offices in Dallas, having not eaten anything that day, I was totally exhausted. I walked into their reception area, and there behind the receptionist was the conference room, totally visible through floor-to-ceiling glass walls. And beyond those walls was the conference table covered with all manner of food (which now was pretty much all scattered about from having been picked over by those who had enjoyed a great lunch without me). And worst of all—and I see it now—in the middle of the table was what was left of a now-melted and dripping ice sculpture that was carved and placed there to welcome me (several hours before my tardy arrival). Actually, it was approaching dark, so they kindly suggested that they take me to my hotel to allow me to freshen up and join them for a business dinner.

My headache was now matched by an upset, stressed-out stomach. In the limo ride from their offices to the hotel, I was positive that I was going to throw up in the car. I sat next to the window and rolled it down for fresh air. Somehow, I made it to the hotel and checked in. It was time for a couple of real business survival treatments if I was going to make it to that dinner.

The first treatment came from my Tennessee grandmother. Lie down, lights out, cold cloth across your eyes and forehead. Drink a cola with crushed ice. Second came from a business seminar I had attended on how to use an HP hand calculator. The instructor taught us to do transcendental meditation for about a half an hour. Since that presentation, I had become interested and studied various meditation methods. Thankfully, that night it

> Meditation is probably one of the most important tools in my business tool kit, if not *the* most important.

worked. Within a half-hour, I was feeling terrific. We had a very successful business dinner, all was forgiven for my tardiness, and we moved on to the next stage of negotiations later that month. (And no, we didn't buy the resort. Damn!)

Meditation is probably one of the most important tools in my business tool kit, if not *the* most important. The science is now clear that it is a great stress reliever and, in my opinion, should be mastered by all, but especially entrepreneurs.

\*\*\*

MY TIME WORKING for Adnan Khashoggi was a time of my maturing and learning from some of the outstanding international experts in the field of business. I observed negotiations that ranged from the price of a watch in Paris to a contract for healthcare delivery systems to an entire country, from the purchase price of a parcel of land to the legal and commissionable fees for multibillion-dollar defense equipment, and even negotiating for where my next assignment would take me as well as when and where he would meet with the President of the United States. Adnan was the greatest salesman that I ever observed.

And it seems to me that, even to this day, his one great sales philosophy was "Always be prepared to walk away from the negotiations table." Any acceptable compromise for a negotiating position should be planned well in advance, and that proverbial "line in the sand" be predetermined as to where one is willing to stop.

Often at the Beverly Hills Hotel in California, there would be several of the bungalows that were being used by various members of Adnan's teams in negotiations with other companies. When negotiations seemed to hit a snag and tempers would warm up, I often witnessed Adnan come into the room with a smile on his face and those brown eyes beaming.

"My friends!" he would say. "Why are we arguing about this? Nothing is worth such tension and unkindness. We are friends, so let's just forget about this deal. It is not worth these problems among friends. Let's just end our discussions. Come on, I will buy lunch."

And he was indeed serious and sincere. If the negotiations were not going to accomplish what his team had been instructed to do, then it was time (and perfectly acceptable) to "walk away from the table." Often, and sometimes too late, I have failed to remember to walk away. But when I have remembered how easy he seemed to walk away, I attempted to do so as well—and with a smile. At those times, the burden seemed much lighter for having done it his way.

So, that was the beginning and the end of my employment with Adnan. The last time I was with him was his 50th birthday celebration at his home in Majorca. I was able to visit his Arabian horse facilities (another story about how I lost a king's ransom personally getting into that business). That evening at the party, I sat next to Uri Geller, the fellow that became famous for his supposed ability to bend metal things with his mind. I watched him take my watch off my wrist and make the hands spin. I also watched as he picked up some of the silverware off the table and bend it with his mind. I can't tell you how long it took me after I returned home to learn to bend a spoon with my mind (NOT). It was a star-studded evening with royalty from the Middle Eastern countries, New York, San Francisco, and Los Angeles business celebrities and, of course, numerous stars and starlets from Hollywood. We were transported to and from the city up to the villa by helicopter.

It was certainly a night to remember.

# *Chapter 12*

## BET ON BRIGHT

SOON AFTER I finished my graduate work for my MBA at the Stanford Graduate School of Business, the entrepreneurial bug could not be suppressed. I had an excellent job working in the Triad world of Adnan Khashoggi, but I wanted to see if I could start up a small business "on the side."

Generally, I understood that most start-up companies needed sufficient overhead capital to grow a small business. While Steve Jobs, Hewlett and Packard, and many others were able to utilize their garages to "get it going," others did not have that option, and were therefore faced with the task of finding small office space. Additionally, these entrepreneurs would probably also need secretarial assistance, office equipment such as fax machines (remember those?), copiers, a central telephone service, and more. Today, those services are plentiful through companies such as WeWork, Regus Office Space, and others. But no such services were available at the time—or at least that I could find in Silicon Valley.

I decided to see if I could jump into that service niche. I rented a large office space in a new, one-story "garden" office building. I was able to negotiate an excellent, three-year lease including tenant improvements (TIs), creating about 15 small office spaces of varying sizes, a conference room, receptionist area, restroom access, and secretarial services that could be hired by the hour.

Thinking I had a clever marketing idea, I named the company Executorial Services, combining the words *Executive* Services and *Secretarial* Services. It worked well enough, with little expense being incurred in marketing.

The contractor did a beautiful job with the TIs. I hired an excellent secretary/administrator and was able to offer office furnishings if the subtenants needed to rent them.

Business started off quickly with several excellent tenants signing up, paying a reasonable deposit upfront with first and last months' rent included. The spaces were filling up, and everything looked great.

And then the "fall." The owner of the building started having financial troubles, resulting from his inability to lease up the rest of the building and pay his mortgage. Soon, my leased space started suffering from a lack of landlord-contracted services. The heat was not always on; one day, we had no electricity, and I heard from the secretary one morning that there was no toilet paper in the restrooms!

Since I was not receiving all the services promised to me as contracted in the lease agreement, I stopped paying the rent (as I began to lose subtenants who also stopped paying me *their* rent). The owner/landlord then sued me for not paying the rent. This would not be the last time that I suffered losses because of circumstances that were not of my doing and totally beyond my ability to correct the challenges.

I had to hire an attorney to represent me in this matter (whoops, there go the profits). The attorney reviewed the contract, as well as my contracts with the subtenants. Surprise! I was absolutely right in not paying the lease amounts since the services were clearly not being provided. Good so far. Then came the lesson!

"Max, the amount that the landlord is demanding for you to pay and be released from the remaining time on your lease is almost certainly less than it will cost you to go to court, defend yourself and your new company, and pay my legal fees and court costs. You will win, and the result is… you will lose."

I did not want a lesson in lease agreement defaults. What I wanted was my losses reimbursed from the landlord's failure to perform! Sometimes those situations are referred to as "legal blackmail." It is not a bluff. It is what it is. You win the lawsuit, and it costs you more than the other side is willing to settle for. This was a lesson which, fortunately, I learned very early in my entrepreneurial journey, one without an easy solution.

If you are a small entrepreneur and you face these large legal fees you may incur, while the other side may well have corporate attorneys on the payroll whose fees are already being paid through salaries, you are often in this untenable position: "Pay me now, or pay your attorneys over the next months or years. Produce documents and show up for depositions. Face lack of income in the interim, and maybe even a jury trial with enormous costs to you, a small business entrepreneur."

So, what is the lesson, and what is the "bounce back"? The easy answer is one to always remember, whether in a legal blackmail situation or a venture that turns sour:

**Bet on bright and cut your losses early.**
**Take your hit. Lick your wounds.**
**Live on to fight another day!**
**Sometimes you just have to pay the piper.**

By the way, that also applies to hiring employees and picking partners.

The bounce back was that with my new entrepreneurial experience (and lessons learned from a not-so-great track record), I invested in another similar venture, did far more vetting of the individuals involved, including their financial strength, AND brought in an attorney as a partner. His investment was zero dollars,

> Sometimes you just have to pay the piper.

but a piece of the action in return for his legal services, pro bono. And it worked big time. No attempt was ever made to legally blackmail us because we had a sunk cost in an attorney on board. With that new team, we invested in an already established French restaurant, which took the new investment money and expanded into a new second location.

\*\*\*

WHILE WORKING FOR an attorney in Khashoggi's offices, I learned another valuable lesson about legal errors to avoid. I had been asked to review a file that contained numerous legal documents. My job was to review the business consequences of some of the language in those contracts, communication papers, and notes. I had assembled all the relevant documents and put them in a manila folder. The senior attorney buzzed me and asked me to bring the folder to his office for us to review together. I threw everything together, stacked it nicely, and put it in that folder.

I walked into the attorney's office and handed him the folder. I stood there thinking we would go to his desk or a conference table with the folder, but that did not happen. Instead, he opened it up and promptly stared at me with eyes that would pierce a tank. Without a word, he closed the folder, held it by both edges, and vigorously snapped it open. My mouth dropped to my chest. *What the hell is he doing?* Every document in that folder was tossed wildly into the air, some almost reaching the ceiling. And they landed all over his office carpet, his desk, and other furniture. I'm certain the legal secretaries could hear him shouting at me.

"James, don't you ever put a document in a folder without securing it with the little metal fasteners! Do you have any idea of the damned consequences if we lost a legal document, an original document or even a certified legal copy? Do you think we create these papers so some lame brain like you can treat them so haphazardly, resulting in our possibly losing a serious lawsuit or settlement agreement?"

"Yes, Sir—I mean, no, Sir. I mean, I understand."

"Now, I'm going to lunch. And by the time I get back, you will have picked up all these papers. And you will have reassembled them into the proper order so I can review your work. And they will be attached to the manila folder with the metal clasps! You got it? And I will never *ever* see a folder on your desk or in your files that does not have the papers secured by clasps. Understood?"

"Yes, Sir!"

Well, I missed lunch that day, but I can promise you that I never lost nor misplaced a document while in his employ. Nowadays, one has mostly computer data files. But securing those documents into the proper files on your computer is no less critical. And you need to back them up in a secure cloud. You can't trust the servers in your office or home to never go down. I have seen it happen, but fortunately so far, not to my files and records. But I certainly have had my servers go down, resulting in all the data stored in the clouds being reloaded to a new or repaired server.

He also taught me another really important lesson. There was a gentleman who often brought business opportunities to our firm to analyze whether we thought it was worthy of investment by our clients, particularly the Khashoggi companies.

The attorney called me into his office to introduce me to this man who had brought one of these "deals" for us to look at. After the introductions were made, we went over the basics of the invest-ment. It was a paddle wheel boat that would be launched at Lake Tahoe on which tourists could buy tickets to ride and eat and drink. It could also be rented for special occasions.

Actually, it sounded like a fascinating idea, and it would be a fun thing to be a part of. I took all the materials back to my office (and put them in folders with proper metal fasteners). But as I reviewed the presentation materials, I discovered several major flaws in the business plan, especially the projected number of riders on board and the number of trips that could/would be made per day. The numbers were wrong! And they grossly exaggerated the revenue and profit as a result. The plan actually had this one boat in two separate places at the same time, as though there would be revenue generated from two boats (one was a ghost ship, I guess).

I wrote up a full, business-school-like analysis. My conclusion was that this was one of the worst investments I had ever seen. It made no financial sense. The risks were enormous, and the financial part of the presentation was so bad that the math was not even presented accurately. I would not recommend this investment if it were the only one on the planet!

A few days later, the attorney called me into his office again. The gentleman who had brought us this investment was there, and I was asked to present my findings.

I built up a head of steam and launched into my review. I said all the things that I had put into the written analysis. I felt 10 feet tall. I had done a fantastic job of stopping our client from investing in a terrible deal. My MBA studies and experience had paid off.

Everything was quiet, and the attorney did not look happy.

He simply said, "Thank you, Max. I'll catch up with you later."

I wasn't sure what the silent treatment meant, but I expected that I would probably join them for lunch to continue the discussion or perhaps be rewarded for such a good job.

Into my office roared the attorney. He slammed the door and immediately began yelling.

"What the hell were you thinking! Telling him that he had made a major mistake bringing us that investment! You tore him to pieces. You did not just present it as not being an okay investment, but that it was his fault that we spent time looking at it. That doesn't matter. He is not an investment specialist. He sells insurance and knows everyone in this town. He has more contacts and access to deals than anyone I know. And because he trusts me, he brings them to me before he shows them to others who have investor clients. Now I have to go and smooth things over, explaining to him that you are a new, wet-behind-the-ears analyst who doesn't look for the possibilities or ways to fix what may have been overlooked!"

I felt like I was a cadet Doolie back at the Air Force Academy, braced at attention and sweating my shadow against the wall. I had fallen from a huge, self-boosted ego to a humiliated failure.

"Damn it, James! The next deal he might bring in could be a super winner. But I can't imagine him wanting to be put through the wringer ever again like you did to him. What you have to realize is that we never meet with someone that brings us an opportunity without giving something back to them. It could be a referral to someone else who might be able to make a deal or make an investment. It might be someone who can add to fixing the business plan faults. It might be suggestions from us on how to correct the math errors and numbers. Let me tell you one more time, and only once: *No one* who brings us an opportunity will leave here empty-handed!"

> I had fallen from a huge, self-boosted ego to a humiliated failure.

Not only did the lesson stick, but the attorney was able to retain this gentleman as a source for more deals, some of which were very prosperous.

Oh, and guess what? That paddle wheel boat has been operating on Lake Tahoe from about 1972 until the time of this writing.

In fact, today, there might even be two of them.

**Dad and Mom** and "Little Max" on the first farm 1942

**Looking for my** next chore as the "Son of a Sharecropper"

**BMOC, Jack of** all trades and "Master of None" Voted "Most Likely to Succeed

**Started in the** 3rd grade. Learned so much that prepared me for the military/Air Force Academy. Worked hard to make the TN All State Band

**Pilot Training,** 1964-1965
Helicopter Training was next, then working with the astronauts recovery program, and then off to war

**One of the Cadet Leaders** for a tour of all the South American countries' air force academies 1963

**Jolly Green Headquarters,** Udorn Thailand With co-pilot Billy Privette

**Dad and Max** contemplating where to go next

**Sometimes you just** have to take a stand and go with your gut

**Warrior Ethos: Warrior** ethos is the embodiment of the warrior spirit: tough minded-ness, tireless motivation, an unceasing vigilance, a willingness to sacrifice one's life for the country, if necessary, and a commitment to be the world's premier air, space and cyberspace force

**Attending one of** the philanthropic charity events. Linda has been on the CEO Advisory Board for many years

**A great picture** of the Center for Character and Leadership Development, Polaris Hall, winter at the Air Force Academy

**My Dad called** me the "Eagle Man", my collection of eagle memorabilia and research of the history of eagle symbolism. This is outside my offices at AKM 2017

# Chapter 13

## NEVER BURN YOUR BRIDGES BEHIND YOU

WELL, JUST A few years out of Stanford, as well as the initial stages of my learning how to conduct business in the real world, I experienced the lesson of the old trite expression, "Never burn your bridges behind you."

Travel, especially when working for Adnan's international companies, could be exhausting as well as potentially damaging to one's family life. It seemed that every time I was asked to go on an international business trip, most often to Europe or the Middle East, it was scheduled for about a week's duration. However, most trips ended up being extended for at least two weeks, and sometimes considerably longer. This was a tremendous burden on a wife with two young children back home in California. And I sure didn't want to miss out on so much of the children's activities, not to mention my responsibilities as a husband and father.

Spending a year away from home during the Vietnam war was vastly different. A passion for serving one's country in time of war helped mitigate the sacrifices of being away from family. Plus, while not on missions from your home base, you were in one place with your own housing and personal effects, i.e., not living out of a suitcase.

Before I left the United States for Vietnam, we celebrated my daughter's first birthday a couple of months early so I would not miss that singularly important occasion. Just in case I didn't make it back, there would be the pictures and memories of Dad. But even going away on business trips seemed like an emotionally damaging event for me, and even more so for the family. There were the missed swimming lessons and meets, the merit badges earned in scouting, dealing with homework, and attending school events. And how about the emptiness of not sitting down together around the evening dinner table and hearing all about that day's activities—ouch!

One of the Triad group's clients was a real estate professional with a vertically integrated company there in Silicon Valley. My time and experience had been primarily focused solely on analyzing real estate investments and presenting those to investors. It was a wonderful experience but limited compared to all the other opportunities possible in the real estate industry. This particular client's businesses included various real estate ventures such as property management, residential and commercial development, residential resales offices, investment property sales, and syndication. The owner had told me that if I ever decided to leave Adnan, he would like to talk to me about joining his company.

Well, I took the opportunity to do so. To my surprise, he offered me the job of president of the company that was the conglomerate of his numerous holdings. *Clearly, I thought, "I might well be going in way over my head.*" When I expressed my appreciation for the offer (and my reservations), he assured me that he was not going anywhere and that we could work together.

Wow! My ego was so large at that moment, you could not have fitted it into a gymnasium. And of course, I said "Yes." The Triad executive group expressed their disappointment that I was not staying but also their support and encouragement for me in my new venture. Plus, they told me that if it did not work out, to come on back.

The owner turned out to be a highly effective mentor. He gave me significant responsibilities and an incentive to grow the companies. We built a real estate investment brokerage and management team with projects ranging from syndicating a 1,200-unit apartment building and several garden office buildings, to increasing the residential real estate offices to 10 locations and continuing to present investment opportunities to the Triad group and other Silicon Valley companies (sale leasebacks) and individuals.

As we expanded the operations, I was able to hire two fellow alumni from the Stanford GSB. We made a great team and were able to create some great investment opportunities.

But doggone it, the owner of this company called me in one day with bad news. Some of his personal investments were not performing as well as he had hoped, and he needed to cut back on expenses and reduce the sales and investment forces. Additionally, he was selling the corporate offices to one of our investors and had decided that he could save money by putting one of his long-term residential realtors into the management position with a reduced number of locations, closing several of the real estate offices I had opened.

How much clearer could the message be?

"Max, I'm sorry all our plans have to change. Take all the time you need, but I think maybe you are going to need to seek a position with another company."

*Damn!* That hurt.

So, I called my former direct boss in the Triad group. "Wonder if maybe you'd have time for a drink at Mac's Tea Room after work today? It'll be like old times when you drew all our new organizational plans on cocktail napkins and paper placemats." (I am pretty sure I still have some of those placemats to this day.)

"How about 6 this afternoon? I've been expecting your call."

What! How had the word gotten out to him so quickly? The owner of the company I was leaving had already made sure that the old bridge didn't need any repairs. He had called to let the Triad group's founding CEO know that he would appreciate his taking a call from me if it happened.

> Never burn your bridges behind you.

And apparently, his response had been to ask why. When told that I might call to get caught up on how the real estate world was progressing in the Triad ventures, he told him there probably could be an interest on my part in finding a new opportunity.

Never burn your bridges behind you.

*Nice. Great. Thanks!*

The result was that a few days later, I had a new position with Triad. I would continue to search out real estate investment opportunities. However, remembering why I left him in the first place, I insisted that I would only be responsible for the United States, and NOT international real estate deals that required travel out of the country!

This was mutually agreed upon, but five days *before* I officially started the new position, can you believe it, *FIVE DAYS* before I officially started, *I* was on an airplane headed for Beirut.

So much for my entrepreneurial self-control.

# *Chapter 14*

## WHAT MIGHT HAVE BEEN

ONE OF THE new ventures I was invited to look at was an entity that we formed for Adnan called Triad Entertainment. Since the team seemed to find themselves often in the company of Adnan at New York and Hollywood social functions, it was not hard to understand why various entertainment ventures and opportunities were presented to us.

I was asked to try my hand at working in this new business (at least it was new to *me*) with a very well-known Hollywood actor, Mel Ferrer, who was married to Audrey Hepburn. Mel became the President of Triad Entertainment, and I was his VP. Why me—I can only guess! But it was greatly exciting to be tossed into the "Tinsel Town" industry.

My first "assignment" was to begin reading movie scripts that were submitted to Triad to determine whether or not we should invest in them. It was a real learning experience, and I must admit that I had great difficulty in making that imaginary leap from the pages of a written script to what it might look like on the big silver screen. And from all the failures of movies at the box office, I suspect I am not the only one with that difficulty. So, here go a couple of failures that I participated in.

If my memory serves me right, it was a movie to be made with Richard Roundtree following his major box office success in *Shaft*. To help protect the downside, we loaded up the cast with famous and popular actors and actresses. They included Broderick Crawford, Chuck Connors, Marie-José Nat, Max von Sydow, Ray Milland, and maybe some others I don't remember. The movie was in the popular genre (at the time) of international spy thrillers. It was shot largely in Beirut, and even the Air Force cooperated in some of the flying and airport filming. What an exciting adventure for me. And then the cotton really got tall for this country boy—a London premiere for the first showing!

Uh oh! The film did not play well with the movie critics. I wasn't involved in the decision as to what to eventually do with the movie. But the next time I heard about its showing, it was featured in a drive-in movie somewhere in a not-so-affluent neighborhood in Florida.

My next venture in the movie world was a bit more up the talent scale of an MBA. Two young men from Los Angeles brought us an idea for a new movie script. It seemed that they had taken their newly developed computer skills and utilized them to compile data from the most popular movies, analyzing what the features were that were common to the most successful ones. What they had discovered was that the following were prevalent in many of the most popular movies:

- Doctors
- Animals

- Airline travel, especially involving stewardesses (whoops, I mean flight attendants)
- Major cities
- Romantic entanglements

So, they took their computer analysis and hired a writer to put together a screenplay that contained those ingredients. The story became one about the San Francisco Zoo, where there was a horribly ill hippopotamus. Only a veterinarian in New York had the experience and education to treat this particular animal. On the back-and-forth flights from San Francisco to New York, the vet met a beautiful flight attendant based in San Francisco, with whom he later became engaged. But alas, the hectic schedules created conflicts which set the scene for drama that was difficult to resolve.

That is, until the hippo miraculously healed, the flight attendant was relocated to New York, and all three lived "happily ever after."

Well, the movie did not make it to the big silver screen. But here is a bounce back: It became a made-for-TV movie. I know this because late one evening, I was surfing channels and stopped on one that played old movies. At first, it seemed like maybe I had seen this movie before, but then it dawned on me that this was the screenplay set to the small black-and-white TV screen.

I want to share one last hard fall in the entertainment business. We negotiated the rights to Laura Ingalls Wilder's *Little House on the Prairie* books to be made into a series of movies. This was when the idea of creating a series of movies one after the other, such as *Star Wars* and *Indiana Jones,* which were having great success, was popular. However, the attorney that was put in charge of these negotiations failed to find the necessary team to complete bringing this venture to fruition. What a great idea it *might* have been! But the rights were subsequently sold to another organization, and you probably know how that turned out. *Little House on the Prairie* turned out to be one of the most successful television series ever made. Somewhere along the checkered path of Triad Entertainment, the entity was put up on a dusty shelf. I rarely saw Mel Ferrer after that, usually to have a cocktail and laugh about our failed ventures. But the lesson learned by me was clear: The next (and *only*) investment in movies I ever made was to buy tickets and popcorn!

> It's probably good to remember not to stray too far from your field of expertise.

**It's probably good to remember not to stray too far from your field of expertise.**

# Chapter 15

## STORIES FROM MY DAYS
## AT DAYS INN

AFTER I LEFT Adnan's organizations the second time, I chose to move to Sacramento, CA. The competition was tough in the San Francisco Bay area, so I thought perhaps in a smaller city like Sacramento, I might be able to become a "bigger fish in a smaller pond," i.e., less competition than with those who choose to stay in the areas of Stanford, UC Berkeley, and San Jose State. I listed my home in Los Altos and quickly bought one in Sacramento. Much like a lot of my failed financial decisions, this one led to a mess.

I bought the Sacramento house before the Los Altos one sold, and it was on the market for almost a year before it did. There were also lots of maintenance items that had to be taken care of in my absence. So, there I was, carrying two mortgages—two sets of upkeep and maintenance expenses—with equity tied up and cash unavailable in a home I no longer needed. And the real problem was that I had no income.

At first, I rented an office from a law firm and put my real estate broker's license to good use. At one point, I recall having a possible project list of 70 plus, but none of them seemed to have a high degree of probability of success. In fact, I would sometimes become so frustrated and depressed that I would play backgammon against myself just so I could get a win!

Finally, I moved one of the possible real estate transactions I hoped to broker a little higher on the list. A friend told me that one of his clients wanted to buy an apartment complex in Colorado Springs, CO. Since I had gone to school there at the Air Force Academy, I thought maybe I might be able to participate as a real estate broker. So, with a strong recommendation from the friend, I was able to sign an agreement to be the broker. It was a 1,200-unit complex with a substantial sales price. I needed the money badly, so I negotiated a commission agreement, much reduced from the then-current market rates.

Hurrah! It closed. We flew in a private jet to Colorado Springs to close the final documentation and then to Santa Monica, CA, to celebrate. The client's partner had a Learjet, but it had not added the necessary noise-reduction modifications necessary to fly into the Santa Monica airport. That didn't seem to bother the two partners, so in we went, louder than permissible. I remember that as we deplaned, the ground crew was hooking up a towing vehicle to the front of the plane. I assumed they were taking it to an area to park it.

The owner later called me in my hotel room and advised that I should get myself a commercial airline ticket from Los Angeles back to Sacramento. Seems the FAA had grounded his jet and levied a very significant fine. One of the partners, the world's largest tomato grower, didn't seem upset at all. I was impressed.

But I was definitely unimpressed when I had great difficulties collecting my fees. Weeks went by with threats and counterthreats and legal actions initiated by me until finally, without prior notice, I received a check in the mail for tens of thousands of dollars. You can just imagine how fast I drove from the mailbox to the bank to deposit that check and make doubly sure that it cleared before some other controversy reared its ugly head.

> Sometimes when you are crawling up the mountain of success, you may fall off, slide way down, or even hit the valley floor below.

Sometimes when you are crawling up the mountain of success, you may fall off, slide way down, or even hit the valley floor below. This can even happen after you think you have planted your flag on the mountaintop. The remedy is to grab hold of whatever you can on the way down and reclimb some of the territory you have already been through. The path to the top is never a straight line!

But that was a one-time deal. I still needed a steady income (very important for a risk-taking entrepreneur). Again, a friend came through with a salvation lead. *(Always remember to network constantly and keep records and frequent communications with your contacts.)* A local very successful residential real estate office wanted to expand into the commercial real estate brokerage business. Given my experience with Miller Properties in Los Altos, CA, and the solid credentials of my real estate experience since leaving Stanford, I was hired.

Actually, things went very well in the beginning. I closed a couple of deals with new agents that we hired, and I was able to teach classes to the residential agents, which were sufficient for them to begin to bring in some of their clients to explore investment opportunities.

I suppose I shouldn't have felt too guilty at the time, but another far more promising opportunity was presented to me. With "hat in hand," I met with the owner of the firm and explained that I needed to resign from the new venture. She was extremely kind and understanding, and so off I went to a new world of "hotels and motels."

*What?! Where did that come from, and why?*

Well, when I was with Adnan's organizations, one of my responsibilities was the Chairmanship of the Triad project in Salt Lake City, The Salt Lake International Center. This was a 1,000-acre industrial park near the airport. During that time, I met some contractors from Atlanta who were seeking construction contracts in Utah. They were two great guys with whom I enjoyed my time, especially since we could talk about what it was like living in the South. One day, I received a call from them suggesting that I should contact the owners of Days Inns of America, headquartered in Atlanta—a company for whom they had built hotels and motels. The Day family was planning on expanding into the Western states and needed someone with experience to help with site selection, mainly for the existing East Coast franchisees who wanted to expand principally into California. It was too great an offer to be turned down.

So, off to Atlanta I went to spend a month learning all about the hotel-motel business. I wasn't sure I could even spell motel correctly, so this was a great opportunity to venture into another venue of real estate. I quickly learned that the hotel business wasn't really a real estate business, but truly an *operational* business. After all, how much the land cost had little to do with how much to charge for coffee in the restaurant. And once the decision to build was made, the coffee became even more important!

> The climb up the hotel mountain started with a great personal fall.

The climb up the hotel mountain started with a great personal fall. I received a call from home indicating that by the time I could get there, most of the furniture would be gone, the moving van would have already been there, and I could pick up my two children (my 11-year-old daughter and 9-year-old son) at my mother-in-law's home. The call included a message not to try to find their mother (my wife). That was a blow!

I flew home, picked up my children, and we started a "team." I had virtually no idea how to be a mother *and* a father, starting with cooking! Being from the old South, if my dad had caught me in the kitchen doing anything but eating, he might have taken a plow line to me. That was a role reserved for Mom. I don't remember any of my male friends in high school ever enrolling in home economics. We chose auto shop instead. But thanks to a couple of wonderful children, we made it.

Well, sorta.

It was a time in our culture when the roles of men and women were changing. In fact, the magazine of the Stanford Graduate School of Business decided to do an article about our now family/ team of three. It was to reflect the new changes occurring in family makeups. The article was titled "Bachelor, Father, Executive: Pride or Panic."

It was a humorous look at my attempting to balance work and parenting. Every paragraph was a phone call from my children to me at work. For example:

"Dad, there is about a foot of water in the laundry room. Should we call somebody?"

*Panic!*

"Dad, I just was elected cheerleader!"

*Pride.*

"Dad, the principal of my school said he needed to have a meeting with you right away."

*Panic!*

"Dad, I got a B+ in Math!"

*Pride.*

"Dad, I brought home my report card. I don't think you are going to be very happy."

*Panic!*

And a big one that required much more than just one line:

"Dad, the graduate student that you hired to stay with us while you are in Atlanta has taken off. She left a note for you. I'll read it for you."

*Mr. James, I have totally lost control of your children. I am leaving to catch a bus back to San Diego to live with my mother!*

"That's all it says, Dad. Not sure what she means by it. But don't worry Dad, I'm pretty sure we'll be okay until you can come home."

*Yikes! OMG! Call their Grandmother! Call a neighbor! Pray!!!*

\*\*\*

AFTER THAT FALL, we seemed to find ways to be a successful team, but in no small part without the help of friends and relatives. I still had to travel in this new job and that meant finding some other ways to keep our little family together. With more help and more experiments, we made it for a few years.

As I found great hotel building sites throughout California and began presenting them to Days Inn headquarters executives for their approval to be presented to the potential franchisees, the decision was made that these sites needed to be kept in-house to become a place for a company-owned Days Inn facility. That quickly led to my becoming a partner in Days Inn, and I was assigned the Western states as my territory to develop. The company had divided the United States into separate territories that several men were awarded the responsibility to build and operate hotels and motels. At that time, Days Inn was the sixth-largest lodging company in the world. I was honored to be brought into the executive ranks and was fortunate to start a partnership which was called "Days of the West." There were lots of falls and bounce backs in building what eventually became 18 hotels and motels in California and Nevada, which my team built, co-owned, and operated. My hope is that some of those hotel and motel stories will be interesting and entertaining, and most of all, beneficial to you.

I was on the road looking at sites when I received a call from the man who was in charge of construction for me.

"Max, you need to get here as quickly as you can. We have a big problem!"

Within a few hours, I arrived at the site. There I found the head of AIM (American Indian Movement) in full war dress doing a war dance on the construction site. He claimed that we had to stop work because the hotel site was on an ancient Indian burial ground.

*Oh no.* Just what I needed *after* having bought the land, contracted with numerous construction companies, and put the financing in place.

The short story is that we negotiated a settlement. We would hire the University of California Berkeley to "do a dig"—i.e., a full, ancient archeological excavation. Many months of delays and many thousands of dollars later, we received the full report. *Yep!* The site did hold a problem for us. The report said there were three separate areas that had to be considered. The first was whether or not we would be prohibited from building on the site at all. If so, the second was to what extent, and the third, if we could build at all, was what were the portions of the property we could build on.

The first was, in fact, an ancient Indian burial ground. Result: We could not touch it in any way, and certainly not to construct a building over that area.

The second was an area that contained "ancient Indian artifacts." That included broken pottery pieces, a few arrowheads, and some other objects. The settlement forbade us from building any structures over that area, but we *could* pave over it and use it for parking... on one condition. We had to agree that it could be dug up in 50 years to again look for ancient Indian artifacts.

*Fine. Okay.* I agreed.

The third area was designated as containing "modern-day artifacts." What the hell are those? Soda bottles, beer cans, hubcaps, and plastic dishes. And the restrictions for these "artifacts"? Build anything we wanted. *Whew.* So, we built our hotel and our parking lot and satisfied AIM.

\*\*\*

I NEEDED ONE very special permit to build a 10-story hotel at the intersection of Century Blvd. and the 405 Freeway at the Los Angeles Airport. The Redevelopment Agency finally agreed to cooperate with me in securing the various parcels of land needed to complete the project. If I agreed to purchase two service stations, they would close a street connecting some residential houses to Century Blvd. I agreed. Additionally, there was one older house that I needed to purchase to complete the combined parcels for construction. The agency said that one was up to me alone; I should not expect them to get involved until I had completed the acquisition.

The home was owned by an elderly lady, originally from Texas. And she was Texas tough! She had learned what we were up to and that we needed her house (or her "home," as she was quick to correct us), so we arranged an appointment to visit with her there. After we introduced ourselves, she invited us in and asked that we sit on her living room couch. On the coffee table in front of us—in plain and obvious view—lay a fully loaded revolver. I got the message.

> Know your opponent and respect their advantage, (and hopefully, it won't be a loaded gun).

The negotiations went quietly and respectfully. Bottom line? She agreed to sell but at a price about three times what the house would have sold for on the open market.

*So, what is the lesson here? Know your opponent and respect their advantage, (and hopefully, it won't be a loaded gun).*

Another time, we were building a 180-room motel at the confluence of the American River and the Sacramento River about two exits from the State Capitol building in Sacramento. Hoping to hold the construction costs down, we decided that we would *not* build the project with union labor only. Instead, we would use both independent contractors (nonunion) as well as union labor. The system that is utilized in this arrangement is called a "two-gate system," meaning that union workers come into the fenced construction site through one gate, and the nonunion workers come through a separate gate. The union was very unhappy with this decision, especially since it was occurring within a couple of miles of the elected state officials at the Capitol Building and the lobbyist who represented the unions. Regardless, we started the early phases of construction, which were mainly ground preparation. Our construction office was within the fenced area of the construction site.

One afternoon, I received a panicked phone call. It seemed that some people had gone onto the site and turned over the construction trailer… with all our construction team gathered inside. Our construction manager was in the trailer, which was now lying on its side. He called the police for assistance, who quickly told him that there was an officer on site. What we found out was that was indeed *almost* true. There was one policeman sitting in his squad car on the adjacent property, a service station. He was taking pictures but never left his vehicle! Rumor had it that sometime later that afternoon, at some remote location in Sacramento, "there was quite a brawl, baseball bats and all." Amazingly, no one went to jail.

That same site was protected from the two rivers overflowing by a very large riverbank about 10 feet in height. We planned a major celebration for the groundbreaking of this hotel. The widow of the founder of Days Inn attended, as did state, county, and city-elected officials. One of the prominent state representatives was the Lt. Governor, Mike Curb. After a brief ceremony and the traditional groundbreaking and shoveling of the ground by the celebrities, the caterers brought out all the food into the big tent that was set up on the site. Within a few minutes, over the riverbanks from the river side of the levies came a rush of homeless men who apparently claimed the riverbanks at that location as their temporary home—at least for this event. The Lt. Governor jumped into his limousine and beat a rapid retreat before the media cameras could capture his being there. While some of my staff and I attempted to keep the event under control (very unsuccessfully as the food disappeared), Mrs. Day also escaped into a safe vehicle and hastily departed the site. Thankfully, everyone made it home safely. The river "residents" left with a full stomach, and I was pretty sure that I would lose my part-

> Always preplan and pre-inspect whatever venue you are going to use for any type of presentation.

nership interest in this first motel I had built for Days Inn. Fortunately, that did not happen. It did point out another major principle: Always preplan and pre-inspect whatever venue you are going to use for any type of presentation.

**What is even better is to be able to do both,** and that was the case with the Days of the West team. As I mentioned earlier, I knew virtually nothing about the operational side of managing a lodging facility. I mean, who knew the price of coffee was a big deal! Two important executive slots were critical: a person who had experience and skills to operate the facilities, and someone who was tough enough and smart enough to handle the building of the hotels and motels from conception to cutting the opening ribbon. The COO came from a family of hotel owner/operators and international brand executives. When there was an executive meeting at home base in Atlanta, this gentleman always accompanied me (mostly because I had insufficient experience to respond to questions from the committee). To this day, he, Steve Stratton, and I have remained friends and significant business partners in other real estate deals. The EVP of Construction, Jim Hansen, was a master's degree graduate of the School of Engineering at Stanford University. Clearly, these two men were well qualified to take on their respective roles in our new company. They had (and still have) impeccable character and integrity.

After I sold my interest in Days Inn, I started several small companies in the hotel development, management, and brokerage industries. It was a reasonably successful venture, with this company contracting to manage a few properties owned by others. It was an okay business, but nothing like managing your own real estate and operating for your own bottom line with your sole ideas rather than the owners'. We were successful in finding a nice property to develop for another client, but not for our own account. Fortunately, our financial "bacon" was saved by managing to be the real estate broker for a very large hotel property at the San Francisco Airport. We even attempted to own and operate a restaurant that was adjacent to a large golf resort property. Early success, but like four out of five start-up restaurants, we soon started having cash flow problems.

So, we sold it at a loss and moved on.

Somehow, I survived all the trials, turmoil, and failures of my career in the hotel business, only because of my perseverance and hard work, I suppose. However, the industry chose to recognize me with an election to the California Hotel and Motel Association Board of Directors and appointment as the Director of their Political Action Committee. And the governor appointed me to the Governor's California Tourism Corporation's Board of Directors!

> Often, you just gotta keep grinding away, reaching for the next plateau on that climb to the mountain peak.

I hope these stories remind you of this important truth: Often, you just gotta keep grinding away, reaching for the next plateau on that climb to the mountain peak. Remember that many of your falls will result in your eventually planting your flag on the mountaintop. And never stop dreaming and striving for when the day will come that you will be able to proudly walk down from the top, making room for someone else to follow your path to the top, walking the beaten trail that you made for them.

# Chapter 16

## HOW LOW CAN YOU GO

JOHN, A FORMER employee, had set up an appointment with me soon after I had sold my interests in the 18 hotels in which I had been a partner. We had built, owned, and operated these properties throughout California and Nevada, and John had been a desk clerk at one of the hotels in Sacramento. I thought it took quite a bit of gumption for a desk clerk to call up the "big guy" and seek an appointment to present me with an investment opportunity, so I said, "John, why don't you come to my office, and let's see what you have." So, John (and his wife) showed up and made the presentation.

"John, that was an excellent presentation. I don't know if that product will do all you claim it will, but I do recognize the benefits of nutritional supplements. Now, if I understand the deal, you want me to sign up as a distributor with you as my sponsor, right? Everything I sell will result in a small profit for me, but also for you. And I can, in turn, sign up other people to sponsor, and I'll be paid a portion of what they sell. Is that right?"

"Yes, Sir. So, if you sign up two, and they sign up two, and they sign up two more, you could end up making a lot of money from all those various multiple levels of distributors that are in your organization."

*Level one (2 x 2 = 4), and Level two (4 x 2 = 8), and Level three (8 x 2 = 16), and Level four (16 x 2 = 32), and Level five (32 x 2 = 64).*

**2 + 4 + 8 + 16 + 32 + 64 = 126**

"And if they all produce $10 each for your share, you pocket **$1,260 each month** for as long as they keep producing. And Mr. James, what if each sponsored five individuals?"

*Level one (5 x 5 = 25), Level two (25 x 5 = 125), Level three (125 x 5 = 625),*

*Level four (625 x 5 = 3,125), Level five (3125 x 5 =15,625).*

**5 +25 + 125 +625 + 3,125 + 15,625 = 19,530**

"And if they all produce just five distributors each, your $10 share would equal **$195,300 per month!**"

In all reality, this was a distribution system that was not taught at Stanford's Graduate School of Business. I only knew of a couple of companies that used this system, so I had some questions and concerns.

"John, I am not very familiar with Multilevel Marketing. I think some refer to it as a pyramid scheme, and isn't that illegal? A scam?"

"Yes, but this is not a pyramid. We meet all the legal requirements to stay classified as a *network marketing company.*"

"John, what if I said that I think network marketing is a great distribution system, as evidenced by the great success of Amway? They are a great company with great leaders of integrity. In fact, the founders are two of the richest, most philanthropic men on the planet. Their products are outstanding and well received by their customers."

"Then I'd say you are going to love this company."

"Okay. But John, what if I said to you that I don't like network marketing companies? I hear that they trick you into going into a big meeting, lock the doors, and do a hard sell. They promise that everyone will get rich if only they buy a lot of product, resell it, and convince other suckers to do the same. I also hear that people have gone bankrupt by buying way too much product to qualify for luxurious trips to places like Hawaii, resulting in their going broke, even losing their home, and filing bankruptcy. What would you say to that?"

John's response was classic.

"Then I'd say you are going to love this company!"

Yep, I signed up. And I immediately bought quite a lot of the product to share with "friends and family" to see what the results would be. The product was a liquid mineral drink strongly based on potassium. It tasted horrible. But I was a pretty good salesman, concentrating on the benefits and presenting them in a scientific way. I traveled to the company's distributors' many meetings and events. I learned how to hold meetings and presentations in someone's living room or a large hotel conference center. I learned how to explain the marketing program and the structure of the distribution system. In fact, one *could* make a great deal of money, but recruiting a distribution team and helping them do the same was and is not an easy task. Most recruited distributors give up pretty early, but some stay. And many continue purchasing the products if they are good buys.

I did well, but not great. I did, however, really enjoy the sales and leadership roles necessary to succeed in the network marketing business. So, when an opportunity came along to jump ship from doing that full-time and to get back into real estate investments, development, and brokerage, I left the MLM world. (For the time being, at least.)

After this initial run with MLM, I went back to my interests in real estate and hotel management. That lasted for a few years, with some successes and some failures. However, it was after the last failure as a lodging company consultant, building a motel in Davis, CA, that I really ran into financial problems. But following that fall, I was given a chance to get back into an MLM, and I attempted one desperate effort to make another successful run in network marketing.

A previous associate distributor from the first MLM called me and said he was in on the ground floor of an exciting new distribution enterprise. It had a great compensation program, and it was a product in an industry that was very stable with widespread demand.

It all sounded okay, so I asked him to come out to my house with a sample of the product, and we could further discuss it. The next day, he shows up at the house and rings the doorbell. When I asked him to come on in, he said, "First, let's go down to my car, and I'll show you the product."

*I was a little surprised he didn't just bring it in with him, but okay.* So out to his car we went. He opened up the trunk, and there lay a 25-pound sack of dog food.

"So, where is the product?" I asked.

"That's it," he said, matter-of-factly.

"What? Dog food?"

"You have a dog, don't you, Max?"

"Yeah."

"Do you feed him dog food?"

"Of course."

"And I bet you know lots of folks who also have dogs. And there is an almost certainty that they feed their dogs dog food, too. So think of the size of the marketplace! We can sell them this quality dog food at a price that will be hard to beat—even at competitive retail pricing. Plus, we can sign them up as distributors so that they can buy it at the wholesale distributor price, and they even get it free if they sign up distributors underneath them in the compensation plan."

Now, let me rewind. Actually, I shouldn't describe this as a "chance" to get back into MLM, but rather that I *needed* to get back into MLM. Reluctantly, I signed up as a network marketing distributor under him. As is typical, a new distributor needs to use the products themselves and have enough on hand to demonstrate the product to potential customers and potential distributors.

Always being the optimist, I ordered the dog food. I don't remember how I was talked into the amount of product I ordered, but late one afternoon, the doorbell rang again.

"Mr. James?' the truck driver asked hesitantly.

"That's me."

"Where do you want me to unload your dog food order?"

"Unload? Can't we just set it there on the driveway? I'll move it into the garage from there."

"Sir, I don't think you are going to want to leave it on the driveway. First of all, there is way too much. It will block your drive.

And second, it has a smell to it that's… well… it's going to attract not only a lot of dogs, but probably squirrels. And, maybe more importantly, you're going to attract some rats."

"Why will it block my drive? How many sacks are there?"

"Sir, I have a full pallet for you."

*Egads!* That was about a stack of four wide, four long, and four high. Yep—34 sacks of 25 pounds of dog food. 750 pounds! I moved one of the cars out of the garage so that he could back up to the garage door and offload the pallet of 750 pounds of dog food.

The next morning, I went down to the car garage, only to be met by an overpowering smell of dog food. I opened the garage door and discovered about six of the neighbors' dogs sniffing around. I closed the door, went around to the outside, and discovered the large oak trees were also full of squirrels. Lastly, the next night, I listened to what had to be mice and rats rummaging through the garage. I knew that this was not going to work unless I could sell this mess quickly. Remember, cut your losses early!

My friend set up the first presentation, and I was thinking that getting up on stage in front of a group of dog owners in a hotel conference room with a sack of this smelly dog food was going to be a problem. I wondered if he had told them in advance what the product was. I sure hoped so.

So, I loaded up my Mercedes trunk with three sacks and headed off to meet him.

"Which hotel are we presenting in?" I asked when I arrived to pick him up.

"Actually, we are going over to someone's home that my veterinarian said might be interested. They have a couple of dogs, and the vet said they were nice people and could probably use some extra money as distributors."

We pulled up in a not-so-great neighborhood, with dogs from several houses, including the prospect's, growling and barking. The front yard was fenced in with that popular sign hanging on the gate:

"Beware of Dog. He bites!"

I blow the car horn from the street, and the owner comes out and invites us in after assuring us that the dogs were locked up.

*Here I am, a financially falling and failing now ex-multimillionaire, visiting in a home with my smelly, 25-pound sack of dog food, trying to sell it to folks who probably know far more than I about how to feed their dogs good nutritious food.*

The presentation was a total bust. They didn't buy, didn't think we knew what we were talking about, didn't like the smell of the dog food, and couldn't understand how the distributor compensation plan worked (how they could possibly make any money or even get the dog food for free).

I left with my tail tucked between my legs like an old, wounded hound dog. I dropped my friend off at this car and drove home to my garage—nay, animal farm.

The next morning, I called the network marketing company, and my associate and I demanded, upon the threat of fire and brimstone raining down on them, that they remove the pallet of dog food from my garage that day. Apparently, I was not the only dissatisfied distributor. The company was never really able to make a go of it in network marketing.

*Just how hard can I fall?*

Being without any liquid assets and owing lots of money to not only creditors but to family and friends, the effort to sell stinky dog food in a network marketing system had to be *the lowest point of my entire career.*

# *Chapter 17*

## SOMETIMES IT JUST AIN'T YOUR FAULT

WHEN IT BECAME apparent that I was not the one to continue consulting (no equity) on the building of that motel in Davis, CA, I thought maybe it was time for me to go back to what I thought was my first love, real estate. After all, that is what I had focused on in biz school and had started my career in with Adnan, the Salt Lake International Center, Miller Properties, and building, owning, and operating 18 hotels. For the client in Davis, we had obtained all the necessary permits, purchased a hotel franchise, finished the interior décor selections, and started construction with the site owner, who was a contractor.

During that time period, I had spent many hours with the motel owner's son. Jim was bright and obviously wanted to begin to move out from under his dad's supervision and start his own business. He had been approached by the franchise seller for RE/MAX to see whether he would be interested in opening a RE/MAX franchise operation in some of the areas not yet taken in Northern California. Since Jim knew of my past experience opening and running, residential retail sales offices in the San Francisco Bay area, he invited me to participate in looking at this venture.

RE/MAX was booming, growing in leaps and bounds. We formed a partnership with Jim running the administrative side of the business, and my role was to locate new office facilities, recruit agents, and work with those agents as needed. This all sounded so good that instead of buying one franchise territory, we bought seven!

*After all, isn't it true that "if one is good, seven is better"? Absolutely not!*

Even the franchise saleswoman suggested that we did not need to start that ambitiously. We, on the other hand, felt that we could protect one and all of the territories if we controlled our "neighbors." And we did not want to lose the opportunity in those additional areas to competing franchise owners.

> Isn't it true that "if one is good, seven is better"? Absolutely not!

The cost of opening a new office for real estate agents was heavy. First, you had to locate a great facility in just the right area with curb appeal and access feasibility. Negotiating a lease almost always included significant tenant improvements (walls for private offices, cubicles for semi-private offices, electrical for all the office equipment, plus telephone lines for numerous locations throughout the facility). After running out of personal investment funds, I hit the streets to find investors who wanted to join us. Fortunately, we were successful. The pitch to investors went something like this:

RE/MAX is growing very rapidly as a brand name. The company's success has been its ability to attract many of the very top real estate sales producers. That success simply came from their system. Instead of the normal compensation system of paying the agent about 60 percent of the sales commission and charging them nothing for utilization of the office facilities, RE/MAX sought out the most successful agents and paid them 90 percent of the commission *but* charged the agent what was called a "desk fee." The desk fee varied, depending on whether the agent chose a private office or a semi-private cubicle. The more productive agents could earn considerably more commission revenue by taking a bigger cut of the sales proceeds and paying a set monthly "desk fee." From many of the existing real estate offices, successful agents took the bait and came over to our RE/MAX offices, paid the flat "desk fees," and took home more of the sales commissions from their listings and sales.

To finance opening all these offices, I had invested all of my remaining personal liquid assets and was able to obtain a Small Business Administration Loan, putting up the equity in my home as collateral. But we still needed more money, so I called on my "friends" who knew me and my business successes and background. Most investors funded via a convertible note with a very attractive interest rate. And, as we met with some real early success in attracting top agents in the seven territories in which we had purchased franchises, we were able to "go back to the well" to borrow more money from those early-in investors.

The overhead was enormous, as most everything was financed: long-term office leases, equipment leases for copiers, telephones, computers, furniture for all those agents, and the list goes on.

And we bought each of the franchises from the Master Franchise Holder for California.

Those purchases were made with down payments and monthly payments that were a percentage of sales and a fixed payment.

Administrative secretarial staff, escrow employees…

All times seven!

But the fun was equivalent to the overhead! We had residential resale offices with great agents. The franchise territories were contingent on each other, and they ranged geographically from (but not including) the San Francisco area up the Pacific Coast to the wine country, then back eastward and down through Sonoma, Napa areas, and up to (but not including) Sacramento.    While I was still living in the Sacramento area in my "dream home," I would often stay overnight in the wine country so that I could attend the weekly realtor breakfast meetings and tour the new available listings with some of our agents (and set up recruiting sessions with agents I was trying to attract). I stayed at the Sonoma Mission Inn, Silverado Country Club, as well as a few other great bed-and-breakfast facilities.

Everything was looking good. But "into each life, a little rain must fall." Yeah, okay, but is that a cloud burst, a thunderstorm, or 20 days and 20 nights?!

Our stormy weather was a recession. Interest rates during the '80s recession went through the roof with CDs up to 20%. Housing sales plummeted. Agents who had marginal revenues quit the business in droves. But what about those very successful agents whom we had recruited? The attractive formula stayed the same, but the input number that killed the golden goose was the gross sales commissions. The great agents knew and felt the result immediately.

Why incur a heavy desk fee when the reduced gross commissions received on their high split didn't even cover the fixed fees? Why not go back to a very low-risk situation, i.e., no fixed costs, but still more net revenue with the lower commission rate percentage?

*But what if I host a party and nobody comes?*

And that's what happened. It seemed to happen overnight. First, the good but not great agents went back to their prior offices to weather the housing recession storm. As the storm continued, the better agents crossed the breakeven line for net income, and they, too, headed back to a lower commission, no-fixed-desk fee system. The competing real estate offices saw the opportunity to get back their good agents and began to aggressively recruit, offering higher commission rates than before but without desk fees. The result was that we lost most of the superior agents rather quickly.

Our negative cash position quickly resulted in our losing some of the franchise territories back to the master franchisor, and we were unable to pay the rent and monthly leased equipment charges. Then there were the note payments to our investors. And finally, making payroll for our employees became almost impossible. Bottom line, giant fixed costs grossly exceeded our commission revenue and desk fees paid by the remaining agents. My partner's dad gave up on us as a business to invest in, took his son back to the new motel as an employee, and wrote us off as a bad business but a good tax deduction.

*Party's over! Turn out the lights!*

I really thought I was going to have to declare bankruptcy. I finally sold my dream home after having it on the market for 14 months, taking a greatly reduced sales price and settling up with the Small Business Administration for the loan. That left me with almost no net equity from that sale. I took the money and paid the moving company to take my personal property to a rental house in Napa. While living there in that house, I often did not meet the full monthly rental payments, but thanks to a couple of really wonderful senior lady landlords, I was not tossed out on my ear. My wife worked in a poorly heated Quonset hut, selling weightlifters' gloves on cold telephone calls to gyms and fitness centers. We did what we had to, trying to make ends meet.

I actually met with a bankruptcy attorney about the situation. I took my accountant, a Stanford classmate, with me to the meeting. After a somewhat brief session, the attorney said that it would probably be a fairly straightforward procedure, and he would need a $5,000 deposit to get started.

*What?! If I had $5,000, I wouldn't need to be in his office!*

After we left, my accountant bought me a cup of coffee and gave me the following advice.

"Max, I don't think you are going to need to file bankruptcy. You'll be able to work with most of your creditors and reach some sort of settlement with discounts and time payments while you bounce back. But here is what you do need to do: Picture yourself down on your hands and knees, pushing a peanut across the floor with your nose. It will be a slow and difficult process. But just keep pushing, and only every once in a while, lift up your head and look back at the progress you've made. Then put your nose right back down and keep on pushing that peanut. Eventually, you'll reach the other side of the room."

I have never forgotten that story, now 40-something years later. And he was right. I did reach the other side of the room, maybe with holes in the knees of my trousers and a bloody nose, but I made it. I bounced higher as a result.

I learned another great lesson during the "harder I fall" phase of this entrepreneurial venture. I went back to one of my top investors to ask him to make another investment in our business. This was months before the final fall. As I began explaining where we were, how many new locations had opened, and how many top agents we had hired, he stopped me.

"Okay, I'll write you a check just as soon as you have the paper-work ready."

Ready I was, and I put the necessary documents on his desk.

With a big smile, he said, "That kind of preparation is why I am confident that you will do everything you can in a professional manner to make this work for both of us."

While he was filling out the check, I kept talking about how great we were doing and how well he was going to be rewarded for his confidence.

Suddenly, he stopped writing and looked up at me with a stern face.

*Oh no, he has changed his mind!*

"Max, here is an important lesson for you. I have been in the automobile dealership business for a long time. That voice you hear but probably don't recognize on the TV and radio commercials about buying cars from my dealerships is me. I know a thing or two about salesmanship.

*"Never forget this: Never sell past the close.*

"You got your money, so shut up, take the money, and leave. It is possible that after a buyer/investor has said yes, if you keep talking, you might just say something they hadn't thought about that they consider a negative. And you have just killed your deal."

### *NEVER SELL PAST THE CLOSE!*

Guess what? I zipped my lips, took the check, jumped in my car, and left his offices in a hurry. And if the car phone had rung, I wouldn't have answered it for hours.

Sadly, he lost his investment. But we stayed friends, played golf together, and he even invited me to his home for a small private cocktail party with his house guest, Arnold Palmer!

Again, the lesson here is this:

**Don't burn any bridges behind you if at all possible.**
**There is always a chance you may need to retreat across them.**

While I was living in the rented house in Napa and licking my wounds over the failure of the RE/MAX adventure, I experienced one of the most unpleasant business systems in the world: the bad debt collection industry. It was always my intent to pay off all my creditors in full. While I would sit at the dining room table, doing everything I could to pay as many bills in full as I possibly could, the phone would constantly ring with calls from the collection departments of creditors, collection agencies, and, of course, law firms that had been engaged to collect debts with their threats of legal actions, reputation smears, and worse.

One day, I had to drive to Sacramento from Napa because AT&T refused to accept payment by mail with a check. I purchased a money order and went to an industrial park where the AT&T

collection offices were housed. I entered the building and walked down a very long hallway to a reception window at the end of the hall. It was a bulletproof, thick glass window with a small opening at the bottom, so small that you had to bend over to talk to the person on the other side of the glass. The young but tough-looking male receptionist asked what I wanted, took my money order, and disappeared, presumably to check my files back in some other room. While I waited, I could hear the young employees talking and laughing from some room away from the window. They were laughing about how they had treated a creditor who was on a phone call trying to work out a payment plan.

I was appalled but not surprised, as I had experienced the same treatment over the phone with bill collectors. Here I was, having been a multimillionaire just a few months earlier, a very successful businessman, on the Governor's California Hotel Association's Board of Directors, a veteran of the last war, and a graduate of two prestigious universities. And I was being treated like a derelict—a fraud or a thief, a bum, a damn, deadbeat swindler—someone somehow deserving of their spite and disrespect.

It brought up the old movie scene of the woman tied down on the train tracks with the man standing over her, pulling on his mustache as the train is approaching. He repeats over and over, "You must pay the mortgage!" And she repeatedly screams, "But I can't pay the mortgage!"

And still, the train keeps coming.

The collection industry was cruel and performed in an inhumane manner. Maybe they still do.

Clearly, this venture is in the category of "the harder I fall."

So how did "the higher I bounce" come about?

# Chapter 18

## ONE MORE TRY FOR
## THE BRASS RING

SOON AFTER I sold my dream home in Sacramento, leaving me as close to broke as I ever wanted to get, I moved to Napa, CA, where I was somehow able to rent a house (for which I had trouble meeting the monthly rental payments). Each day was filled with responding to creditor calls while I also sought to borrow more money from friends and family. Those loans were not to invest in any new venture, but rather to simply survive by keeping a roof over my head and food in the belly. It was truly one of the worst and most miserable points of my financial career.

One morning, I received a call from one of the executives I had known from the previous MLM. He told me that he and a few others were back into a new MLM launching and asked me to drive down to Oakland to attend one of their first presentations. It was an evening in which they would present the product lines and business opportunity to become a distributor.

"Thanks for the offer, but I have already proven that while I did okay in the previous venture, I certainly am not well qualified to be an early leader. Why would you want me to join?" I asked.

"Look, Max. You actually were in one of the top achievement levels, but you quit too early. You chose to go back into what you thought was a better opportunity. The downline that you built did really well with the surviving distributors in your group."

(A downline is an organization built by recruiting other distributors/sub-distributors into your organization from whom you receive a commission on their sales.)

"Yeah, okay, but it was not the level of income that I was accustomed to earning, so I sought out greener pastures."

"I know. I remember what you jumped into. More real estate opportunities. But now that we've all suffered because of this current recession, rumor has it that you might not be doing all that great. True?"

"Ouch! You really know how to hurt a fellow. But yeah, you're right. I have to admit, your rumor mill has got it right. I had to close down all of the real estate offices that I'd opened throughout Northern California."

"Max, tell you what. If you'll come down tomorrow night to the Hilton at the Oakland airport, I'll buy you dinner, and you can just listen to what's presented."

*Hmmm! Free dinner, and maybe even a glass of wine! And a chance to get out from under all these overdue invoices for an afternoon and evening? Maybe I can even mooch a free room from the hotel I had built, operated, and owned there at the airport.*

"Alright, you got a deal and a dinner companion. See you tomorrow night."

And so off I went for a free meal and some camaraderie with old associates, and what the heck, maybe even a business opportunity. The meal (and wine) were great, and the dinner conversation was light and certainly not a pressured sales pitch. Dinner ended, and down the hall we went to a small meeting room to hear the presentation. There were probably 15 or 20 people in attendance.

The products were nutritional supplements, an industry I was very familiar with. I was impressed with what these start-up executives had put together, or so it seemed. Then there was the business opportunity presentation. Wow! They had done their homework and created a very lucrative distribution plan and compensation program. I was totally taken in and very impressed. About halfway through the business program, I got out of my chair, left the room, and gave the receptionist outside the door (who was responsible for signing new distributors) the cash necessary to become a new distributor. When the executives finished up and came outside the meeting room, I remember saying to them with a grin, "These products are going to have to be really ineffective for this distribution plan not to work. Congratulations!"

In MLM, the larger the distribution organization you build and the larger the sales volume you and your team create, the more positively it impacts the "commission percentage" you receive, as well as the larger the "downline" from which you receive these commissions or overrides.

In this case, the first significant level of increase that one could reach was called the "Diamond" level. Since I needed cash flow badly, I flew into the recruiting mode with full afterburners engaged. Friends and some family, former business associates, and MLM team members trusted my decision that this was a company with a great chance to make money either full- or part-time and enjoy the benefits of buying and using the products at a wholesale price.

The result was that I achieved Diamond level in 15 days. Apparently, that was somewhat of a record, so the MLM company asked me to make an audiotape as to how I accomplished that level. Not surprisingly, the tape was titled "Fifteen Days to Diamond." I was told that it sold well.

With a great start to a new venture, it was time to expand at a rate that would yield maximum profits. Napa was (and is) a wonderful community in which to live. The weather is terrific for outside activities, golf especially, for me. I loved the early mornings, often with cooling fog rolling in from the San Francisco Bay. There are fabulous dining experiences throughout the valley, and, of course, there are the unbeatable wineries with international award-winning wines.

But Napa is a relatively small town with a limited population. I decided to move back to Sacramento so that I would have a much larger population available to me from which I could recruit distributors. Again, my financial resources only allowed me to rent a home. I found one that was centrally located, with several hotels nearby where I could hold meetings to present the product lines and business opportunity. Additionally, Sacramento had been my distributor base in the previous MLM. It was where I had developed relationships with many friends and business associates when I had lived there before. The lesson here was that you are only going to appeal to a limited percentage of the population in your marketing efforts, and therefore, the market size from which your percentage of success will be achieved needs to be large in order to result in significant profits.

And it worked. MLM presentations were made in living rooms and kitchens to a small number of prospects, or in a hotel ballroom to hundreds of potential "partners." Handling disappointments when these presentations were made required a positive attitude. When the living room presentations ended up being made to a very small group (which were sometimes only the hosts), many of us adopted an attitude that was essential:

"Those that are here are the ones that are supposed to be here."

In these small settings, we also found that we could discuss additional recruiting strategies, more detailed benefits about the products, and ultimately leave knowing that the evening had been well worth the effort.

These presentations turned out to be very successful. Within a few years, I had a downline of over 30,000 distributors. My monthly income was in an upper five-figure category. I was able to attend conventions, meetings, and award ceremonies all over the United States, including several in Hawaii. In fact, our group even held a several-day cruise around the Hawaiian Islands with a large group of distributors. We had tons of fun and held several training sessions during the cruise. MLM can be a business that offers great financial rewards as well as creating deep friendships and business associations that are entertaining and rewarding.

So, once again, my life experience proved that *the harder you fall, the higher you bounce*. I had gone from the lowest of low financially, borrowing money to survive, to a wonderful life provided by an income approaching seven figures a year—the satisfying success of a serial entrepreneur.

But how long would it last?

# Chapter 19

## ZIT CREAM?!

THE THIRD MLM did not last but a few years. This could be one of those stories that belong in the chapter, "It Ain't Always Your Fault."

Here's what happened. There was a college basketball player in Florida who had a heart condition and was taking this particular product. During a game, his preexisting heart condition resulted in his having a cardiac emergency. Once the medical profession discovered that he was taking a product that contained ephedrine, that became an issue with the FDA. A Vanderbilt University study indicated that the ephedrine in the product could possibly raise the metabolism by four percent. Nevertheless, the product was suddenly banned, and sales and distributor income stopped almost immediately.

The San Diego company then produced essentially the same product—but without the ephedrine. That product did not sell nearly as well, but for reasons that were not disclosed, at least to my knowledge, a multinational pharmaceutical company bought the

San Diego one. The owners made the decision to share the proceeds of the sale of their company with the distributors who had not filed any claims against them related to the distributorship contracts. The distribution amount was based upon the percentage of revenue each distributorship had contributed to the company. Fortunately, my distributorship (which was held in my company, American Kiosk Management, or AKM) was near or at the top of that list. The only requirement was that each distributor had to sign a consulting agreement for a two-year period. On a monthly basis, the requirement was to inspect the retail outlets which were selling these products in a specific geographical area. These surveys required compliance with proper product merchandising, such as checking for proper shelf location, cleanliness, and adequate product on display.

During that two-year period, AKM continued to search for other products that would fall into one of the following three categories of "mall cart/kiosk opportunities":

1. **Products that were easily demonstrable.** A classic example was the cooking demonstrations whose products resulted in a delicious aroma wafting throughout the mall, especially as you walked close to the kiosks. And the "cook" always had a microphone attached to his apron. Another more current example was the "Zoom Copter." This was a plastic helicopter-type model that was hand-cranked, resulting in the copter flying upwards, high over the carts almost to the mall ceilings and remarkedly returning within an arm's length of the demonstrator. Now, I am an old helicopter pilot with over 5,000 hours of flying time and hours and hours in classrooms studying rotary aerodynamics. And I was *still* amazed at the flying envelope of the toy!

2. **Products that everyone already had one or more of**. A good example of a product like this was sunglasses. Perhaps you needed another because you left yours in the last store you were in, or you sat on them and broke them, or the colors of the ones you own didn't match your outfits.

3. **Products that had a very high "brand-name recognition factor."** This category was my favorite. These would be products that everyone already knew about. The first example that I became involved with was the diet pill that was marketed heavily on local radio stations.

While looking for additional products to market on carts and kiosks in the mall, I decided to look at products being sold on television infomercials. A company named Guthy-Renker Company seemed to be the king of the infomercial industry.

While I was looking for these opportunities during my nutritional supplement businesses, I approached that company to see if they would be interested in allowing me to be a distributor of the line of nutritional supplements they were selling. The interest on their part was strong enough that we flew in their corporate plane to the headquarters of the nutritional supplement company I had represented to discuss the possibility of some sort of arrangement to try infomercials and a combination of both companies' nutritional supplements.

From that point, the decision was made for me not to jointly represent both companies, but to fully examine creating a new MLM within the Guthy-Renker organization, selling their line of supplements. But the barriers turned out to be too risky. The main one being that the carts/kiosks would be manned by employees of the

MLM distributors. It was judged to be too great a risk to ensure that none of these distributors or their employees would make "medical claims" about the non-medicinal supplements, thus exposing the already profitable infomercial sales to possible regulatory violations, and therefore risking a well-established business's reputation (and profits) for an unproven and risky venture.

But I had given the Guthy-Renker executives a taste of what could happen in a successful mall kiosk retail operation. Certainly, it was a new distribution channel that they had not experimented with at any previous time.

I continued to stay in touch with the two owners of the Guthy-Renker Company, or at least I tried to contact them frequently, but not always successfully. My goal was to convince them that one or more of their products being marketed via infomercials could be successfully marketed and sold through the distribution channel of carts and kiosks in shopping malls.

That industry had grown to a $25-billion market and had become known as the "Specialty Retail" industry (later also referred to as the "Auxiliary Retail" industry). I felt that their products would be well received in that venue, particularly since they were spending millions of dollars on television promotion. And the promotion was not just a 60-second or less exposure, but rather a full 30-minute ad, often using celebrities as the spokespeople.

Eventually, I decided to be more specific in my solicitation of becoming a "specialty retail" distributor for one or more of their successful products. I had a cart in a mall in Nashville, TN, selling a nutritional product that was doing extremely well. So, I decided to send them a financial profit and loss statement of the current month's operations of just that one mall location. That month, the cart had gross revenue of just over $150,000 for just the 30-day period. In fact, one of the salespeople had sold over $100,000 by herself!

That was the tipping point. And legend has it that just as I sent the P&L statement, they sent their plane to bring me to their headquarters.

And what a meeting that turned out to be! I walked into one of the conference rooms to talk about just what I was looking for if they decided to "give her a try." We had a detailed discussion on how it might work. I suggested that I would buy the product at a wholesale price from them and then resell it at a price that, while they could not control it, e.g., price-fixing, they would not object to a reasonable price. They also would be sent pictures of exactly how the carts were merchandised. They wanted a complete breakdown every month on what products had sold and at what price per product, as well as the totals per product and totals per location. Lastly, they would have the sole right to terminate the agreement at any time for any reason.

They explained that their main concern was that if the sales at the carts were very successful, they could possibly cannibalize their infomercial sales in that market area to such an extent that they would lose money. They clearly had a breakeven sales number necessary to hit in order to cover the direct marketing expenses of the television time they were purchasing, plus, of course, their corporate allocations and product costs.

While I was not overly thrilled with some of the possible restrictions, I was so sure about AKM's ability to sell their products at retail that I agreed… which led to another conversation.

"Okay, Max. So exactly what do you need from us to get started?"

"Great! First, I need the products of course. And I assume that I can purchase them on a 'Net-90-Day' basis?"

"No, I think we would require a 'Net 30 Day.'"

"Okay, so how about a 'Net 60' to get me started?"

"Fine, we will start there and see how it goes."

"I also need the brochures and any other marketing materials you send out when you receive inquiries from your TV ads, in addition to the materials you include in the fulfillment orders you send to your customers."

"No problem; we can provide you all you need."

"Oh, and I would like to get a copy of the TV infomercial on a closed-loop video. I will set up a small television on the cart to replay that video constantly. That way, potential customers will see it playing, recognize that they have seen it on your infomercials, and therefore be much more willing to stop and ask about the products. Simple, brand-name recognition. So, any problem with providing the cosmetic line spokesperson's video?"

"Why would you want a copy of *that* video?"

"Again, so that customers will see it playing on the cart and be drawn to the cart to see the spokesperson talk about the cosmetic line of her products."

"Max, we're not talking to you about selling that cosmetic line on shopping mall carts. We do *not* want to experiment with those products at retail competing with our TV spots."

"What?! If that isn't possible, then why am I here? I thought that is what all our communications have been about, including the last few hours of discussions?"

"No! We are talking about you selling Proactiv."

"Proactiv! What's that? I never heard of Proactiv."

"It's an acne skin care treatment."

"Zit cream! Are you joking? How am I going to sell zit cream on a cart? As a customer comes up to the cart, I'm supposed to say something like, 'Let me put this on that pimple on your face. I'm sure we can make it disappear.' I can't believe I'm sitting here talking about zit cream sales to someone in a very public space like shopping mall traffic and discussing a very personal appearance issue. Wow! And just how much of this Proactiv did you sell last year?"

"About $125 million."

"Really? You sold $125 million of zit cream on television in just one year?"

"Yes."

**As I raised my hand high, I said, "I can sell it!"**

And so began the rewards of a lifetime of being a successful entrepreneur: the Proactiv road to $1.7 billion in gross revenue from carts and kiosks in malls.

# Chapter 20

## MY FAVORITE BUSH

MOST OF US have probably read or heard about the Bible story about the "burning bush" through which God spoke to Moses. I also have a story about a bush. While the bush didn't verbally speak to me, that bush may have just saved my life.

I was playing golf in Sedona, AZ, and on one of the par 3s, I pushed my golf shot off to the right into some thornbushes. The ball was easy to find and was in a somewhat open spot where I could attempt to hit it out onto the green. I took a pretty good swing at it and actually got it out and onto the green!

But as I started to walk out of those thornbushes, just below my Bermuda shorts, one of my legs was cut by a very sharp thorn shaped like a hook. The hook dug into my calf and managed to make a pretty deep scratch about six inches long. It wasn't very painful, but it began to bleed quite a bit. I pulled a dirty wet rag off of the golf cart that I normally used to clean the dirt and mud and grass off of my golf clubs. As I found out later, that wasn't a very smart choice. After a few minutes, the bleeding had pretty much stopped, so I continued playing.

When I got home, I cleaned the scratch-up more thoroughly and put Neosporin on it to prevent any infection. I continued to clean it and apply Neosporin for the next couple of days, but it seemed to be getting worse with the infection spreading around the scratch.

After another day, following a restless night with my heartburn bothering me, I decided to go to a hospital clinic to have a doctor look at the infection. It took me about 15 minutes to drive there in my car. As I was driving, I thought, *Man, I should have taken a couple of antacids to get some relief from this heartburn.* I parked the car in the lot adjacent to the hospital clinic and walked into the reception area, happily finding that there were no other patients waiting. I stepped up to the reception counter to speak with the nurse on duty.

"Good morning. How can I help you?"

"I recently scratched my leg on a thorn out on the golf course, and it doesn't seem to be getting any better. I think it may be infected, so I'd like to have a doctor take a look at it."

"Okay," she said slowly. "But I notice you are rubbing your chest. Are you having chest pains?"

"No, ma'am, not really. Just suffering from a little heartburn. I have GERDS."

"Very well. Just come on through that door, and we'll let the doctor know you are here."

With that, she escorted me back into one of the rooms which had a hospital bed, and she instructed me to lie down. *What the heck is going on? I just have a scratch on my leg!* Shortly after I lay down, the doctor came in, introduced himself, and said, "I understand you are having some discomfort in your chest. Tell me what's going on."

"Just a little heartburn. I have GERDS. Actually, I'm here to have you look at my leg. I scratched it with a thorn, and it seems to be infected, even though I have routinely applied Neosporin after cleaning it thoroughly."

"Okay, I'll check that out, but first, I want to check on your chest pains. So, here is a nitroglycerin tablet for your heart. I want to run some quick checks to make sure you are not having a cardiac event. In fact, let me also give you some morphine for the pain."

"Nitroglycerin! Morphine?! Doc, I have heartburn!"

"I understand, Mr. James, but let's just be sure you're okay."

Next thing I know, I am being put through all manner of tests: EKG, blood pressure, X-ray…

The doctor came back in shortly and let me know, "Well, everything looks okay, but you're obviously still having some discomfort in your chest area. So, I recommend that you see a cardiologist right away."

> This is all really beginning to get tense. I came in to have a scratch checked out, and now I am being told I need a cardiologist!

*This is all really beginning to get tense. I came in to have a scratch checked out, and now I am being told I need a cardiologist!*

"Alright, I suppose. But I don't know one here in Sedona, so if you'll give me the name of one, I'll call and make an appointment."

"You don't get it. You need to see one NOW!"

With the little hairs on the back of my neck beginning to stand up, I must have shouted, "What?! I just have heartburn!"

To which he replied, "I don't think so. I am concerned it may be more than that."

"Okay, well, can you call a cardiologist and tell him I am on my way over? And would you write down the address for me?"

"You still don't get it, Mr. James. You are going in an ambulance."

"Ambulance! I told you I have heartburn. And besides, I can't go to the main hospital in an ambulance."

"Why not? What would keep you from going in the ambulance?"

Thinking quickly, I said, "My car is parked outside in the parking lot."

I must admit that seemed like a pretty lame excuse, but I truly *was* experiencing a rapid heartbeat now—from panic and anxiety! Ambulance! Emergency Room! Cardiologist! Geez, that was enough to give a fellow a heart attack!

The next thing I knew, I was strapped into an ambulance, wired up to several monitors, and talking to a couple of paramedics who were watching all the monitors. Both were ex-military combat medics. Since I had flown rescue in Vietnam and Laos with pararescue airmen, we had a lot of mutual experiences. The ride to the main hospital was about a 20-minute ride, so we had time to share some war stories. But about five minutes before we reached the hospital ER, I asked them if they would go ahead and begin to get things ready for a quick transition from the ambulance. The discomfort in the chest had changed to some fairly intense pains.

In the ER, they moved me from the mobile gurney to a bed and began more tests. After getting the tests run and receiving the results, the cardiologist showed up.

"Mr. James, can I call you Max? Alright, good. We can't find anything negative from the tests we just ran, but there is clearly a problem. So, we're going to run a camera into your wrist and up into your heart to see if we can determine what's going on in there.

This won't hurt because I am going to give you a little anesthetic before we take you up to surgery."

*SURGERY! I have a thorn scratch on my leg that may be infected. I have heartburn. My car is parked in the parking lot. And now I am in the emergency room with a cardiac surgeon who is taking me to surgery! What the blue blazes has happened in the last couple of hours?*

I get the shot to deaden my wrist (or so I thought), and the next thing I know, I wake up in the operating room with a really bright white light shining into my eyes. *Uh oh. Dead and Crossover? Bright white light? I'm pretty sure they don't have these in hell, so where have I landed?* I roll my head over to the left, and thank God there is a nurse.

"Welcome back, Mr. James. Let me get your cardiologist to come in and talk to you. Just relax. I'll be right back."

My first thoughts were really powerful, and for me, a powerful life lesson.

*I now know what death may be like. If my faith is right, I will wake up in a wonderful place I call Heaven. If my faith is wrong, I simply don't wake up. There is nothing! It's just all over.*

And so what goes on my tombstone? Well, my epitaph is not going to change:

The Harder I Fall
The Higher I Bounce
This Time Into Heaven
I Pray

In comes my cardiologist, who repeats, "Welcome back, Max," and then continues.

"We really were lucky. The problem was your left anterior descending artery, more commonly called the 'widow maker.' It was 100 percent blocked! At any time, you could have suffered full cardiac arrest."

Wow! I vividly remember the emotions that surged through my body and my then-irrational mind. *I almost died. My existence could have been over.*

And then the good emotions came like a flood. *But I didn't. I am still here, at least for some unknown period of time. But that was true when I came in here, the unknown time frame. Thank you, Lord. I sure dodged another bullet.*

The cardiologist then asked me, "Max, do you remember talking with me while we were looking at the pictures that the camera in your heart was transmitting to the big video monitor up there?"

I was sorta caught off guard by the question. "No, I don't remember that."

With what sounded like he was somewhat irritated with

> You honestly don't remember telling me that I was the world's greatest surgeon, and that I should charge you more?

me, he asked, "You mean you don't remember our conversation while we were inserting the stents?"

With a bit of my own irritation, I answered quite loudly, "No! I don't remember anything from the time the nurse gave me that anesthetic until I woke up here on this surgery operating table."

And lastly, he asked, "Are you serious? You honestly don't remember telling me that I was the world's greatest surgeon, and that I should charge you more?"

Only then did I begin to realize that things were probably going to be okay. I had found a cardiologist (that probably should have been a stand-up comedian) with the phenomenal skills built over a highly successful medical practice who could provide some humor into my emotional state.

*Thanks, Doc!*

Before leaving in the ambulance, I had called my son, who lived in Sedona, and told him that I was going to the hospital for a checkup because apparently a doctor at a clinic wanted to make sure my heartburn wasn't something worse. Oh, and I asked if he could pick up my car from the hospital clinic parking lot. Later, when I was headed up to surgery, I asked one of the orderlies if she would call my son and let him know I was going up to surgery to determine what was wrong with my heart and ask him to call my wife in Las Vegas to let her know.

Yeah, I hear you thinking, "Why didn't you call your wife yourself?" And you would be correct to ask that. I hope it was because, at that time, I still wasn't concerned that I was having a heart attack and would talk to her after the tests. In any event, it was a mistake not to let her know. The result was that she immediately found one of her employees to drive her from Las Vegas to Sedona, and it was a trip the drivers in the Daytona 500 would have been proud of. I woke up in recovery, and there she sat in a chair next to the bed. What a great blessing to have her there!

So back to the burning bush. If I had not scratched my leg on that bush, I most likely would not have gone to the hospital clinic because of my "heartburn." And with my having the "widowmaker" 100 percent blocked, there is a realistic chance that I would not have made it.

When I play golf on that course, and I get to that Par 3 hole, I always go over to that thorn bush, tip my hat, and say a little thank you prayer to the Man upstairs for using a little bush to send an important message once again—this time not to Moses, but to *Max.*

Still skeptical? Well, guess why that thorn bush scratch was looking so infected, thus sending me to the hospital clinic? Ready? I am allergic to Neosporin!!

Without the thorn bush, without the scratch, without the Neosporin, without the heartburn, someone else would be telling this story.

Cardio rehab was an essential element in the recovery and cardiac improvement process. One day, while I was working out in the hospital rehab center, my cardiologist showed up. I was on the treadmill, hooked up to the various wireless cardiac monitors. He stepped over to where I was walking, slapped me on the bottom, and said, "So how are you coming along?"

"Fine, I think. I don't seem to be setting off any warning bells or red lights." I recall also saying, "Doc, you gotta be making a fortune. Look at all these folks. This cardio rehab fitness center is packed with heart patients. Bypass survivors, heart transplant recovery patients, and a bunch like me with new stents."

With a serious expression, he quickly corrected me. "No, Max, they're not all my patients."

Then with a big mischievous grin, he added, "Not all mine make it."

I told you he should have been a stand-up comedian.

And there is a lesson here also. **Make friends with folks you enjoy being with and always look for common interests you can share**.

After a few weeks of cardio, I begged to do something physical besides show up at the rehab in Sedona and Las Vegas. He was reluctant, reminding me that I had suffered a serious cardiac event. But I persisted, wanting to get back to the more enjoyable and outside exercise of playing golf. Finally, he said, "Okay. But on one condition."

I'm thinking, *What could be a condition to carefully not overdo physical exercise on a golf course? Maybe only play a few holes? Play when it isn't too hot? Or how about don't keep score? That would reduce the stress, I suppose.* But nope, I hadn't guessed the one condition he was imposing.

"You have to play with me!"

> So, not only should you not burn your bridges, but when you can, you should take your friends and allies and partners across the bridges with you!

Now, there's a deal. I had some anxiety about getting back to normal, including playing golf. And my cardiologist, who had saved my life, insisted that he be with me on the golf course.

And that is how I got back to chasing that little white orb.

That was several years ago, and today, as I write this note, he came to Las Vegas this weekend, and off we went to play a round of golf.

So, not only should you not burn your bridges, but when you can, you should take your friends and allies and partners across the bridges with you!

Do all you can to stay healthy. Remember what my dad said? "None of us are going to get out of here alive."

But he should have added, "And while you are still here, enjoy all the time given to you on Planet Earth."

# Chapter 21

## PEAK TO PEAK

HAVING REACHED A "mountain peak" with my company's first venture into an MLM, we continued to experiment selling other products in this same venue so we could climb higher to yet another peak.

Success often seems to come as one builds foundations block by block, brick by brick. Sometimes the right block fits perfectly into the solid base you are building. And sometimes, when you are building the foundation of success, you don't know exactly what the final building or success will look like.

That was certainly the case in my putting blocks and bricks into the dream foundation I was building. And, as I wrote earlier, many of those bricks were defective, and the blocks didn't fit! It even seemed that I often had to tear down the foundation I had built and start all over. But though that is how it may have seemed, that is not how it works. When you fall, you take some of the tools you have been using down with you. Then, they will get to be used again and again... Therefore, you are not "starting all over." You have a tool belt now filled with loads of useful tools, many of which have been sharpened and improved over time. (Also of note here: Rarely is it the tools that cause the problem, but rather the user—the mason.)

Looking back at all my failures and some limited successes, I see that each failure gave me experience and knowledge of what *not to do* next time, as well as what to do differently.

The MLM experience with a nutritional supplement, operating multiple locations throughout the United States, gave me a solid foundation to take on the task of introducing Proactiv directly to the customers of shopping malls by using the cart and kiosk business and distribution model.

Two of the earlier restrictions put on American Kiosk Management by Guthy-Renker were that the number of locations would be restricted AND that none could be located in the best malls, known as "A" malls. AKM could only open in the "B" mall category. This, again, was not only to test whether we could sell the Proactiv products on carts and kiosks in shopping malls but also to test just how much cannibalization of the infomercial sales would be created. Would customers stop buying online and instead buy directly from the carts?

Fortunately, it became evident that most of the customers at the shopping malls had different buying preferences than those who were purchasing online. The actual cannibalization was less than five percent, which meant that 95 percent of the cart sales were additive to the total sales online—a different market altogether.

When AKM started selling Proactiv in the malls, many of the potential AKM customers still did not feel comfortable giving out their credit card information for a retail purchase there, especially at a kiosk. Much of that reluctance was diminished when dealing face-to-face with the salesperson at a kiosk. Additionally, the experience of buying the products at the kiosk allowed them to touch, feel, smell, and experience the products BEFORE buying rather than after. This eliminated the hassle of having it sent to their homes and only then deciding whether to keep and use the products or return them to the online seller. Buying directly also allowed the customer to immediately begin using the product rather than waiting for an online order to arrive through the mail or by other delivery services. Lastly, in our situation, we were able to pass on the savings from no shipping charges.

With those advantages being marketed by our sales staff, we were able to prove that direct retail did *not* detrimentally cannibalize the infomercial sales *and* that we were able to operate the carts and kiosks at a substantial profit. Nevertheless, AKM tested in only five B shopping malls before we were allowed to expand into A malls. At the end of about two years, AKM was greenlighted to expand to a few A malls. There was no increase in cannibalization from the infomercial sales. And, as expected, the sales in the A malls were indeed higher than in the B malls. With this overall concept now proven, it was "Katie, bar the door."

Because shopping mall customers do not visit them often, certainly not like they do grocery stores, we often heard, "Oh, I didn't know I could buy the product here. I thought it was only sold online." For our sales revenue totals, that meant that it sometimes took up to 90 days for sufficient customers to discover our locations and that they could now buy directly at retail locations. That, of course, meant that it sometimes took that 90-day startup period to reach profitability.

So, a major question (which almost all entrepreneurs face) was how to fund a rapid expansion. The first answer was, as mentioned earlier: Pay for the product *after* it has been sold. We had negotiated "Net 60," meaning that payment was due to Guthy-Renker within 60 days of their shipping the product to us. Since not all locations were able to produce sufficient profits to allow for reinvesting in other locations, we needed outside funding.

The method we used went something like this: I would find investors who were interested in looking at low-risk, small-business opportunities. And, as I had learned, those likely to look favorably on putting money into one of my ventures would be that old, trusted standby: family and friends.

My "offering" was to find those potential investors and offer them this program: They put up all the funds required to open and operate a cart, to include but not necessarily be limited to the lease deposit for the location in the mall, the initial product orders, the cost of merchandising the cart with brochures, a television display, computer and a point-of-sale machine, the payroll for the sales team at that location, and other as-needed items.

For making that funding available, the investor would receive a full 70 percent of the profits, and we would retain 30 percent. That is, UNTIL the investor had received all of their investment back. At that point, the percentages switched from 70/30 to 30/70. The investor would now have zero investment in the operation but still be receiving 30 percent of the profits. We would now be retaining 70 percent of the profits, which would allow us to cover a portion of "corporate overhead allocation" and hopefully funding for future carts that would not need investor funding.

This methodology worked so well that the patient investors who understood the startup period were receiving more than 10 percent *per month* on their initial investment. Utilizing this method, AKM grew to about 40 mall locations.

In order to keep growing, I needed more investors or one large venturer. An individual whom I will name Jim called and inquired about the rumor that I was looking for an investor because the business was growing rapidly and successfully. I explained that I was not selling an interest in my business but selling a profit participation loan deal. I went through the details, which apparently sold him on taking the next step. He said his attorney would make an appointment with me to finalize the details and draw up the necessary documents.

After making the appointment, his attorney showed up in my office to do just that.

"Max, Jim is quite excited about doing this deal. He tells me that your current investors are all quite happy with the return on their investments. Is it really hovering around 13 percent? I mean, really?"

"Yes, Sir. That's about right, although there is no guarantee on that number, and some have taken longer than others to reach it."

"Is it also true that you want to fund another $2 million?"

"That is the amount that we think we need to continue on our current pace."

"Well, okay then. I have a list of the things I need to see before we move to the next step. I want to go over your profit and loss statements and the balance sheets you have with your other investors. I'd also like to see the same things for those carts that you funded internally. Now, as I understand it, you are a distributor for Guthy-Renker Company, with an exclusive for shopping malls. Is that right?"

"That is all correct."

"Then I am going to need a copy of your legal Distribution Agreement with them. I need to know that you are authorized to resell Proactiv."

*Uh oh! Here comes a major problem.*

"We started this all with the concept of testing a few locations. Once that test proved successful, we shook hands and just kept going. They are truly honorable men, with integrity beyond reproach. And I also am a man of character. There have never been any problems."

"Max, I gotta tell you, you aren't getting $2 million of Jim's money without proving to us that you are legally a valid distributor of the Proactiv products for me to review! And until you can produce such evidence, we are not interested in proceeding."

"Okay. I don't think that is a problem. They are extremely pleased with our operations. They like the manner in which we are representing them and the product line. And, of course, they are also happy with the sales and the amount of product that we are purchasing from them for resale."

My next step was to secure such "evidence" that we were operating with the full consent and approval of Guthy-Renker. So, I called Greg Renker, explained the situation, and asked him to please provide me with the evidence. He indicated that would not be a problem.

A day or so later, I received an email that read something like this:

*To whomever it may concern, Max James and American Kiosk Management, LLC, are authorized to sell Proactiv products.*

Great! I called Jim's attorney and relayed the email showing our authorization to sell the products as a distributor.

"Max, are you kidding me? You think I am going to advise my clients to loan you $2 million based on a one-sentence email? I need a fully drawn legal Distribution Agreement between the parties, fully executed by their authorized corporate executives. Then—and *only* then—should you bother to come back to me."

*How long could that take?* I wondered. *How long before we could continue our rapid expansion?* I called Guthy-Renker's in-house Legal Counsel and Development Officer. (Let's call him Ben.)

"Ben, I am raising some additional growth funds for our expansion. I have a significant investor who is willing to loan up to a couple of million dollars on a profit participation basis. Naturally, we are excited about bringing him into the fold. Everything looks great so far, but his attorney is insisting on a formal Distribution Agreement between Guthy-Renker and AKM. I suppose you have boilerplate documents that you can utilize to memorialize our distribution arrangements?"

"That sounds like great news. I will jump on it and get back to you quickly."

Now, all I had to do was wait for the Distribution Agreement to arrive, review it for approval, have it signed, and then get it back to Jim's attorney. But nothing happened—at least that I was aware of! After a few weeks or so, I called Ben.

"Ben, I really need that Distribution Agreement. I think this investor is the answer to my being able to continue building this Proactiv retail business, both for you guys and for me. And I don't want him slipping away with his investor funds, potentially to another deal. What the hell is going on? Is there a problem?"

"Not that I am aware of. I finished up the documents over a week ago."

"Then, where are they?"

"I gave them to the Executive Committee for their review and approval. And I haven't heard of any negative feedback."

"Ben, aren't you on the Executive Committee? Has this been on the Committee's agenda?"

"No, not while I was there. So, let me follow up and see where we stand."

Again, no rapid response. About a week later, I receive a call from Bill Guthy.

"Max, we received the Distribution Agreement that Ben and you have worked out. I'd like you to come down to our offices in Los Angeles so we can discuss it."

"Thanks, Bill. I'd be happy to do that. How soon can we meet? I could fly down this afternoon."

"No, I can't make that happen on this end. How about next week? Are you available then?"

"Of course. Just have someone let me know what day and time. I'll be there."

I was not only disappointed that there was at least another week of delay but now somewhat anxious about the necessity of a meeting with them for further discussions. They had already told me that there didn't seem to be any problems with our operations.

I arrived at their offices, expecting to meet with Bill, maybe Greg, and probably Ben. I waited in their lobby until I was asked to join them in a conference room. What a surprise! The room was full of their executives, including the EVP of Finance, the Proactiv Brand Manager, Bill, of course, and a few others... but not Ben.

*Uh oh.*

But before the meeting actually convened, in walks Ben, who sits down directly across the conference table from me.

Ben leaned across the table, shook my hand, and said, "Welcome back, Max. This is going to be a great meeting."

I sorta leaned over in his direction and asked him, "Ben, are you sure? Why are all these execs here?"

Ben then shared these great words of wisdom.

"It is always a great meeting when everyone shows up that is involved. If it were going to be a bad meeting, you would be meeting just with Bill and me."

**Good to remember. If you show up for an important meeting, and there is a crowd in the room, you are probably okay. But if there are just a principal shareholder and an attorney, watch out. Gird your loins; you're in for a ride!**

And that would begin one of the most important business meetings of my career. Bill Guthy started off the meeting with some comments about my operations.

> If you show up for an important meeting, and there is a crowd in the room, you are probably okay. But if there are just a principal shareholder and an attorney, watch out. Gird your loins; you're in for a ride!

"Max, you have exceeded all our expectations. Congratulations! I'm told you have about 50 locations up and operating now, and you feel like you have lots of room for growth. That's great. However, there are a few concerns we want to discuss with you. Image is very important to the success of our brand. We spend millions on the packaging and choosing the right promotions, as well as celebrity endorsers. You've told us that you don't have sole authority as to how you merchandise the kiosk or carts, that the shopping malls have 'design merchandisers' on their staff that have to approve or even participate in the design of the cart presentations. I think you told us of one particular cart that you opened for another product line that was pretty much controlled by the mall's merchandiser. You said that she insisted that you have a lot of greenery and plants as the theme, which you opposed. In fact, there were so many plants on the cart that you sold about as many plants as your prime product."

"Well, that might have been a bit of an exaggeration, but yes, it did look like a plants-for-sale cart. But Bill, I have given you pictures of every cart we have opened so that you could object if you thought we failed to meet your standards. Have you had any problems with how they look?"

"No, not at all. They really look great. Better than we expected."

"So, do you have other concerns?"

"Well, pricing of our products to the consumer is really critical. And, as you know, because of price-fixing laws, we certainly are not able to dictate to you what prices you charge for the Proactiv products at your carts."

"Yes, but I have submitted my pricing lists to you for your 'suggestions,' and I understand there have been no problems with those prices."

"Well, yes, you're right. I think you are pricing everything reasonably for your profits and to no detriment to our sales online."

"Are there other concerns? What are they?"

"No, that's about it. But because we cannot control what you do or whom you take on as partners, either equity or debt, we could be exposed to individuals, groups, or entities that might not meet with our approvals. I'm sure we also told you that we generally do not take on partners, that you are among the very few with whom we have done so. I understand that you have someone who is willing to put up around $2 million to support your operational expansion. That has the potential to possibly be harmful to our company and even the Proactiv brand. So, we have decided to shut your operations down. I'm sure you recall that we agreed that we could close you down for any reason whatsoever at our sole discretion."

At this point, I am sure I turned a pale white, with sweat breaking out on my forehead and rolling into my eyes as my stomach worked its way up into my throat.

"Bill, if you do that, I will be upside-down financially. I owe Guthy-Renker for product that is still sitting on the carts, I have mall leases for my locations that cannot be terminated immediately without severe penalties, I have employees that have built-up paid time off, and much more. I am quite sure I would have to file bankruptcy on this company."

"Max, there is one alternative to all that is having to occur."

"I can't imagine what that might be, but I am all ears."

"Sell us half your company. Actually, 50.5 percent. You don't need to borrow money. We have money to invest in you and your company that will give you what you need for expansion."

*Sounds both good and possibly bad. Too good to be that easy and totally without major restrictions.* The 50.5 percent already suggested that the control was out of my hands and into theirs, so I raised that point.

Bill's response included two things: First, he explained that he had already demonstrated that he had control, i.e., he could shut us down at any time of his choosing, which was more controlling than owning 50.5 percent of an ongoing company. Second was the fact that we were the experts in mall cart and kiosk operations, and he would have to seek out new expertise and personnel to duplicate what we had already accomplished, and there was no guarantee that the effort would be successful. And that was not in-house at that time. It was his intent to have us continue operations as we were, not to add any new restrictions or changes.

"I suppose you will want more financial and personnel reporting and maybe want to add some of your staff to our corporate organization."

"No, not at all. We will ask that you come down to our L.A. offices on a regular basis to meet with Greg, Ben, and our Financial Exec Kevin."

"How often do you expect that meeting to occur: weekly, monthly? And what reports will be required?"

"I suspect quarterly meetings will be sufficient, as long as you continue to perform at such a successful level. Or if you want our help in supporting your efforts. As to reports, I would think updated monthly and YTD P&Ls and balance sheets. We would not be buying into this operation unless we were confident that it would be a good investment in your people and your business plans."

Feeling somewhat better after the initial shock, I realized just what the "bad and the good" were: I had lost sole and total ownership and control of my company but had become a partner with a multibillion-dollar company!

Somewhat of a dream, I suspect. Going from one single little mall cart in the corridor of a mall to now being very profitable and having sold 50.5 percent of my company and being supported by the owners and staff of a multibillion-dollar enterprise.

From that meeting, the acquisition occurred. What the new structure became was North American Kiosk, LLC, owned 50.5 percent by Guthy-Renker Company and 49.5 percent by American Kiosk Management, LLC. The meetings in Los Angeles did occur no more frequently than quarterly. Our Las Vegas corporate group grew quickly as we expanded to over 400 manned carts and kiosks in the United States, Canada, Australia, New Zealand, and Puerto Rico. We also added "automated retail" machines in over 800 locations. These were once called "vending machines" but are now far more technically sophisticated.

The result of all this expansion with a great product line, Proactiv, with great support from a company of unmatched integrity and a corporate staff of individuals who were not only of unquestionable integrity but also friendly and supportive, became a company that in 15 short years accomplished revenue of over $1,700,000,000.00. (That's one billion seven hundred million for those of you who got dizzy looking at those zeros!)

There were many tough problems to solve along that journey, ranging from criminal misconduct by staff and vendors and customers to some of the most hilarious situations you can imagine.

Stay tuned. There's lots to follow about climbing to that billion-dollar-plus peak.

# Chapter 22

## FROM FOUR TO FORTY TO FOUR HUNDRED CARTS AND KIOSKS

WITH THE FINANCIAL backing of a multibillion-dollar company, the newly merged company NAK (North American Kiosk, LLC) moved to another gear of growth. In fact, this speed was Mach 1 at least, maybe even "warp speed." When we created the new company, NAK, we had grown to about 40 locations, which meant we had grown 10x, or *1,000%*. A great start no doubt, and certainly a start that attracted the Guthy-Renker Company to initiate the merger. The sky seemed to be the limit with their backing and their partnership, and soon, we would strive for an even bigger percentage.

None of this growth would have been possible without a great team led by that extraordinary, performance-oriented leader, Linda Johansen. She came on board in 2002, when there were only six locations. Her initial role was Vice President of National Recruiting and Training. But very shortly after that, the then-existing Chief Operating Officer was not performing up to a standard that was required.

Linda had shown that she was born to lead. I clearly remember asking her if she thought she could handle moving into that COO position. Her answer was an extremely vocal and aggressive: "Of course." And she was certainly not exaggerating! At one point, Linda and her teams were opening a new location *every other day!* And she never looked back.

*One principle that helped us manage that very rapid growth was what I termed, "Go like hell, then pause and clean up the messes. Then again: Go like hell, stop, and clean up the messes."*

> The enemy of excellence is perfection.

It was okay to make some mistakes, remembering that the enemy of excellence is perfection.

Here is a portion of an announcement about Linda's performance that was made at AKM:

**"To the friends and associates of Linda Johansen-James:**

**For the second week of January in 2002, when Linda came aboard AKM, the weekly sales totaled only $29,380.
Just one week later, the sales rose to $36,267.
That seems to have been the beginning
of our rapid expansion.**

**And exactly nine years later for the exact same date,
the second week of January in 2011, the weekly sales
totaled *$2,021,240!* That's from $29,380 to $2,021,240!!!
A *6900% increase.***

**She has led our field operations in a variety of roles, earning two of the top leadership positions: President and Chief Operations Officer.**

**Today, I am happy to announce that Linda has a new title and additional responsibilities. I know you will join me in congratulating her and wishing her continued success in her leadership of the greatest specialty retail company on the planet.**

**Linda is today the new CEO of American Kiosk Management. Max James, Executive Chairman**

So, from the first four locations to the next tipping point of forty locations, there was the growth of *1,000%*. And to the next tipping point of four hundred locations, there was the growth of *6,900%*. Those were not goals and "tipping points" that we worked hard to achieve. We just worked hard to achieve all that we could. Sometimes it's okay to overachieve. Wouldn't you agree! Oh, and did I mention that we also opened and operated about 800 automated retail machines with our Guthy-Renker product line?

Linda continued in that role with great success, driving the company to that $1.7 billion ($1,700,000,000) in total sales from 2002 until 2017.

However, being the CEO of the world's largest owner-operated specialty retail kiosk company was not the end of Linda's accomplishments. She also obtained the distinction of holding the Certified Retail Executive (CRX) and the Certified Leasing Specialist (CLS) designations. She is recognized as a highly sought-after speaker for the International Council of Shopping Centers (ICSC). And Linda *still* finds time for her significant contributions to various philanthropic organizations. She supports Steve Young's Forever Young Foundation, the Alice Cooper Rock Teen Center, and she has served as the Chairwoman of the Camp Soaring Eagle Foundation for chronically and terminally ill children. For over 20 years she has supported St. Jude Children's Research Hospital and has been on the CEO Advisory Board for over 12 years. Clearly, Linda believes that to whom much is given, much is expected.

> Linda believes that to whom much is given, much is expected.

Today, Linda is a very successful entrepreneur, continuing with her extraordinary talent, experience, and drive. She is the sole owner of several ventures, most under the umbrella of her company, International Retail Management and Consulting Group (IRG). That company now has its own magazine, *International Retail Magazine,* which Linda produces. She continues to share the successful experiences that she has had in the world of specialty retail with numerous clients who are greatly benefitting from this deep well of knowledge that she has attained.

I have now retired, but I did not leave the great relationship that I have had with Linda. We are married, and I am proud that she chose to include me in her new name, Linda Johansen-James, and in her personal life. What a great bonus this partnership has created for us!

You know, my dad once told me, "A partnership of two is one too many!" Well, that is certainly *not* the case for the partnership that Linda and I have enjoyed since she joined AKM and that we continue to enjoy today. Creating business partnerships is always a challenging task, and almost always a necessary one. Great books have been written on all the nuances of forming, building, and maintaining partnerships. It will always remain a critical risk that every entrepreneur must face.

Along the way, there have been many challenges. On par with the rest of the content you've read thus far, many of these challenges taught us significant entrepreneurial lessons, and many were downright hilarious events. At a certain stage of growth, such as the success we attained, I continued to be somewhat of an entrepreneur. However, when you are a CEO or Executive Chairman of a company this size, you must take on the role and responsibility of a corporate leader. I suppose you could say I was an "entrepreneur in corporate clothing."

> Hire for character and train for skills. Bet on bright and cut your losses early."

The point here is that I never strayed from my entrepreneurial attitude and operational strategy even though the company was now a very large corporation—hardly a startup venture. The vision and principles of an entrepreneur stayed focused on each separate location, each department of the corporate office, each new idea, and all the personnel we hired and managed.

We focused on policies created by Linda like these: *"Hire for character and train for skills"* and *"Bet on bright and cut your losses early."*

When someone failed to demonstrate good character or integrity or complete their responsibilities while maintaining moral standards, there was always a price to pay. It might be extra training and a second chance, but it was never ignored, and it often meant immediate termination and criminal charges filed and prosecuted. I believed in the "rotten apple in the barrel" example. For instance:

Every evening when the location closed for the day, cash deposits had to be taken to the bank's night deposit boxes, as well as writing out a sales report that included cash received, checks, and credit card receipts. All of those could be checked by our corporate finance department every morning. If there was a discrepancy—let's say in cash deposited—then a phone call would be made to that location to determine what caused the difference in reported amounts and actual deposits.

But what if an employee discovered that they needed money for gasoline to drive home that night? They might think, "I'll just borrow $5 for tonight and pay it back tomorrow." Well, it could also happen that the next day, they simply (and innocently) forgot to "pay it back." If that amount wasn't questioned by the corporate finance department, next time, the employee might need $25 to pay the babysitter or buy some groceries on the way home. Unfortunately, if the first $5 had not been questioned, then maybe the employee might think less about using the company's money for another "short-term loan."

What if no one from the company asked about that shortage? Might the employee think, "Wow!" This is too easy. I think I'll take $100 next time, and if that doesn't create a problem for me, maybe I can get away with even more."

Maybe that seems unlikely. However, my experience is that a few of our employees—only a tiny number of the 1,800 we employed— spent a lot of time trying to figure out how to beat the system. It ranged from $10s and $20s to the most outrageous being a system to steal $80,000! That employee was eventually caught and prosecuted. Another made off with $20,000 but was also caught.

And how about this one? At one time, expired product was sent to a warehouse to be destroyed. So, the warehouse put this product in bins to be transported to the appropriate destruction process facility. However, an employee was able to steal the product out of the bins, take it home to a garage, and attempt to sell it online. They also were caught and prosecuted.

So, what is the point here?

Inventory control can be a major issue. One must design a system that reduces inventory loss and prevents inside personnel theft. These examples illustrate the principles of what I mean when I say, "Hire for character and train for skill," as well as "Bet on bright and cut your losses early."

I would also add that the prosecutions should, to the extent possible under the appropriate laws, be made public to all your employees. This will discourage others from going down the wrong path. I would argue that these prosecutions should be done even if the legal costs outweigh the direct benefits.

I suggest that all entrepreneurs consider theft prevention (or shrinkage as it is most often called in retail) with at least two possible options.

It has been said that virtually everyone can be tempted under certain conditions. So, how can an entrepreneur prevent those conditions?

There are two schools of thought. First is a belief that has been described above, i.e., leave the objects of the temptations visible and easily accessible, and when the employees (or customers) are enticed to take advantage of the opportunity, notify the proper authorities and prosecute fully.

The second school of thought suggests that the temptations should be removed so that there is less opportunity for theft. This was the policy and procedures that were utilized in our organizations. I would rather not entice anyone to violate ethical and moral standards concerning theft.

*\*\**

WHEN OPERATING FROM a kiosk or cart in shopping malls, typically, the staffing consists of three or four individuals. Ninety percent of the time, there would be only one employee manning the location. The staff consisted of a manager and two or three part-time employees. One of the questions most often asked of us was, "How in the world do you manage and supervise a retail location when there is only one part-time employee on the job at least 50 percent of the time?"

Managing multiple locations of any business is an art form, yet absolutely critical to the success of the location. Excess labor can destroy what otherwise might be a profitable location. In the previous paragraph, one management practice was described, i.e., financial systems that were able to be monitored by the central corporate staff utilizing technology and direct communication. There were also numerous daily reports on personnel, cash flow, product inventory, sales performance, and more.

A lesson I had learned in earlier ventures that helped me form management practices with these kiosks was described by Harvey MacKay as "walking the manufacturing floor." Simply put, don't spend all your time at corporate headquarters, but rather get out into the field. Much can be learned from being on the front lines.

In my experience, it works well to have each of the corporate staff members spend at least one day working the remote locations. There are many details they are not aware of since they are remotely located in the corporate offices. They might discover how difficult the job is in the field, e.g., standing all day without a chair to utilize at the sales locations. Or maybe how difficult it is to deal with an irate customer who is unruly for no apparent and logical reason. Perhaps they would've had a lack of understanding about how to correct a malfunctioning piece of technology or the home office not being able to respond to the field's issues in a timely manner (and how important timely responses are).

When a certain number of locations are up and operational, it is wise to consider hiring a "regional manager" to visit the locations on a consistent basis (to walk the manufacturing floor) on behalf of corporate leadership. It is also wise to hire a "mystery shopper"— someone who will not be recognized as working for the corporation. These inspection reports, when communicated back to corporate, can be highly beneficial. Now, it is not always necessary to hire a mystery shopper from outside your organization. That person could be someone on the corporate staff or from another region/location that would not be known to the location being shopped.

Looking back, there were many unusual situations when I visited as a mystery shopper. Though some seem humorous now, they were highly irritating at the time, and correcting the problems was imperative to the efficiency of the operation.

When I would mystery-shop a location, I would stand away from the unit and observe the employee's actions in assisting (or not assisting) customers that would stop at the unit. It was additionally informative to then walk up to the location and pretend to be interested in the products. The following are a couple of examples of what happened on these trips.

Once, I was shopping at a location in Memphis. The young employee was chitchatting on the phone (no personal phone calls were allowed). It seemed like at least 15 minutes had passed with her still talking, and it was obviously a personal call. I could no longer just observe. So, I went right up to the facility where the employee was sitting and talking and pretended to be a new customer. Sadly, she did not stop her phone call when I approached. I wandered around the kiosk, picking up the various products, pretending to be reading the packaging information. *STILL* her phone call continued.

*Now, this is getting ridiculous!*

At this point, I moved right up next to where she was sitting. Still, she paid no attention to me. *That's it*, I thought. *This has gone far enough.*

"Excuse me," I said.

To which she replied, "Do you want something?" as she cupped her hand over the telephone mic.

"Yes, could I get some help?"

She then uncupped the phone but did not hang up! She said to the person she was talking to, "Hold on just a second. Don't hang up; I have a customer wanting something. I'll be right back. This should only take a second."

*WHAT! Now I have passed my patience limit.*

I handed her my business card, which had my company name (the one she worked for), my name, and my position: Chairman and CEO.

"Hang up the phone, now! Who was that you've been talking to for at least the last 30 minutes?"

"That is none of your business!" she replied haughtily.

"You may be right, but guess what? My business is none of your business either because you no longer work here! Take your personal things and leave. You will be contacted by the HR department tomorrow."

A similar event happened in Nashville, where I was, again, mystery shopping a cart. But this time, there was no one at the cart. My hope was that they were on an authorized 15- or 30-minute break. So, I sat down away from the location, anxiously waiting to see when they would return. I waited 30 minutes, and finally, I wandered up to the kiosk. Standing about 10 yards away were two young men. One was dressed nicely in a college-preppy sorta look. The other was dressed very poorly in a grubby set of clothes; sleeves rolled up on a very wrinkled, ugly shirt, with the shirttail hanging out over an even grubbier pair of wrinkled jeans. His hair was long and appeared not to have been washed in quite a while. No shoes… but he did have on sandals.

The preppy fellow came up to the kiosk and asked me if he could help me.

"No," I replied. "I'm waiting for the salesperson to show up."

"Okay," he said. "I'm the manager, but I'm off duty. The man standing over there that I've been talking to is the salesman. Hey Joe, come on over and see what this guy wants."

*You gotta be kidding me! That man is the on-duty salesman? Surely not. I can't think of a thing about him that complies with our dress code!*

"Seriously. You work here? Dressed like that?"

"Yeah. I reckon I do. What's a matter? You don't like my looks?" he says with a bit of a threat in his voice and posture.

"No, and on two counts. I don't like your looks, and secondly, you no longer work here," I said matter-of-factly, And I handed him my business card.

Now here comes preppy, who informs me I can't fire his employee. So, I handed him my card. He glances at it, clearly now getting the message that I am the owner and CEO. But he obviously doesn't grasp the concept of a chain of command.

"I don't care who you are; you can't fire my employee!"

*Now I have lost it!*

"You can join your buddy Joe over there on your way out the door. And I will be notifying security that you are no longer to be allowed in this mall until you have been officially terminated! You can start walking now. I'll escort you out personally! Now move!"

Probably good for me that they did. But within about 20 minutes, back comes Mr. Preppy. He boldly sticks out his arm, hands me a business card, and says, "My uncle is a lawyer. This is his card. You'll be hearing from him real soon."

"I sure hope so! Now you have just a few more minutes to vacate this mall. Understood?" And he left, never to be heard from again. Whew.

Now, one last example.

I was on the second level of a shopping mall corridor, observing one of our locations on the first floor. The manager was talking with several people a few feet away from the cart. It looked like the "customers" were a family, but the manager never escorted them back to the cart to talk about the products.

After about 30 minutes of watching them visit, I left the upper level of the corridor and went down to the cart. Again, I pretended to be an interested customer, and the manager just continued talking to the family. Finally, I stepped over to the manager and asked if I could get some assistance. Reluctantly, she agreed, telling the family to just "give her a minute to talk to this customer." After she rushed through a presentation of information about a couple of the products, she asked me to just look around and come over to where she had been talking if I had any questions.

*OUCH!*

"Well, it just so happens that I'm the owner of the company you work for, and you've been visiting with this family for far too long. You've been ignoring customers, and it needs to stop. NOW."

"They're my relatives, and I'm gonna talk to them if I want to!" she snarked back.

I reiterated that customers were her first priority, and then she went too far.

"I don't care who you are; you got an attitude!"

*What! Did I really hear what I thought she said to me?*

However, in a way, she was right… but not by what she meant. I *did* have an attitude, and it was that she was not qualified to be a good manager for our company.

***

THERE WILL ALWAYS be disappointments an entrepreneur faces in building an enterprise for profit. The challenges can sometimes seem like asking a mountain to move. To survive those times, it always helped me to try and look for the humor. Often the humor was the height of ridiculousness. But it kept me going.

# *Chapter 23*

## WHEN IT'S TIME TO GO

AS A SERIAL entrepreneur, there are times when, for whatever reason, you will disagree with those who hold your current business position in their hands. That can occur to an executive in a company reporting to someone up the line; or certainly to an entrepreneur who owns less than a majority of a company that he founded and built and who is responsible to a group of investors or a lending institution; or even to a CEO reporting to a Board of Directors.

I know that there is a long list of executives that have found themselves in that position, e.g., Steve Jobs, and even little old me. In fact, the average tenure of a CEO is only about eight years and seems to be shrinking every year.

A close friend of mine was forced into just such a situation. His board had decided there were better options to fill his position since, in their collective opinion (though not the majority), he had mishandled an external matter with other entities, judged by the board to be damaging. He, on the other hand, disagreed with that analysis and insisted he had managed the situation properly and effectively.

He eventually accepted the executive committee's recommendation and remained on the board. That allowed him to continue to offer the board and the organization the benefits of his talents and experiences. A great, though disappointing solution for any entrepreneur. At some point in situations like this, it may be wise to consider other options rather than losing the debate and being summarily and often publicly dismissed. Yes, even for entrepreneurs. Maybe even *especially* for entrepreneurs.

My experience is to make your case strongly and back it up not just with your opinion but hopefully with some others who will support you. And additionally, look for data that supports your recommendation. But if the "boss," owners, board of directors, or others that control and will make the final decision on your recommendation still disagree, then you have to make choices. Is the direction that you are now required to go one that you truly believe you can't live with? Then negotiate a separation from the entity and/or those who control it. Resign? Maybe. Negotiate a "buy-out"? Maybe. Best of all, perhaps there is a common denominator that can be reached via a compromise.

> Your being "right" is not always the only or even the best choice.

If at all possible, as did my friend, perhaps you can resign from your position but continue in a meaningful role without loss of reputation and financial loss. Again, try not to burn those important bridges behind you. After all, your being "right" is not always the only or even the best choice. I have learned, painfully, that my position of important matters was too often the wrong position to die for. I know you have heard that sometimes you need to stop making your point to where it becomes an argument and step away even though you are 100 percent sure you are right.

Like has been said before in the cartoon about the beat-up old knight who lost the battle: "Some days the dragon wins."

# Chapter 24

## PUT YOUR MONEY
## WHERE YOUR HEART IS

IN AUGUST 2007, Mark Hille, from the development office of the USAF Academy's Endowment Foundation, contacted me about making a significant donation to the Academy. He didn't talk about an amount, but he asked, "If you were to make a major donation to the Academy, where would you want that money to be used?"

I told him that, in my opinion, the Academy had not invested enough in public relations funding to demonstrate to the general public, the graduate community, cadets, and the Academy staff that character development was a major program being emphasized at the Air Force Academy.

The Academy had received some bad press as a result of cheating scandals, sexual abuse reports, and other incidents that reflected poor character and morality. Because of an emphasis on religious diversity, the chapel, which had been the primary place for religious and moral instruction and training during the first decade of the

Academy's existence, was no longer the beacon of good character that it had once been. New facilities were needed to emphasize character development programs, activities, and events.

I asked Mark this hypothetical question: "What is the most iconic building you see in photographs of the Academy?"

Before he could respond, I said, "It's the chapel and its spires. It was under construction when we were there and opened in 1962. We were required to attend church services, stay awake and learn morality, and so forth. But today, you don't have to go to chapel. There is little or no morality teaching, and the only subject taught about ethics and character development is the honor code."

I then explained that, based on the results, the honor code alone has not been sufficient. Just a few years ago, a first-string football player was benched because of alleged sexual abuse or sexual harassment. Any honor scandal at the Academy makes the national headlines, and many people will simply pounce on any character issue that arises and beat it to death. The Academy isn't putting enough emphasis on teaching character development.

Mark suggested that I come to the Academy to meet a guy by the name of Erv Rokke and share my thoughts with him. I agreed to do so and also told Mark that I wanted to know more about the Air Force Academy's Endowment Foundation.

"The Endowment Board includes some people I think you might know—Harry Pearce, Bart Holaday, and Bill Wecker. And there are other Founding Board of Directors members who have had successful professional and military careers," Mark said.

Eventually, I became one of the first 12 members of the Founding Board of Directors of the USAF Academy's Endowment Foundation. My interest in character development up to this point had been all talk and no action. But now, my commitment needed to be a leadership gift to start the ball rolling. I was blessed to be able to make the first seven-figure donation that the Endowment had received. My first gift was a restricted gift to be used only for the construction of a building for character and leadership development.

Soon, I made that trip back to the Academy and was introduced to Lieutenant General Erv Rokke, a former Dean at the Academy (and now a retired Lt. General). Mark had told me that Erv was working on a full mission statement for the Center for Character and Leadership Development department. When we met in Erv's office, we talked about the need for expanded facilities for the Department of Character and Leadership Development, and it didn't take long to realize that we were on the same page. He showed me a very attractive brochure that had been produced and presented to the Board of Visitors at their last meeting, which contained the mission statement that he envisioned for the Center for Character and Leadership Development. It was both a strategic and implementation plan for character and leadership development; one that would conduct research and share that research with cadets and the Academy staff, as well as the greater Air Force and beyond.

When I looked it over, I was impressed. Erv asked me what I thought about it. I suggested that the Academy needed to create a new structure on its campus, one that people could relate to and appreciate—especially the cadets, of course. It would be an important and relevant place where cadets would talk and learn about character and leadership development, instead of having the program buried in Vandenberg Hall dormitories.

Erv said, "Max, that's very interesting. John Regni's office is right next door. He's already initiated plans for such a building." John, a lieutenant general, was then the Superintendent of the Air Force Academy.

John viewed a new home for character and leadership development programs much like the Kennedy Center, with a serious national and international appeal. He stepped next door into the Superintendent's office and asked John if he had time for a brief conversation. The Superintendent came into Erv's office, and after a brief introduction, he confirmed that plans were underway and that the civil engineers had already designed a building that would be located between Arnold Hall and Vandenberg Hall.

"If you have an artist rendering of the building, I'd love to see it," I said.

He went back to his office and brought out the rendering of the building. It was a rectangular box constructed with steel, glass, and aluminum that looked like all the other buildings in the cadet area.

"I think it's one of the ugliest buildings I've ever seen. Not to mention it doesn't represent the building's purpose and significance, and it's located in a terrible site." (Well, I said something to that effect, probably in an unprofessional military manner.)

John put his head back and said, "Really?"

I could tell that he didn't appreciate what I had said after all the work that had been done so far. He shrugged and sharply asked, "So what would you do?"

I thought the building needed to make a statement. I told him that architectural firms all over the world would be interested in designing the first new major building in the cadet area at the United States Air Force Academy. There should be a solicitation for design—an architectural contest. The building should be an **iconic** structure, one that would rival, but not overshadow, the chapel. This new building would demonstrate that the Air Force Academy had a major focus and commitment to the development of character and leadership for the cadets.

To his credit, John Regni decided the idea of an architectural contest was a good one. But he ingeniously modified that idea and presented it to Skidmore, Owings, and Merrill, LLC (SOM), the architectural firm that designed and master-planned the USAFA in 1954. Skidmore said that to ensure that the design of the new building complemented the original plan for the Academy, the contest should be internal to Skidmore. The firm's regional offices in Chicago, San Francisco, and Washington, D.C., were selected to produce conceptual drawings for review by the Academy and presentation to a jury composed of members hand-selected by the Superintendent.

\*\*\*

A FEW WEEKS after the meetings with Mark Hille, Erv Rokke, and John Regni, Regni surprised me by calling to ask if I would serve on the jury to choose the best design submitted from the architectural contest for the Center for Character and Leadership Development. I was truly honored to accept the role. Each juror was given an advisory group to help choose the design. One of those on my advisory group was Terry Isaacson, who chaired the Congressional Board of Visitor's Character and Leadership's Subcommittee at the time.

The design chosen was especially unique. It was selected for its iconic shape (a trapezoidal structure), which was completely different than the other two competitive structures, one being a glass cube and the other a glass cylinder. The unique element was the glass trapezoid structure pointing directly to the North Star, better known as Polaris. Polaris appears to stand almost motionless in the sky because its axis is perfectly aligned with Earth's axis. All the other stars in the night sky seem to revolve around Polaris. Thus, it has been used for navigation by adventurers for centuries, often called the "Compass in the Sky."

For purposes of the CCLD building, it was presented as a symbol of a "moral compass" for character. When a cadet stands in front of the Honor Board, a panel of his cadet peers, the North Star is visible through the apex of the building. The symbolism is significant because one's moral compass must be consistent and ever-present. Right is always right. The integrity of one's actions should never waver, just as Earth and Polaris are never wavering in their relationship with each other. Character and morality should always be connected without variance.

There's a very important point to make when reflecting upon the need for the Academy's emphasis on character development. When our class entered in 1960, what the Academy and the Air Force expected and demanded of us was not far from the character culture that we came from. Who were our heroes? John Wayne. Chuck Yeager. Douglas MacArthur. Dwight Eisenhower, even Roy Rogers, Flash Gordon, and Steve Canyon.

However, many of today's young adults have heroes who are sports and entertainment celebrities and make as much as $50 million a year but think it's acceptable to assault their fiancées in an elevator or watch animals fight for fun and profit. Some of these kids come from an environment where cheating is acceptable. For others, ratting on a friend for lying, cheating, or stealing is not judged as wrong. The gap between the culture in today's society and the culture needed at the Academy to prepare cadets to become "Leaders of Character" in the Air Force is wider than it has ever been.

Today, there is a much greater need to focus on character development. The new and very much iconic building, the Center for Character and Leadership Development, has made a significant impact at the Academy, not only on the physical landscape but also on the Academy's ability to accomplish its mission as stated today:

The mission of the United States Air Force Academy
is to educate, train, and inspire men and women to become
**Leaders of Character**, motivated to lead the
United States Air Force in service to our nation.

**AUTHOR'S NOTE:** For more on the CCLD building and my passion for character development, you can find an interview with the *Journal of Character & Leadership Development* in the appendix of this book.

\*\*\*

BEING A SUCCESSFUL entrepreneur has many wonderful aspects, as seen here in the CCLD building through the ability to be a part of something that will live well beyond yourself and benefit many. First, there is the satisfaction that "you built it." It may have been a relatively short climb to the top of the peak, or it may have been long, weary, difficult, and exasperating. But you made it. And hopefully, the financial rewards have allowed you to enjoy many of the material things you have dreamed of doing and owning.

Some of the rewards that have fallen my way have entailed playing golf at some of the finest resorts in the world. One particular trip was the "dream trip of a lifetime"—playing golf in Scotland, including St. Andrews, and attending The Open in Ireland, among other experiences. I also take an annual trip to Pebble Beach to play many courses there and stay in the Jack Nicholas Suite right next to the crashing waves against the rocks, the waters creating a beautiful scene on the 18th green. We were also able to buy a beautiful second home in Sedona and own a partnership interest in a private jet. And so much more that has left phenomenal memories to enjoy as I look back over this serial career as an entrepreneur.

But perhaps more importantly, in our entrepreneurial ventures, there has been another factor we felt was important: creating a culture of giving back. I've found this to be true time and time again—if you give, it will be returned to you tenfold, and sometimes, a hundredfold. When one gives without expecting a reward, the emotional benefits to a team of people are extraordinary.

We have been long-time supporters of St. Jude Children's Hospital. Linda has served on the Advisory Board for several years. We were even able to sponsor a fundraising golf tournament for St. Jude called the Liberty Bowl Golf Tournament.

We also created Camp Soaring Eagle, a camp in Arizona for critically ill and, unfortunately, sometimes terminally ill children. And what a pleasure it was to have Jane Seymour as our spokesperson. We have been able to host 7,000 campers!

Additionally, we were able to participate in the Air Force Academy Foundation's success in building a major architectural award-winning facility at the Academy to service the Center for Character and Leadership Development, now called Polaris. This included serving as the Chairman of the CCLD Committee for nine years during the planning, funding, and construction of this structure. I have also been fortunate to be able to continue to donate to several other programmatic initiatives such as the *Journal for Character & Leadership Integration* (for which I now sit on the Editorial Advisory Board), the editor-in-chief for that journal, and an individual "character researcher" position.

I have often said that I have been blessed with two categories of philanthropy. First, there has been the instant gratification of seeing those young children at camp, some who had only been out of their homes to see the doctors or stay in hospitals, now laughing and playing, finding new friends who, like them, were battling with courage.

And the second category is "legacy" gratification. This includes being a major participant in creating Polaris, an iconic structure to stand not only as a facility to research adolescent character development, but also to be a commanding symbol of the level of "excellence, service, and integrity" the Academy cadets aspire to achieve.

I am proud to have been a part of those two accomplishments, neither of which could have occurred if I hadn't taken the risk to become an entrepreneur and, instead, played it safe. Additionally, every nickel of the millions that I've given to the Air Force Academy has been donated for the improvement of character development.

So, I'm proud to say: **"I've put my money where my heart is."**

# Chapter 25

## LOOKING FORWARD

I BELIEVE THAT the challenges of "developing leaders of character" that face the Air Force Academy (and all institutions of higher learning) in the years to come will continue to grow. The social culture that exists today in modern America (and other countries) is far different from the culture that existed when the Air Force Academy became operational, with the first class of cadets promoted into their second lieutenant's rank in 1959.

The gap that existed between the standards of ethics and character performance that the USAF required in the '50s and '60s vs. the standards of the culture and society of that same era has widened immensely. Today, the USAF has the same level of character requirements as in the earlier years, but the society from which young men and women are now recruited to become cadets and future "leaders of character" has changed and become less ethical and moral.

The Air Force Academy has changed how it has taught character development over the last 60 years. Much more of the learning is experiential, not just blackboards/whiteboards and lectures. An additional change in the experiential category is what is unpopularly described as "second chance." One of the future CCLD policies will continue to be a close examination of the benefits and/or negative consequences of the "second chance" program. I believe that character can be developed, that young men and women can experience and learn what the results of failure of poor character, attitudes, and actions can be. I don't need to give all the examples that can occur on the battlefield and in the combat air war if a lack of trust exists.

Experiential learning while at the Academy might mean that a young man or woman becomes a true leader of character by being given a chance to correct their errors in poor choices of character. In fact, one year at the Academy, the Cadet Chairman of the Cadet Honor Committee was a "second-chancer." Or how about the cadet who, during his last year at the Academy, could no longer keep his honor code violation bottled up inside him. He went to his AOC and confessed that he had been lying to his mother about how well he was doing in his academic classes when, in fact, he was barely getting by. His mother was so proud of him for being at the Academy; he just could not tell her that he might not make it academically as each testing period came and went. He became a second-chancer as well.

Additional continuing research will need to be conducted on how to handle the issues of the conflicts resulting from loyalty to a team vs. tolerations of character failures. It seems that the most difficult of the three requirements in the Honor Code is this: "… nor tolerate among us those who do." Team loyalty, loyalty to a close friend, classmate, or even roommate often morally and emotionally conflicts with being a "rat." For example, "I just couldn't

rat on my intercollegiate teammate the week before the big game."
Or, "My roommate had worked so hard for over three years to meet
the academic challenges he was having. All his life, he had wanted
to fly jets in the U.S. Air Force. His parents were so proud of his
making it at the Academy. I saw him glance at a fellow cadet's test
paper in class. Somehow, I just couldn't turn him in for cheating
to our Squadron Honor Rep." This is a really tough one, and I
was personally told by an Honor Rep that he did not believe in the
Academy's no-tolerance requirement.

Depending upon how egregious the violation of honor is, perhaps the second chance has been a good one. All honor violations
are punished, often severely. And many honor violations still result
in immediate dismissal from the cadet wing.

We need to continue to understand that if we believe we can
teach aspects like honor and character, then that should have an
impact on how we deal with violations in future years. If we want
cadets to experience growth in their character as individuals, then
we need to provide the space for them to do so. And if that is a
valid means to teach character, then we ought to become the best in
the world at doing so. The Academy is a unique crucible in which
testing on how to achieve character development can be accomplished in the best ways. We need to continue to do more research
on how you can best teach and develop adolescent character. That
is my opinion. And real-world examples for some have empirically
shown that the second chance leads to a lifetime of solid character
development and strong character performance.

Today, there is that iconic building that houses the future policies and training programs for the cadets and CCLD professionals
to build upon the great history and accomplishment of the Long

Blue Line. The graduates of the Academy feel strongly about character and honor. They proved it by donating the most money ever for a program or project during the Academy's history. The goal for the funding of the Polaris facility was greatly exceeded. Future years will undoubtedly find continuing support from grads and all those who believe that character and leadership should be inseparable.

I believe adolescent character development will continue to be improved over the next ten years with outstanding results in developing "leaders of character" for the United States Air Force and this nation.

# Conclusion

## YOUR TURN

SO, STILL THINK you want to be or continue to be an entrepreneur? I truly hope so. I have tried to demonstrate through my many and varied stories the really great times I have enjoyed, battling my way up one mountain, falling down sometimes painfully, and then the thrill and great satisfaction of climbing up another. And I didn't always fall off the mountain, but rather looked around and spotted another mountain to climb, that great "peak-to-peak" mentality that led me to voluntarily leave one peak, go down into the valley, and begin the next climb.

> The only successes worth attaining were those that I could do with total integrity and strong character traits.

The rewards of climbing these mountains have been enormous. I always felt that the only successes worth attaining were those that I could do with total integrity and strong character traits. In making this journey, I witnessed many whose character was not acceptable, at least to me. Every time I thought I could deal with these character flaws, not only was I in for serious disappointments, but the businesses sooner or later, usually sooner, failed miserably. I think that is why, in my latter business ventures, working only with those of high integrity was a choice I made. And certainly, in those many cases where I witnessed poor character, I was wishing I could have avoided those individuals. I can see the great benefits of adolescent character development and how it produces a legacy of high integrity. My wish is that as integrity and character increase, the number of times entrepreneurs have to deal with the consequences of poor character *decreases*.

Has the journey been worth it to my family and me? You bet. We have been able to witness the benefit to others that our resources have provided. We have loved being a part of the charitable events that we have been involved in, so that witnessing those who benefited became very personable and satisfying.

> Your dreams can only be shattered by your lack of desire and determination.

We know that when you give, the benefits come back to you at least tenfold.

Having achieved some modicum of success was, of course, its own reward, but the real reward in being an accomplished entrepreneur is what it allows you to do for others, your family, and those you will never meet.

So entrepreneurs (and others), go do it, get to it, enjoy the journey and the rewards. And remember one last thing: "Your dreams can only be shattered by your lack of desire and determination."

"Far better it is to dare mighty things,
to win glorious triumphs, even though checkered by failure,
than to take rank with those poor spirits who neither
enjoy much nor suffer much because they live
in the gray twilight that knows not victory nor defeat."

**—Theodore Roosevelt**

# If You Try Your Best, That's Success.

# ABOUT THE AUTHOR

Max James is an Air Force Academy graduate and pilot who was shot down in Vietnam twice. He went on to become the founder, CEO, and Executive Chairman of American Kiosk Management, a billion-dollar global presence worldwide with 54,000 employees.

Through personal stories and business adventures, Max James delivers insightful business lessons within the pages of his new business memoir, *The Harder I Fall, the Higher I Bounce* (publisher: Made For Success, 2021).

In recognition of his groundbreaking contributions to the specialty retail field, Max James became the first inductee into the $25 Billion Specialty Retail Hall of Fame. Max has also been featured in *Fortune* magazine and dozens of media publications and television appearances for his work in business and charitable contributions.

Mr. James has spent the past decade leading the charge as the Chairman of the Air Force Academy Foundation committee for the CCLD (Center for Character and Leadership Development), now called Polaris Hall.

Max and his wife Linda Johansen-James reside in Las Vegas.

# *Appendix*

## AN INTERVIEW
## WITH MAX JAMES

Interviewed by Dr. Douglas Lindsay of the *Journal of Character & Leadership Development* (JCLD)

**Mr. James's Background:** After graduating with honors from the United States Air Force Academy, Mr. James flew with the astronauts in the Astronaut Recovery Program at Cape Canaveral. He then volunteered for Combat Air Rescue duty with the Jolly Green Giants in the Vietnam War, followed by an assignment as a combat instructor pilot. After his time in the military, Mr. James earned an MBA from Stanford University's Graduate School of Business. He then started his business career in the real estate industry as an international investment analyst, which led to a lucrative stint as a real estate sales executive and eventually a real estate developer. Along with a corporate partner, Mr. James's company built, owned, and operated 18 hotels in California and Nevada. He became an Executive Vice President of Days Inns of America, CEO of "Days of the West," and served on the Board of Directors of the California Hotel Association and the California Governor's California Tourism Corporation. Mr. James later returned to the world of real estate and developed several RE/MAX Real Estate territories in Northern California. The retail industry beckoned, and Mr. James developed the world's largest chain of owner-operated kiosk retail stores. This involvement in the Specialty Retail Industry led Mr. James and his wife, Linda, into numerous product lines, ranging from his American Yoyo Company to the cosmetic world of Avon, Revlon, and Proactiv Solutions. Many other company product lines followed: Solar City, Hess Energy, ABCmouse, Harry & David, and others. Total revenues in just one of those ventures exceeded $1.8 billion. Mr. James was selected as the first inductee into the Specialty Retail Hall of Fame. Currently, Mr. James, who is attempting retirement, retains his position as the Executive Chairman of American Kiosk Management, LLC, which operated over 1,000 retail kiosks in the U.S., Canada, Australia, and New Zealand. He is the Founder of Camp Soaring Eagle, a camp for chronically and terminally ill children, now having served over 7,000 campers. Mr. James, a 1964 graduate of the United States Air Force Academy, received the Academy's Distinguished Graduate Award in 2010.

**JCLD:** Thank you for your time to talk about your involvement with the Academy, the *Journal of Character & Leadership Development* (JCLD), and the Center for Character & Leadership Development (CCLD). Could you share a little bit about that involvement over the past few years?

**James:** In August 2007, Mark Hille, from the development office of the USAF Academy's Endowment Foundation, contacted me about making a major donation to the Academy. He didn't talk about an amount, but he very smartly asked, "If you were to make a major donation to the Academy, where would you want that money to go?" I told him that, in my view, the Academy had not invested enough in public relations funding to demonstrate to the general public, the graduate community, the cadets, and the Academy staff that character development was a major program at the Academy. The Academy had received bad press as a result of cheating scandals, sexual abuse reports, and other incidents that reflected poor character and morality among a few individuals in the cadet wing. Because of an increased emphasis on religious diversity, the chapel, which had been the primary place for morality instruction and training during the first decade of the Academy's existence, was no longer the beacon of good character that it had once been. New facilities were needed to house and emphasize character development programs, activities, and events.

I asked Mark the hypothetical question: "What is the most iconic building that you always see in photographs of the Academy?" Before he could respond, I said, "It's the chapel and its spires. It was under construction when I was there and opened in 1962. We were required to attend Sunday morning church service, stay awake and listen to morality teachings, and so forth. But today the cadets don't have to go to chapel. There is little or no morality teaching, and the only subject taught about ethics and character development is the honor code and classes in philosophy and ethics with a sprinkling of character issues presented in other academic classes."

I then explained that, based on the results, the honor code alone seemed not to be sufficient. Just a few years ago, our first-string quarterback was benched because of an honor violation. Any honor scandal at the Academy makes the national headlines, and many people will simply pounce on any character issue at the Academy and beat it to death. In my opinion, the Academy isn't putting enough emphasis on teaching character development.

Then Mark asked, "Do you know Erv Rokke?"

I told him that I didn't, so Mark suggested that I come to the Academy, meet Erv, and share my thoughts with him. I agreed to do so. I also told Mark that I wanted to know more about the Air Force Academy Endowment Foundation.

Mark said, "The Endowment Board includes some people I think you might know—Harry Pearce, Bart Holaday, and Bill Wecker. And there are other Founding Members of the Board who have had successful professional and military careers."

I said, "Mark, I'd be happy and honored just to sit at the table with those accomplished guys and learn something from them. So yes, I'd be willing to make a trip out to the Academy to find out more about the Endowment Foundation and to meet with Erv Rokke."

Eventually, I became one of the first 12 members of the Founding Board of Directors of the USAF Academy's Endowment Foundation. My interest in character development up to that point had all been words and no action. But now, my commitment to act needed to be a leadership gift to start the ball rolling. I was blessed to be able to make the first seven-figure donation that the Endowment had received. My first gift was a restricted gift to be used only for the construction of a building for character and leadership development.

Soon, I was introduced to Lieutenant General (retired) Erv Rokke, a former Dean of the Faculty at the Academy. When we met in his office, we talked about the need for expanded facilities for character and leadership development, and it didn't take long to realize that we were on the same page. He showed me a very attractive brochure that had been produced and presented to the Board of Visitors at their last meeting. It contained the mission statement that he envisioned for the Center for Character and Leadership Development. It was both a strategic and implementation plan for character and leadership development, one that would conduct research and share that research with cadets and the Academy staff, as well as the greater Air Force and beyond. Erv explained that John viewed the home for character and leadership development programs much like the Kennedy Center, with a serious national and international appeal. Erv explained that he viewed the home for character and leadership development programs much like the Kennedy Center, with a serious national and international appeal.

When I looked it over, I was very impressed. Erv asked me what I thought about it. I suggested creating a new structure at the Academy, one that people could relate to and appreciate, especially the cadets, of course. It would be an important and relevant place where cadets would talk and learn about character and leadership development, instead of having the programs and the CCLD staff stealthily buried in Vandenberg Hall dormitories.

Erv said, "Max, that's very interesting. John Regni's office is right next door." (John, a Lieutenant General, was then the Superintendent of the Air Force Academy.) "He's already initiated plans for such a building." Erv stepped next door into the Superintendent's office and asked John if he had time for a brief conversation. The Superintendent came into Erv's office, and after a brief introduction, he confirmed that plans were underway and that the civil engineers had already preliminarily designed a building that would be located between Arnold Hall and Vandenberg Hall.

I said, "If you have an artist rendering of the building, I'd love to see it."

He went back to his office and brought out the rendering of the building. It was a rectangular box, constructed with steel, glass, and aluminum that looked like all the other buildings in the cadet area. I thought it was one of the ugliest buildings I'd ever seen and certainly didn't represent the building's purpose and significance, and I thought it was located in a terrible site. Probably in a somewhat unprofessional military manner, I said something to that effect.

John put his head back and said, "Really?" I could tell that he didn't appreciate what I had said after all the work that had been done so far. He shrugged and sharply asked, "So what would you do?" I told him that I thought the building needed to make a strong statement. I added that architectural firms all over the world would be enthusiastically interested in designing the first new major building in the cadet area at the United States Air Force Academy. There should be a solicitation for design, a worldwide architectural contest. The building should be an iconic structure, one that would architecturally rival, but not overshadow, the chapel. This new building would demonstrate that the Air Force Academy had a major focus and commitment to the development of character for the cadets.

John Regni decided the idea of an architectural contest was a good one. But he ingeniously modified that idea and presented it to Skidmore, Owings, and Merrill, LLC (SOM), the architectural firm that designed and master-planned USAFA in 1954. Skidmore said that to ensure that the design of a new building would complement the original plan for the Academy, the contest should be internal to SOM. The firm's regional offices in Chicago, San Francisco, and Washington, D.C., were selected to produce competitive conceptual drawings for review by the Academy and presentation to a jury composed of members hand selected by the Superintendent.

A few weeks after the meetings with Mark Hille, Erv Rokke, and John Regni, Gen. Regni called me to ask if I would serve on the jury to choose the best design submitted from the architectural contest for the Center for Character and Leadership Development. I was truly honored to accept that role. Each juror was given an advisory group to help choose the design. One of those on my advisory group was my classmate Terry Isaacson, who then chaired the Congressional Board of Visitor's Character and Leadership Subcommittee.

The design chosen was especially unique. It was selected for its iconic shape (a trapezoidal structure) which was unlike the other two competitive structures, one being a glass cube and the other a glass cylinder. The unique element was the glass trapezoid structure pointed directly to the North Star, better known as Polaris. Polaris appears to stand almost motionless in the sky, because its axis is virtually perfectly aligned with Earth's axis. All the other stars in the night sky seem to revolve around Polaris. Thus, it has been used for navigation by adventurers for centuries, often called the "Compass in the Sky." For purposes of the CCLD building, it was presented as a symbol of a "moral compass" for character. When a cadet stands in front of the Honor Board, a panel of his cadet peers who have the responsibility of judging his honor violation, the North Star is visible up through the apex of the building. The symbolism is significant because one's moral compass must be consistent and ever present. Right is always right. The integrity of one's actions should never waver, just as Earth and Polaris are never wavering in their relationship with each other. Character and one's actions should always be connected without variance.

There's a very important point to make when reflecting upon the need for the Academy's increased emphasis on character development. When my class entered in 1960, what the Academy and the Air Force expected and demanded of us was not far from the character culture that we came from. Who were our heroes? John Wayne, Chuck Yeager, Douglas MacArthur, Dwight Eisenhower, even Roy Rogers, Flash Gordon, and Steve Canyon.

However, many of today's young adults have heroes who are sports and entertainment celebrities who make as much or more than $50 million a year but think it's acceptable to assault their fiancées in an elevator or watch animals fight for fun and profit. Some of these kids come from an environment where cheating is acceptable, even encouraged. For others, ratting on a friend for lying, cheating, or stealing is not judged as wrong. The gap between the culture in today's society and the culture needed at the Academy to prepare cadets to become "Leaders of Character" in the Air Force is wider than it has ever been. Most recently, as I write this, there have been numerous suspensions of members of the hockey and swimming teams for improper conduct by some toward their team members for "hazing."

I've heard graduates complain that the Academy has changed and that the old standards from when they were cadets have been compromised. In my opinion, the Academy has changed out of necessity. The Air Force, and the military in general, had to change what they were focusing on in terms of character development. Those entering the Academy today come from a society with very different norms of ethics and morality than when I entered as a cadet.

Today there is a much greater need to focus on character development. The new, and very much iconic building—Center for Character and Leadership Development—has made a significant impact at the Academy, not only on the physical landscape, but also on the Academy's ability to accomplish its mission as stated today:

> The mission of the United States Air Force Academy is to educate, train, and inspire men and women to become Leaders of Character, motivated to lead the United States Air Force in service to our nation.

I'm fortunate to have been able to make contributions to improving the Academy's emphasis on character development. I have also been fortunate to be able to continue to donate to several other programmatic initiatives such as the *Journal for Character & Leadership Integration*, the editor-in-chief for this journal, and an individual "character researcher" position.

Every nickel of the millions that I've given to the Air Force Academy has been donated for the improvement of character development. So, I'm proud to say, "I've put my money where my heart is."

**JCLD:** That's quite the investment. Thank you for sharing that background and context. You have had a lot of experience both in the military and outside of the military. Why is character important when we start thinking about developing leaders?

**James:** The old expression is "Character counts." And it counts both ways. Bad character creates destruction, and good character creates success. If you have someone in a leadership position that makes decisions without thinking of what is right or wrong, what is good or bad, you are going to end up damaging whatever it is that they are leading. They don't just damage themselves. I truly believe in a moral compass. There are gray areas always, but right is right, and wrong is wrong. My experience in the military showed me that bad decisions, be they falsehoods or outright lies, even trimming the truth, can lead to death, especially in a war. You just really need to know that the character of the people you are working with, and working for in particular, is not going to get you killed because they are going to trim the truth. In the business world, you can destroy a company in a hurry, and you can certainly destroy departments. It can all be destroyed by someone that says, "You know, if I cut this corner, I don't think anyone will find out. I think we can take a shortcut here." It will blow up in your face, and the next thing you know, you have lost the war, the job, the project, or the money. If you are in a philanthropic area, you have damaged the people you are trying to help. It's rare, in my opinion, that you get away with character flaws in action for very long. And even if you do, there's guilt spread all around the area where you have committed the flaw. Guilt, then, causes all kinds of personal problems even if you aren't the one who created the initial effort. If you were guilty by not saying something, then you are going to hurt. I don't know how you can get away with becoming a good leader without having a solid base of good character.

**JCLD:** We seem to see a lot of leader failure now. Some of that is due to social media as we have access to videos of people doing things, both good and bad. Do you think it has gotten worse over time, or has it always been there, and we are better at recognizing it now?

**James:** I actually think it has gotten better. I'm not sure how far you want to go back. If you look at war, the reason we fought some wars was because of bad characters in leadership positions in the enemy organizations. There is also the bad character of our history inside this country… discrimination, civil rights, prohibition, etc. One of my favorite authors is Zane Grey. He writes about how cowboys killed each other and rustlers. That was kind of the norm. So, for lots of reasons, I think that certainly for this country, the display and action of character has improved dramatically. I think it has improved in our Air Force Academy. We found ways to improve character within the cadet ranks as well as in the other professionals there… academic, athletic, and so forth. We have found ways to harness bad character and eliminate it in many cases, which is a positive result for the cadets. So, I would say, character in the United States has gotten better over the decades. However, there are notable and very public (because of social media) examples of bad character, whether it is in the entertainment industry, the political environment, the business world, or the military. But I think there is less bad character than there used to be.

**JCLD:** You brought up the Air Force Academy. How would you describe the value of the Air Force Academy?

**James:** First of all, I think there are a lot of advantages that the military academies and the prep schools contribute to our nation. Let me share a story. When I was selected, as an alternate, by the way, to attend the Academy, there were three things that made me choose to accept the appointment. Number one was the honor. No one from my little hometown of Humboldt, TN, had ever gone to a military academy. To be chosen to go to a brand-new military academy with all of the spires and all of that, was a tremendous honor. Number two, it was an education. It was clear that the other military academies produced tremendous academic programs for their students, and the presumption was that the same thing would occur, and I would get a great education by going to the United States Air Force Academy. Thirdly, the reason for going was that flying jets sounded pretty cool, and I could become a jet pilot like Steve Canyon in the comic strips. Those were my reasons, in that priority. In truth, they are totally upside down. If you are going to a military service academy, you should first want a military career to serve your country. Lots of schools have good academic programs, and for lots of schools, it is an honor to go there. So, that's the first reason one should have for going to a military service academy. Secondly, it's because you get a great education. It's proven. Look at the stats every year when university rankings are published; they are always near the top in all the categories. That's the second reason you should choose to go. The third reason you should choose it is that it is an honor to be selected to prepare you to serve your country. You get a free education, and in fact, they pay you.

Now, what convinced me to go was there was an article in *Life* magazine when I was a senior in high school. There was a cover story about the United States Air Force Academy. There were all these pictures of airplanes, of the spires on the chapel, and it was modern and in the mountains. It just looked fantastic. But the one picture that really convinced me was the social center—Arnold

Hall. They had a spiral staircase. They had these cadets in these stunning dress uniforms and sabers and beautiful women standing by their sides. I said, "I need some of that." So, I went for all the wrong reasons to the Air Force Academy. But why is it important? There isn't an educational institution in the United States comparable to the military service academies that gives you the opportunity to experience growth, character growth, an honor code. Where you can trust those around you to be truthful and loyal and be given a chance to be a leader. You don't have to be the best at the Academy to get leadership experience. You can be an Element Leader, Squadron Exec, on an intercollegiate team, or an intramural team. It was a chance to experience growth in a controlled environment where character was critically important and you could trust that those around you wouldn't be taking advantage of this little farm boy coming out of Humboldt, TN. There's a reason to take some of America's best and attract them into a military environment where they learn through experience as well as teachings and a professional education.

**JCLD:** Thank you for sharing that. So how did your time at the Academy influence your trajectory over your life? What did you take away from that experience that has endured over time?

**James:** We have an expression that I have used in my companies that is, "Hire for Character... Train for Skills." The predominant reason for hiring one qualified person over another is, what do you think about their character? If they are a little short on the skill levels, we ought to be able to teach them, and they can learn through experience. But character counts. We hire for character. People we could trust to do the things that we would ask them to do. The most successful business that we developed had remote locations without significant oversight. They weren't on the manufacturing floor. They weren't in an office building. They were out by themselves, a staff of three. There was one manager and two part-time people. We needed to be able to trust that manager. So, we hired for character, and then we could train them to operate their particular retail unit. That was also true in the hotel business that I was in. There are 10,000 ways to take money out of the cash register. You need to be able to trust your people. Hire for character... train for skills. The Academy taught me that character, in people you had to depend upon, whether it was a superior or subordinate, character counted, and you needed to know that it was going to work because they had solid character. I took that into the business world with me. If I couldn't trust them, I didn't want to work for them, and I didn't want them working for me.

**JCLD:** Is that a common approach in the business world?

**James:** No.

**JCLD:** At the Academy, our mission is to develop leaders of character. In order to do that, we have things like the Core Values. What were your experiences like regarding character in the business world? Was that a novel approach in the environment you were in, or was it pretty common?

**James:** Both, actually. Which probably isn't a surprise. Fortunately, most were good character environments, but some were not. In corporate America, you can find the same percentages that I found in my business world. There are large corporations that are hugely successful where the CEO goes to jail. It is destructive to employees, shareholders, all stakeholders. The guy may have gotten away with it for a time, but the whole thing implodes and hurts everyone. There are also companies out there where character is at the top of the list. You can think of companies where leadership at the top sets the tone, and if you violate character or morality, you are not going to last, and they will let you go. I had partners once that I didn't choose, in a multimillion-dollar enterprise, that pulled a policy from what had been promised. It resulted in damage to people that worked for me. They did it without my consent. I confronted them about it, and we couldn't settle it. They said it had to be done, so we agreed to disagree, and I left. All of those partners, and their executive team but one, went to jail. There is an example of where your commitment to doing it right requires you need to follow through, and it can cost you personally. You hope, eventually, that bad character will be punished. But it isn't always. To answer your question, I see both in the world of business. Because of social media, a lot more of the bad is being exposed and appropriately punished or eliminated from their negative influences on the people they are responsible for.

**JCLD:** To that point, you see a lot of larger organizations having a focus on character through leadership centers or leader development activities as part of the organization. It seems like they are starting to recognize their role in character.

**James:** In fact, there is a whole industry that is going to continue to grow of consultants who do just that. They go into large organizations and examine areas that need to be improved upon in terms maybe of accountability, to remove the temptations or to discover violations. A classmate of mine from the Graduate School of Business at Stanford who, when he graduated, went right into that… corporate responsibility. He has continued that since 1971. So, for however many years that is, that is all that he has done. He works for large corporations and a lot of municipalities to help them make sure that corporate responsibility is something that everyone understands and understands why, and he teaches that character aspect. Then, he helps them put that into policies and guidelines to help people easily, without temptation or the threat of punitive action against them, do what is right.

**JCLD:** It sounds like the Academy had a very real effect on you, and you have certainly made significant investments of time and money over the years. What is it about the Academy that resonates with you today in terms of your continued support and involvement?

**James:** One of the things that the Academy has been changing successfully is the appreciation of what you have experienced and learned at the Academy. For a lot of us, the bond that kept us going at the Academy was ego. We were too proud to quit. We didn't want to go home and face friends and neighbors and know that they would say to you, "He couldn't make it." So, it was ego, I'm going to tell you. Secondly, another old trite expression was that it was "the common bond of misery." We are all in this together. We will stick it out, support each other, and somehow, we will make it through. I enjoyed the Academy, but that doesn't mean you like everything that you had to put up with. I had some bad experiences there which I have written about before. I was one of the guys, that when I got out, I didn't care anything about coming back here right away. I was tired of that way of life. I loved the freedom of going to bed when I wanted and getting up when I wanted. That said, I loved the military. I loved what I did, I loved the flying, and the mission I had in Vietnam. Somewhere along the way, most of us begin to look back and appreciate what the Academy experience really did for us. Whether it was self-discipline… I have to make this bed every morning… I have to shine these shoes, or whether it was the benefit of following good rules and being a team member. That had been imbued in us and stuck with us, and we started to realize, something like this happened to us at the Academy.

The most important lesson that I learned at the Academy was that you can delegate authority, but you cannot delegate responsibility. It happened to me as a senior at the Academy. A third classman gave some physical punishments, unauthorized and unattended, to a fourth classman. I was the third classman's superior cadet officer. I was the Squadron Commander. The result of that action of the sophomore against the freshman, resulted in my being removed from command. They took away my sabre, gave me a rifle, made me march in the back of my squadron, and moved me out of my squadron area into an isolated area. These punishments resulted because of an action taken by a sophomore against a freshman while I was in my room shaving.

There was a Lieutenant Colonel who said to me, "Max let me tell you a story. I was a Squadron Commander in the China/Burma/India Theater. We were short of supplies as well as fuel and pilots, and we were suffering significant casualties. They sent me two wet-behind-the-ears lieutenants from pilot school. They were good, and they did really well on our combat missions. We came back one day, and they didn't land right away. They stayed up and practiced aerial combat. When they got on the ground, I chewed them up one side and down the other. We can't stand this. We have maintenance problems, aircraft problems, and you can't spend those valuable assets. They said okay. We went on some more missions, and they were fine. Then a bit later, we came back from a mission, and they did it again. Unfortunately, they ran into each other in a midair collision, killed them both, and we lost two airplanes. I was the Squadron Commander. I was relieved of command, sent back to the Pentagon, and that's why I have this lieutenant colonel's leaf on my shoulder instead of something of a higher responsibility. Max, you can delegate authority, but the responsibility for anything that goes on in your command or your business environment is your responsibility."

Everything that I have ever done, I have recognized and tried to teach and share with others, that you are responsible for those people that work for you. That has been a key, I think, to the success that we have had. So, what have I taken away from the Academy, lessons like that that were critical and that you needed the people below you to believe you and trust you, and that you would back them unless they violated character. In which case, it wasn't going to work... the team wasn't going to function that way.

**JCLD:** It sounds like, for some of those lessons that you learned, you didn't recognize them as you were going through them.

**James:** Not true of that one! I cried. I lost my command. My ex-roommate announced from the tower, "Cadet Colonel Max F. James, is hereby reduced to the rank of Cadet First Class." That was announced to the entire Wing. Then the Squadron, that I think appreciated my leadership, suddenly lost their leader, and someone else had to take over. I hated it. But it has proven to be an extremely important principle.

**JCLD:** At what point did you realize that lesson? Did it take some time to think through that? Clearly that example had an immediate impact, but when did you learn the lesson from that?

**James:** I believed that Lieutenant Colonel, who was the Group AOC. I got it right then. It made what I had to go through following that a lot easier. This was a principle that, in the military at least, I was going to stick by. If something happens in your command, you are going to be responsible. You are going to pay for it. You don't just get away with it. So, you better watch out, lead, and be involved in everything that is going on as much as you can. Another business motivational leader has written that you need to walk the factory floor. You can't just sit up on the second-floor windowed office and watch. You have to get down and be fully observant. There is another example. It resonated. Did I think it would be a major part of my leadership philosophy later on? Probably not until I ran into it somewhere along the way in the military. But it happens more often than you want to admit. Things don't always go right within your organization, and you have to step up and say, my bad. I didn't know. In business, I have seen a mistake of $6 million because something happened in my organization. It wasn't because of a lie or because it was illegal, but it was a mistake. A $6 million mistake. I said to the people that made the mistake, my fault. I should have asked more questions and been more involved. The point is, you are responsible. What did President Truman say? The buck stops here. And it does. So, yes, I learned it in more ways than one.

**JCLD:** At the Academy, we talk about it being a leadership laboratory, and we talk about it being an opportunity for people to try things and make mistakes. How do you think the role of allowing people to try and fail fits into the idea of developing future officers?

**James:** I think that the changes made at the Academy in character development have been positive from when I was there. Somebody asked me once in an interview, what was the most courageous thing I have ever seen at the Academy? I assumed they were probably asking me about physical courage. Someone saved someone from falling off a building or something similar. My response was a bit different than what they were probably looking for. There was a classmate who was engaged. He and his fiancé had plans to be married after graduation. Prior to his graduation, she became pregnant. So, at the time, the Honor Code was used, far more than it is now, to enforce regulations. The Academy would ask you if you violated a rule, or if you stayed out too late, and you were honor bound to tell them the truth. There was a thing called "tact," however. You remember tact? For example, if you were in a receiving line, and the senior officer and his wife are there, and she has on a hat, and the officer says, "Don't you think my wife's hat is lovely?" Unfortunately, it could be the ugliest hat you have ever seen in your life. You say, "Yes, Sir. I think it is nice." Which is a lie. It is called tact.

We had a thing called the non-marriage certificate. Before you could graduate, you had to sign a certificate that said you were not married. So, this classmate of mine could not do both: get married to his fiancé and graduate. He wanted to marry her as soon as they discovered that she was pregnant. He could have gone ahead with the marriage and graduate and lie on the marriage certificate. They could have gotten married, and he could have said they weren't married. He chose to resign in order to give his wife and child legitimacy and not sign this little piece of paper that lied by saying he wasn't married. He wanted to fly so badly. He was a warrior-to-be. He had busted his hump to pass all of the academics. He had fought his way through the Academy and made it this far. He gave it up for his honor. That was the most courageous thing I saw in my time at the Academy. They got married, and it is 50-some years later, and they are still married. After resigning from the Academy, he went to ROTC and became a navigator. He lost his eyesight qualification and couldn't be a pilot. He served his country proudly. And he is proud of the time he spent at the Academy. But that is the most courageous thing I saw at the Academy. Today, I don't think he would have been tossed out. I think he would have gone in and said, "Here is the situation and what I chose to do. If you want me to serve an extra six months or year or something, fine, but what can we do?" I believe that today someone would have at least listened with heart, instead of saying that rules are rules, and we don't want to talk to you. And you must be out of here tomorrow because you have 24 hours to pack your bags and leave.

General Wakin, who was at the Academy for 50 years, has seen all that has gone on in culture and how it has affected cadets of today versus cadets of my time. The additional temptations and problems that they have to deal with that we didn't. The culture I came from was honorable and a good old Southern environment. A rough dad who disciplined and had a strong sense of right and wrong. So, the gap between where I was morally, culturally, and character-wise and what the Air Force needed me to be, via the Academy's honor system, that gap was not that great. The Academy did a good job of closing the gap. I got it. The culture that today's applicants are coming out of, with things like social media and changes in morality, that gap from where these future cadets come from and the standard that the Academy needs is huge.

I recognized the gap 10 years ago and wanted to do something about how we could effectively close that gap. How can you close that gap in 4 years? So, I wanted to research the development of adolescent character and see if we could come up with things to close that gap. Now it's not huge for everyone, don't get me wrong, but for the culture in general, it is. Now you can think of examples of heroes that people worship who don't have good character. Professional athletics comes to mind, but it's true in the business world as well. Look at the Madoffs of the world where lack of character has hurt so many people. So, the one thing that stands out in that change is second chances at the Academy, depending upon how egregious the violation of honor is. That's what the honor process is all about. It gets investigated, and then a decision is made. Are there gray areas to developing character? Yes. Are there gray areas to developing honor? Maybe not. Maybe right is right. That's why the CCLD building is called Polaris. That's why it points to the North Star. It's a moral compass. Right is right, and wrong is wrong. But in the development of character, you are going to make some mistakes. That is what Gen. Wakin was saying. If you really want to develop character, the only way you are going to do so is to let them experience character temptations that you can't teach on a whiteboard. You have to teach it though experience. I disagree with Gen. Wakin to this extent. I think you can do both. But I do think that experiencing and living in an honorable environment where character is key. Where you learn to trust up and down, and you learn that doing the right thing is much less painful than doing the wrong thing. If you do the wrong thing, you are going to carry around guilt. But the bottom line is that, if they have had a great education and a chance to experience what is right and what is wrong, they are going to be better off leading than if they never had that chance or experience. So, do I think we are doing a better job? Yes, I do.

A great challenge today is toleration and people tolerating those honor violations among their comrades. It's a tough one because there is an innate conflict with teamwork or loyalty in a sport, e.g., where you see someone violate their honor, and you have to decide whether you are going to report it or keep it so that the team will continue being successful or winning. That's a tough one and not just one that occurs at the Academy. What do you do with the person that tolerates that behavior? We need to understand that if we believe we can teach aspects like honor and character, then that should have an impact on how we deal with violations. If we want to let them experience growth, then we need to have the space for them to do so. If that is a valid effort to teach character, then we ought to be the best in the world of doing that. We have a crucible in which testing on how to achieve that can be accomplished in the best way. We need to do more research on how do you teach and how do you develop adolescent character. That's my opinion.

**JCLD:** Could you talk a little bit more about that research, what that might look like and what role that CCLD has in facilitating that research?

**James:** To answer that question, I have to reflect back a little bit on how I got to the point that I did in supporting CCLD. When I was asked if I wanted to donate back to the Academy and, if so, what

I would be interested in donating to, I explained that my interest would be in continuing to develop a stronger base of honor and making the code work better so that we didn't end up with the Academy's reputation being tarnished by the scandalous behavior of a few cadets. That has an impact on the pool from which we draw men and women of great potential as it gets smaller if the reputation is not as good. I wanted to see if we could fix that. So, I said to the people that approached me that I wanted to help the Center. To help them and support them in some way to eliminate scandalous, dishonest behavior in the Wing. So, as I said earlier, I went back and spoke to the person that was writing the mission statement for the Center for Character & Leadership Development, Gen. (ret) Erv Rokke. He had returned to the Academy to work for the Superintendent (Gen. Regni). Gen. Rokke had written a great pamphlet explaining the mission that they were looking for, and I bought into it immediately. He said we are going to have a separate facility because we can't keep promoting this program with offices scattered within the dorms. We don't have a central place. I told him you needed an iconic structure, which was the first time that term was used. Not to reiterate what I already said about my investments, but if developing leaders of character is that central to the Academy, then I truly felt that you need to say it in a building. So, I said I was in. As a result, I was able to make a seven-figure commitment to the facility. A restricted donation to help build that building. After looking at several options, we settled on the current design. After nine long, arduous years, we got it built. It was the first jointly funded project between the military and the civilian world. We had a monetary goal for donations, and we far exceeded that. Why do you think that was? It's because the Long Blue Line, and others outside of the graduate community, believed that we could do it and that character was important enough. To do what? To continue to build a strong core of Air Force officers that had experienced character development. That they are taught that character development is important. It was a tremendous journey. A tough one to fight. But we did it. I believe it is serving its purpose, and it continues to have an even more important impact as we continue to do research and testing of theories around adolescent character development. We implement what we learn and then spread it to other organizations and universities.

**JCLD:** Along those lines, what message do you hope carries to those outside of the Academy?

**James:** When they look at the Academy, I want them to say, "Wow, this must be important." They have a Center (and building) focused solely on character and its development. A place where they welcome others to come and learn and collaborate on character and leadership development. Why is this building important? It is visual recognition of what we are doing… emphasizing character. To show that cadets are moral men and women who have an honor code. So important that they built a special building to highlight that commitment.

**JCLD:** It's interesting that not only does it have the internal message to cadets and the external message to other organizations and universities that we value character and leadership, it is also a reminder to the Permanent Party personnel at the Academy about our mission, our charge, and what is important to us.

**James:** Absolutely. Sometimes you live in an environment for so long that you just passively accept what is going on around you.

That can happen with this building if we don't have events there that draw attention to its purpose. As an example, the athletic directors of other universities had a major conference there to find out what we are doing to uphold high standards of character in our athletic teams and then took what we shared with them back to their universities. Those kinds of events are critical. Otherwise, it is just an iconic building at the Air Force Academy. People can come here to learn about character, and they can take it back to their units in the Air Force, their universities, etc. That is a worthwhile expenditure of effort, time, and money. Obviously, a lot of people agree with that as they are donating their time, effort, and money to character development. Do I feel good that we got it done? Absolutely. Do I hope that we see more and more demonstrable success coming out of the results of having done this? Absolutely.

**JCLD:** Along those lines, and doing a little visoneering toward the future, what would success look like to you 10 years from now?

**James:** It's not just the building, but this Journal as well. There are journals for industries and professions that are absolutely accepted as the best for that industry. I would hope that this building and the support that we have gotten so far will produce results that will be written up in our Journal and that there will be additional researchers that will come to CCLD for a sabbatical or a specified time that will contribute and collaborate. That we can continue to find ways to improve character development in adolescents. That we will be recognized as the keystone of that research, development, and application. There just aren't that many places where you have a group in a controlled environment where you can see the impact of different programs and practices. Ten years from now, when a discussion of character, or adolescent character, comes up, they will say, "What is the Air Force Academy doing about this?" or "What does their research say about this?" It would be the natural reaction that when you talk about character development in adolescents, to think about CCLD and USAFA. People would say, "Did you read this new article from the Academy?" That's my vision. That we are making a major contribution to character development for the Air Force and the world. That the Air Force Academy Center for Character and Leadership Development will have researched adolescent character development, applied it to test it, discovered what worked, and implemented it throughout the Wing, and then spread the beneficial results to the Air Force, other universities, and the world. That was also my vision 10 years ago, and it hasn't changed.

**JCLD:** Thank you for that vision, your investment, and your time.